THE COMMONWEALTH AND INTERNATIONAL LIBRARY
Joint Chairmen of the Honorary Editorial Advisory Board
SIR ROBERT ROBINSON, O.M., F.R.S., LONDON
DEAN ATHELSTAN SPILHAUS, MINNESOTA
Publisher: ROBERT MAXWELL, M.C., M.P.

BIOLOGY DIVISION
General Editor: G.L. WATT

SPIDERS, SCORPIONS, CENTIPEDES AND MITES

FRONTISPIECE: Head of Solifugid. (*Photo:* Richard L. Cassell.)

SPIDERS, SCORPIONS, CENTIPEDES AND MITES

by J. L. CLOUDSLEY-THOMPSON

M.A., Ph.D. (Cantab.), D.Sc. (Lond.), F.L.S., F.I.Biol., F.W.A.
Professor of Zoology, University of Khartoum
and Keeper, Sudan Natural History Museum
Formerly Lecturer in Zoology, University of London, King's College

THE QUEEN'S AWARD
TO INDUSTRY 1966

PERGAMON PRESS

OXFORD · LONDON · EDINBURGH · NEW YORK
TORONTO · SYDNEY · PARIS · BRAUNSCHWEIG

Pergamon Press Ltd., Headington Hill Hall, Oxford
4 & 5 Fitzroy Square, London W.1
Pergamon Press (Scotland) Ltd., 2 & 3 Teviot Place, Edinburgh 1
Pergamon Press Inc., 44–01 21st Street, Long Island City, New York 11101
Pergamon of Canada Ltd., 207 Queen's Quay West, Toronto 1
Pergamon Press (Aust.) Pty. Ltd., 19a Boundary Street,
Rushcutters Bay, N. S. W. 2011
Pergamon Press S.A.R.L., 24 rue des Écoles, Paris 5ᵉ
Vieweg & Sohn GmbH, Burgplatz 1, Braunschweig

Copyright © 1968 Pergamon Press Ltd.
First published 1958
Published in this Format 1968
Library of Congress Catalog Card No. 68–21100

08 012322 8 (flexicover)
08 012323 6 (hard cover)

CONTENTS

LIST OF PLATES
(between pages 144/145)

PREFACE

'If anybody shall reprove me and shall make it
apparent unto me that I do err, I will most gladly
retract. For it is the truth that I seeke after, by
which I am sure that never man was hurt and as
sure that he is hurt that continueth in any error
or ignorance whatsoever.'

MARCUS AURELIUS

THIS book was conceived largely at the sink, where most
modern husbands have to spend so much of their leisure. My
deepest thanks are therefore due to my dear wife who shoul-
dered far more than her share of the domestic drudgery in
order that I might slip away to jot down my ideas. I would also
like to express my gratitude to my friends and colleagues at
home and abroad who have so generously sent me reprints of
their publications. In many cases I have not been able to quote
these in the bibliographies for reasons of space, but my debt
to the work of others in attempting to cover a very wide field
in a single volume must be abundantly clear to the reader.

April 1957   J. L. C–T.

This reprinted edition has been brought up to date by the
addition of new references and data. At the same time, the
opportunity has been taken to correct a few errors and mis-
prints.

September 1967   J. L. C–T.

ACKNOWLEDGMENTS

I SHOULD like to make grateful acknowledgment to the following for the use of several of the photographs and illustrations within this book: the Editors of *Discovery*, *Naturalist*, *The Field* and *Science News*; G. Fryer, R. F. Lawrence, E. A. Robins, J. H. P. Sankey, Duckworth & Co., Shell Photographic Unit, Zoological Society of London, and to Frank W. Lane for photographs by Richard L. Cassell, Walker van Riper and Hugh Spencer.

INTRODUCTION

'The evaporating power of the air may be the primary factor
upon which the organisation of the entire terrestrial fauna
depends.'

R. HESSE, W. C. ALLEE AND K. P. SCHMIDT

THE Arthropoda is the dominant phylum of the Invertebrates.
In the oceans, minute crustaceans comprise the major component of the zooplankton upon which the food chains of the
whales and larger fishes are based; on land the medical, economic and biological importance of insects and mites especially
can scarcely be over-stressed. These may be very cogent reasons
for their investigation, but they are not the most important.
The little creatures are interesting in their own right, and research into the details of their lives provides mental exercise that
is a source of unending pleasure and interest.

Questions are sometimes asked as to the use of academic
research. The answer may be that it lies in man's nature to explore the secrets of the universe, for comparatively few intel-
lectual and aesthetic pursuits are motivated by purely practical
considerations. Scott did not go to the South Pole in search
of coal, nor did Beethoven write his string quartets for economic reasons. The best excuse for climbing Mount Everest may
have been to get to the top, or simply because it was there.
Perhaps the last word on the subject was written by J. S. Bach:
'The aim and final reason of all music is the glory of God and
the recreation of the mind.' And so for all the arts and sciences!

Many excellent books have recently been written about insects and of all the terrestrial Arthropoda they are the most catholic. Over 600,000 species are known to science and the total number in existence probably exceeds a million. There are more species of beetles in the world than of all other animals put together. One of these, *Niptus hololeucus*, can live on cayenne pepper and thrive on sal ammoniac. This species has been known to live in the corks of entomologists' cyanide killing-bottles and no less than 1547 specimens were taken from a jar of casein that had been stoppered for twelve years. The fly *Psilopa petrolei* inhabits puddles of crude petroleum; and both flies and beetles abound in certain hot springs in the western United States where the temperature approaches 50° C. The largest insects include the African Goliath beetle, *Goliathus regius*, which measures four inches in length and two in breadth, and the Venezuelan *Dynastes hercules*, reaching a length of $6\frac{1}{4}$ inches, while the magnificent butterfly *Ornithoptera victoriae* of the Solomon Islands has a wing-span exceeding one foot. In contrast some of the parasitic Hymenoptera are considerably less than one-hundredth of an inch in length, despite the complexity of their structure.

The diversity and versatility of the insects is nowhere equalled in the animal kingdom, but in this volume I hope to show that the other terrestrial Arthropoda, although somewhat neglected, will well repay further acquaintance.

For many years, the majority of zoologists who have worked on the Arthropoda have tended to concentrate their efforts either on the marine Crustacea or on the insects. Apart from systematists, comparatively few have paid more than superficial attention to the remaining members of the phylum and although increasing numbers are now doing so, there is ample scope for new recruits as the reader will soon realise.

It is now generally recognised that the Collembola are not in-

sects and the same may be true of other Apterygota. Nevertheless, these animals have always come within the scope of the
entomologist and receive attention in many well-known ento-
mological textbooks. I have not, therefore, included them in
this book, even though the Pauropoda and Symphyla have
been noticed. Indeed, it is now believed that the latter are
closely related to the Insecta. Consequently the selection of
groups discussed in the following chapters may appear somewhat arbitrary from a systematic point of view: but it will, I
hope, be found to have practical justification.

Life on land entails a number of problems for animals. Larger
forms require structural support, respiratory organs must
become modified for air breathing and there is no longer the
surrounding water into which toxic excretory products can
freely diffuse, while mechanisms for the conservation of water
and the maintenance of a constant internal medium must be
evolved. That these problems are by no means easily overcome
is shown by the fact that several invertebrate phyla are almost
entirely marine while others as yet possess few terrestrial species. Indeed, the Arthropoda have been unusually successful in
exploiting the terrestrial habitat and by adaptive radiation have
succeeded in establishing themselves in nearly all the habitable
corners of the earth. Each aspect of their adaptation to life on
land affects and is affected by other aspects. For example, it
might appear a fairly simple matter for an organism to elimi-
nate water-loss by the evolution of an integument completely
impervious to water-vapour; but such an integument would
also be impervious to oxygen and carbon dioxide. A respiratory mechanism has therefore had to be evolved which permits
gaseous exchange without excessive water-loss. If the integument is rigid and provides support, then growth becomes impossible except by moulting and this limits size. The physiology
of nutrition and excretion too are closely concerned with

water conservation and superimposed upon this basic physiological requirement are the innumerable concomitants of behaviour and ecology.

There are two obvious ways in which small animals can escape desiccation on dry land. One is to avoid dry places and to remain most, if not all, of the time in a humid environment; the other, to evolve an impervious integument. Both methods have been exploited by the Arthropoda and each has its drawbacks and advantages. Indeed, on the basis of this character the terrestrial members of the phylum can be divided roughly into two main ecological groups: the first includes woodlice, centipedes, millipedes and their allies which lose water rapidly in dry air; the second, the Arachnids and insects which are covered with a layer of wax that renders them comparatively independent of moist surroundings.

In the following chapters the significance of this generalisation will become apparent. Forms lacking an epicuticular wax-layer are almost entirely nocturnal in habit, and can wander abroad only after nightfall when the temperature drops and the relative humidity of the air rises. In contrast, most insects, spiders and most other Arachnida are potentially diurnal except perhaps in deserts and other regions with rigorous climates where, anyway, the majority of the inhabitants avoid the excessive mid-day heat and drought by their nocturnal behaviour. (Conversely, arctic animals are nearly always diurnal in habit.) The more primitive groups such as scorpions, whip-scorpions, spiders of the families Liphistiidae, Theraphosidae, Dictynidae, Dysderidae and so on have probably become secondarily adapted to nocturnal habits as a result of competition with more efficient species. At the same time, however, many of them are large and somewhat vulnerable and may need to escape the attentions of potential predators in this way.

On the other hand, liquid water can also be very dangerous to small animals that may become water-logged, or trapped by surface tension. Their environment must be neither too wet nor too dry. This is especially true of species lacking a waterproofing wax-layer. Because they are susceptible to desiccation, they are also susceptible to water uptake by osmosis: consequently they tend to inhabit thick leaf-litter, or burrow deep into the soil where they are less liable either to become water-logged or desiccated.

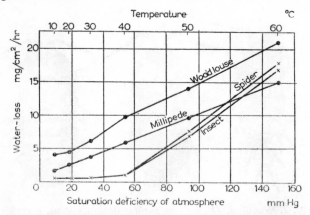

FIG. 1. Rate of water-loss in dry air at different temperatures, and corresponding saturation deficiencies, from a woodlouse (*Porcellio*), millipede (*Oxidus*), spider (*Lycosa*) and insect (*Pieris* larva). In the woodlouse and millipede the rate of water-loss is proportional to the saturation deficiency of the atmosphere, but in the spider and insect it is negligible below about 30° C, the critical temperature at which their epicuticular wax-layers become porous. Rate of water-loss is expressed in milligrams per square centimetre of surface area per hour. (After Cloudsley-Thompson, 1955.)

Rigid, mechanistic behaviour patterns in response to environmental stimuli have been evolved by means of which the animals find and maintain themselves in suitable habitats.

Physiological and morphological adaptations alone would obviously be insufficient to support the life of any free-living animal. Orientation and behaviour mechanisms must also be evolved to retain organisms in environments to which they are suited, to enable them to find food, mate, and indeed to carry out the innumerable functions essential for their continued existence.

The ecology of animals is therefore governed not only by the factors of their environments, physical and biological, but also

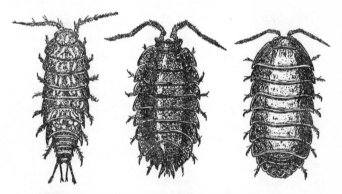

FIG. 2. Woodlice. *Trichoniscus pusillus* (length 4 mm), *Porcellio scaber* (length 14 mm) and *Armadillidium vulgare* (length 15 mm). (After Webb and Sillem, 1906.)

by their own physiological requirements and behaviour. The inter-relationships between living organisms and their environments include both inter-specific and intra-specific factors. These relationships are specific for every organism and continuous throughout its life: they are reciprocal in that the organism is not merely influenced by, but at the same time positively affects its environment, and are indissoluble because the organism cannot exist independently of its environment. Consequently ecology is a vast and complex subject about which comparatively little is yet known. One advantage of this lies in the fact that it is still possible, as Charles Elton pointed out in 1927, for almost anyone doing ecological work on the right lines to strike upon some new and exciting fact or idea.

Ecology has been described as scientific natural history and accurate identification must be made of any animals studied. One of the objects of this book is to indicate some of the innumerable problems awaiting elucidation and to provide a guide to sources for the identification of the British species in particular, as well as to other relevant literature.[†] It is hoped that it will interest natural history workers in this country and abroad: it may also be of use to upper school biology teachers. At the same time, however, I believe that many university students may find in it information, although simply portrayed, that will be of value to them both in the joys of the field and the gloom of the examination hall.

[†] Inevitably this is somewhat arbitrary and no doubt reflects a bias towards the works with which I am more familiar. Both modern and old publications have been quoted, especially where the latter have useful illustrations.

CHAPTER I

WOODLICE

Classification and distribution

Woodlice are included in the sub-order Oniscoidea of the crustacean order Isopoda. They form a reasonably homogeneous group and are of particular interest because there are several common species showing different degrees of adaptation to life on land. The majority are between one and two centimetres in length, and the small size of certain genera such

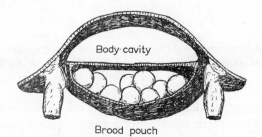

FIG. 3. Fifth thoracic segment of a female *Oniscus asellus* cut across to show the brood pouch with eggs. (After Webb and Sillem, 1906.)

as *Platyarthrus*, *Trichoniscus* and *Sphaerobathytropa* is almost certainly a secondary feature correlated with various regressive characters such as a simplification in the structure of the eyes and appendices, reduction in the number of body segments and loss of pigmentation. An analogous phenomenon is found in the Acari.

The Oniscoidea are somewhat oval in form and their bodies are arched, the curve varying in different genera and species. The head bears two large antennae and a smaller pair of antennules anterior to them. The thorax consists of seven segments which are often considerably broader than the six succeeding ones that form the abdomen. Each of the thoracic segments carries a pair of walking legs and in the female, at the time

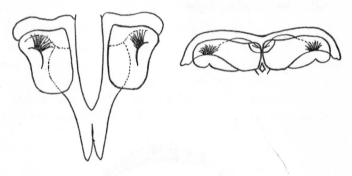

FIG. 4. Pleopods of first thoracic segment of *Porcellio scaber* showing pseudotracheae. Male on the left, female on the right. (Diagrammatic.)

when the eggs are laid, a pair of plates arise on segments two to five. These plates together form a brood pouch in which the eggs are carried until they hatch and in which the young remain for some time afterwards. The appendages of the abdomen are also plate-like, with the exception of the last pair or uropods. The endopodites or pleopods are homologous with the gills of aquatic Isopods and have a respiratory function, while the outer exopodites act as a protective cover. In the male the first two pairs of abdominal appendages are specially modified, their endopodites being long and pointed, while the

uropods are often considerably larger than in the female and
their shape is sometimes of value in classification.

In a comprehensive survey of the Oniscoidea, Vandel (1943)
recognises some 18 families, of which five are included in the
British fauna. These are the Ligiidae, Trichoniscidae, Oniscidae, Porcellionidae and Armadillidiidae. The geological history of the Crustacea is a long one and fossils occur in the Old
Red Sandstone of the Devonian period and in the Carboni-
ferous Coal Measures. Fossil woodlice, however, have not
been found below the Upper Eocene, which might suggest that
colonisation of the land has been achieved somewhat late in
the history of the group. When they do appear, however, they
are generically indistinct from living forms, and Vandel believes that the ancestors of woodlice became terrestrial during
the second half of the Palaeozoic era. He bases this conclusion
on the fact that all the main types of organisation within the
Oniscoidea have a world-wide distribution and consequently
must have a very ancient origin.

The most primitive and at the same time the least well adapted of the woodlice to terrestrial conditions are littoral species
belonging to the family Ligiidae. There are two British species
in this family, *Ligia oceanica*, the largest of the British woodlice
—up to 30 mm in length and rather more than twice as long
as broad—and the smaller *Ligidium hypnorum* which is sometimes found far inland, nearly always in the neighbourhood of
water.

Ligia oceanica has a wide distribution around the shores of
Great Britain and indeed of practically the whole north coast
of Europe. It also occurs in France, Spain, Morocco and America. Although never found far from the sea, it is truly terrestrial and can withstand prolonged submersion in sea water only
if this is well aerated. The normal habitat is in deep narrow
crevices in the rocks just above high-tide level, under stones on

sandy beaches or on the sides of quays: hence the name 'quay-louse' or 'quay-lowder'. In St. Kilda *Ligia* has been found in the crevices of boulders over 450 ft. above sea level, but on that exposed islet spray is often blown to this height (Nicholls, 1931). I have found specimens over a mile inland on the Isle of Man.

The family Trichoniscidae also occurs in very moist places, but the Porcellionidae and Armadillidiidae are found in progressively drier localities. Now this sequence is also one of increasing morphological specialisation within the group, the significance of which will be considered below.

Hatchett (1947) has found that in Michigan *Armadillidium nasatum* does not occur outside buildings, while *A. vulgare* is chiefly found around human habitations; *Cylisticus convexus* prefers rocky regions and *Ligidium longicaudatum* occurs only in very wet situations. *Metoponorthus pruinosus* is somewhat urban in its distribution. *Porcellio scaber* lives on beaches, river banks and other moist situations. *P. spinicornis* requires a habitat where plenty of lime is available and *P. rathkei* is generally distributed but more abundant in deciduous woodlands than elsewhere, while *P. demivirgo* definitely prefers moist woodland situations.

With regard to the British species, Heeley (1941) notes that *Trichoniscus pusillus* is abundant in very moist woodlands, though the animals are frequently overlooked owing to their small size and dark colouring. They can easily be mistaken for young *Philoscia*. They favour the thick sodden layers of decaying leaves which lie beneath the trees throughout the winter and during the summer they live amongst the resulting leaf mould beneath low bushes well shaded from the sun, or within rotting twigs.

Philoscia muscorum is fairly common in moist shady situations in moors and woodlands, particularly amongst the roots of grasses beneath bushes and brambles and at the base of tree trunks, where the soil receives the drippings from the trees and is shaded from the sun. This species is somewhat local and restricted in its distribution and is present mainly in woodland. *Oniscus asellus* on the other hand is the commonest of all woodlice and is found almost everywhere that damp conditions prevail, particularly beneath half-buried stones and bark. It seems to prefer rather more moist situations than *Porcellio scaber* and may often be found with the latter in the same tree, but usually nearer the ground where the wood is old and rotting.

Porcellio scaber is also very common, particularly beneath the dry loose bark of vertical trunks of living trees. It sometimes inhabits damp houses and has been found in heaps of clinker and the nests of wood ants, *Formica rufa*.

Finally, *Armadillidium vulgare* is particularly common on chalk lands, on heaths and slopes covered with low scrub such as are found in railway cuttings and on roadsides. The species also occurs in the neighbourhood of houses and builders' yards where there is loose cement or lime, but is never very numerous in woodland. It can even survive under dry stones warmed by the sun.

Now Heeley claims that it is possible to predict which species of woodlouse will be present in a given habitat by its water-content. In his experiments, however, he provided a moist surface for the animals in the form of a carrot as food. It has since been shown that woodlice of the same species, if desiccated and subsequently kept in unsaturated air, but with access to moist plaster of Paris surfaces, regain their weight by absorption of water through the mouth. These experiments explain how woodlice which are known to lose water in all but saturated air can nevertheless survive indefinitely in unsaturated air provided that a moist surface is available (Edney, 1954).

General behaviour

In different parts of the country there are many curious superstitions about woodlice. For example, in some places their
presence indoors is regarded as unlucky and any food on which
they may happen to wander is considered poisoned. On the
other hand, in certain other districts until very recently a few
live woodlice thrust down the throat of a cow were believed
to have beneficial effects and 'to promote the restoration of
the cud'. No doubt this is why in Shropshire and neighbouring counties woodlice or slaters are sometimes referred to as 'cud-worms'. At one time too, woodlice were pre-
scribed to be swallowed alive as a remedy for scrofulous
symptoms and for diseases of the liver and digestive organs.
It is surprising too how many local names have been given
to woodlice: Collinge (1935) listed no less than 65 ranging
from 'Bibble bugs' (Stafford), 'Cheese-pigs' (Berkshire) and
'Coffin-cutters' (Ireland) to 'Monkey peas' (Kent), 'Penny-
pigs' (Wales), 'Sink-lice' (Lancashire and Stafford) and 'Tig-
gyhogs' (Northamptonshire). In America they are known
as 'Sowbugs'.

Humidity is an environmental factor of prime importance,
both to woodlice and to myriapods, as they all lack a waterproof integument. Woodlice are very sensitive to humidity gradients and aggregate in areas of high humidity. The mechanism by which this occurs is two-fold: firstly, the animals show
a decrease in activity and speed in moist air and secondly, they
change direction more frequently in damp places so that once
they have arrived in a moist situation they tend to remain there.
This reaction to the relative humidity of the air is also combined with avoidance of light and a reaction that causes them
to make contact with as much of their surroundings as possible.
The result of this is that not only do the animals enter narrow

crevices, but they bunch together and consequently protect each other from evaporation.

Kuenen and Nooteboom (1963) believe that, when desiccated, woodlice react positively to the smell of their own species. However, a reversal of the response to light occurs when woodlice become somewhat desiccated, so that if their daytime habitat should dry up they are not restrained there until they die, but become attracted to light and are then able to wander in the open until they find some other damp dark hiding place, where they again become photo-negative (Cloudsley-Thompson, 1952).

Since the normal excretion of woodlice cannot entirely compensate for water-uptake in nearly saturated air, a long stay in such conditions becomes unfavourable and the animals must, from time to time, come out into the open and lose excess water by transpiration. Hence, they climb trees, walls and buildings at night (den Boer, 1961). Nocturnal emergence is, however, inhibited by wind because air currents tend to remove the shell of moist air that surrounds the transpiring animal (Cloudsley-Thompson, 1958).

The clearest adaptation to terrestrial life is to be found in the pleopods. These are variously modified and in the more advanced forms bear tufts of invaginated tubules forming 'lung-trees' or 'pseudotracheae'. Each tree opens to the exterior by a slit-like aperture near the edge of the pleopod, and the minute ramifying tracheae are thin-walled tubes surrounded by blood which carries oxygen to the tissues of the body. When the air is dry, the pleopods are probably kept moist by water that diffuses from the body fluids of the animal.

Like most other woodlice, *Ligia oceanica* is nocturnal in habit and emerges during the night at low tide to feed on seaweeds such as *Fucus* and other algae. The species is strongly photo-negative and tends to remain under cover on moonlight nights. Edney (1954) has recently pointed out that *Ligia* can live on land as a result of wide osmotic tolerance rather than by developing osmotic independence. Since other species of woodlouse can lose much water by evaporation without dying, it seems likely that such osmotic independence is characteristic of the group as a whole. The colour of *Ligia* ranges from a dark greyish-green to a light, dirty brown, while young specimens have two light-coloured patches on the middle of the dorsal side. The British *Ligia oceanica*, as well as the American *L. baudiniana* and *L. exotica*, have been found to show well-marked colour responses due to the expansion and contraction of colour pigment cells or chromatophores, so that they become light when placed on a white background and turn dark on a black background. In addition there is a diurnal rhythm of colour change and they tend to be dark by day and pale by night.

The family Trichoniscidae includes a number of small, elongated woodlice that are fairly widely distributed in damp places under moss, bark, fallen leaves, logs and so on. The Oniscidae are less dependent on moisture, but the common *Philoscia muscorum* which can be distinguished from *Oniscus asellus* by its narrow body and pretty marbled appearance is again usually found in moist situations under rubbish heaps, damp moss and the carpet of dead leaves in woods.

A curious little, white, blind woodlouse is *Platyarthrus hoffmannseggi*. It is easily recognised by its broad flattened body up to 3·6 mm in length with denticulate edges to its segments and short, stout antennae. This species occurs throughout the British Isles and the rest of Europe, and its range extends into North Africa. It is usually found in the nests of ants and the burrows of wood-boring beetles. The species was described in 1833 by Brandt from specimens taken in Prussia and was first noticed in Britain living with several species of ants at Lulworth Cove, in 1859. Although it has no eyes, *Platyarthrus* appears to be very averse to light and quickly hides if disturbed.

A New Zealand species of *Trichoniscus*, *T. commensalis*, has independently evolved the same habit of associating with ants. It is rather larger than *Platyarthrus* and is not quite white, but generally marked with bands or patches of pale brown on a white ground. Moreover, it is not blind but possesses fairly perfect eyes provided with the normal amount of pigmentation.

One of the largest and most common of woodlice is the garden slater *Oniscus asellus* which reaches a length of 15 mm and about half that width. Again the pleopods are without pseudotracheae, but *Oniscus* spp. seem to wander in drier places than any of the species mentioned previously. A number of species occur in the family Porcellionidae, of which *Porcellio scaber* is the most usual and has been recorded from all over the British Isles. It reaches a size even larger than that of *Oniscus asellus* and is very variable in colour, but it is usually a dark slaty grey with irregular lighter markings. It can be recognised by the transverse rows of small tubercles that cover the back of the head and body. This family is better adapted to live in drier conditions than any of the preceding and the pleopods bear well-developed pseudotracheae although a certain amount of respiration also takes place through the integument of the body.

To the same family belongs the remarkable desert woodlouse *Hemilepistus reaumuri* which is not uncommon in North Africa and the Middle East. The animals live together in vertical holes 5–6 cm in diameter and many centimetres in depth. A digging reaction is released by a temperature of 35° C if the soil is dry, and 45° C if it is moist. The head is placed against a small stone or some other rigid body: the anterior legs then lift the sand backwards while the posterior ones throw it away. Sometimes several animals combine to dig a single hole and frequently two woodlice can be seen digging head to head.

The pill-woodlice or Armadillidiidae are so called because of their habit of rolling into a ball like a little armadillo. The ability to do this is by no means restricted to this family however, but has evolved independently in several diverse groups. In forms that can curl up completely the head has become flattened in an anteroposterior direction so that its height is much greater than its length and the front part is covered by the last abdominal appendages or uropods when the animal rolls up. (In other woodlice the uropods project like a couple of small tails from the hinder end of the body). The most common British species is *Armadillidium vulgare*, sometimes called the 'Pill bug', which reaches a length of 18 mm and is a little more than twice as long as broad. The colour varies from completely black to pale yellow, but the more usual shades are light grey.

As already mentioned, woodlice have little ability to prevent loss of water by evaporation and excretion, and although they can regain lost water both by actively drinking and absorbing moisture through their pleopods, they can only survive on land as a result of behaviour mechanisms that keep them in cool, moist places. Woodlice are also able to extract water from their food. In this way they can make up part of the water lost by evaporation. Of the three species that have been investigated in this respect, *A. vulgare* is the most efficient, *P. scaber* comes next and *O. asellus* last. It might have been expected that *O. asellus*, which, of the three, loses water most rapidly by transpiration, would have made up for it by a greater ability to extract water from food. But this is not the case. Adaptation to life on land does not concern a number of isolated characteristics of animals, but their organisation as a whole (Kuenen, 1959).

During the day they normally collect at the moist end of a humidity gradient and avoid the light; it is at night that dispersal to new environments mostly takes place. Changes in behaviour between day and night have recently been demonstrated in *Oniscus asellus* that can perhaps be correlated with the ecology of the species as follows: a fall in the intensity of the humidity response after dark enables the animals for a time to walk in places drier than their day-time retreats, but increased photo-negative behaviour after exposure to dark ensures that they return to cover at daybreak, and thus no doubt avoid the early bird (Cloudsley-Thompson, 1952). The degree of nocturnal activity in different species is correlated with the ability to withstand water-loss by transpiration (Cloudsley-Thompson, 1956).

The daily life of woodlice is regulated by the interaction of their diurnal rhythms or 'biological clocks', humidity and light responses. Seasonal changes also occur in the intensity of their humidity responses, which show a marked rise in spring when the rains bring them out of hibernation (Gupta, 1963). At the same time, seasonal changes occur in the distribution of woodlice. Whereas *Phil. muscorum* remains under stones and litter throughout the year, the tiny *T. pusillus* moves in summer from its winter habitat under stones and litter to dead wood. *O. asellus* is found mainly under stones throughout the year, but in summer it also occurs on dead wood and trees. Finally *P. scaber*, whose winter habitat is at the base of trees, tends to move upwards during summer (Brereton, 1957).

Isopods show a regression in the size of their sense organs which may be correlated with reduction in the rapidity of movement on becoming terrestrial, for the aquatic forms are rapid swimmers. *Ligia* spp. however, which can run particularly rapidly, have retained the big eyes of their marine ancestors.

In a recent review of the adaptations of woodlice to the terrestrial habitat, Edney (1954) concludes that different species can withstand terrestrial conditions of drought to varying degrees, but probably all species spend most of the time in an atmosphere saturated with water vapour and merely differ in the length of time that they are capable of surviving away from dampness. Thus even *Armadillidium* and *Hemilepistus* spp. can venture into dry places with immunity only for comparatively short periods. Edney also suggests that the reason why so little progress has been made toward full exploitation of the land by woodlice may lie in the fact that the conquest of the land by the Isopoda took place via the littoral zone, for *Ligia* and *Halophiloscia* are undoubtedly primitive morphologically. Now animals crossing this zone may well be subjected to extremely high temperatures, and the ability to lose heat by evaporation of water may have considerable survival value in all species.

Food and feeding habits

Woodlice are omnivorous and no doubt useful as scavengers. Some species are of economic importance because they do not confine their attention to dead and decaying matter but sometimes attack seedlings, ripe fruit such as plums, peaches or melons, and mushrooms—indeed they will eat anything that is soft and juicy though they do more mischief by disfiguring than by consuming any large quantities. They are sometimes difficult to dislodge from hot houses as they find shelter in every little crevice.

Nicholls (1931) has shown that although *Ligia oceanica* feeds principally on *Fucus vesiculosus* and other algae, nothing edible comes amiss, particularly if it be in the nature of animal offal, and cannibalism frequently takes place in captivity. The gut contents of one individual were found to include moss capsules and part of a syncytium of *Vaucheria*.

The small, myrmecophilous *Platyarthrus hoffmannseggi* feeds on fungi and their spores, the excreta of ants and other vegetable matter. Some species, especially *Oniscus asellus*, are decidedly more omnivorous than others such as *Porcellio scaber* which confines its diet largely to the bark of trees and *Trichoniscus pusillus* which lives almost entirely on decaying leaves. According to Bristowe (1941)*,[†] woodlice will eat spiders' eggs in captivity, and as they are often to be found in untenanted cells beside empty egg-sacs it can be supposed that they devour Arthropod eggs whenever an opportunity occurs. *Armadillidium vulgare* requires chalk in its diet, and this may be correlated with its exceptionally thickly calcified integument.

Enemies

Woodlice are eaten by birds, reptiles, amphibia, and many other insectivorous animals including spiders, harvest-spiders, mites and centipedes. The number of species of spider which will destroy a woodlouse is, however, somewhat limited. *Armadillidium vulgare* rolls into a ball directly it is attacked, and its hard, thick integument saves it from injury, even from large species such as *Tegenaria atrica* and *Araneus diadematus*. According to Bristowe (1941)* *Porcellio*, *Oniscus* and *Philoscia* spp. secure some protection from the chitin with which their dorsal surface is covered so long as they remain dorsal surface uppermost. In addition they are distasteful to most spiders, which reject them except in times of food shortage when their normal aversion is overcome by hunger. Distastefulness is most

[†] For references marked with an asterisk see the bibliography of general works at the end of the volume.

marked in *Porcellio* spp. and least in *Philoscia* spp. (except for *Platyarthrus hoffmannseggi* whose myrmecophilous habit renders it least likely to attack by spiders). On the other hand the cave and cellar spider *Meta menardi* often owes its survival in subterranean situations to the presence of woodlice, and *Dysdera crocota* and *D. erythrina* have jaws specially adapted to grip and penetrate the crustacean cuticle.

At one time it was believed that certain tegumental glands known as 'Weber's glands' played an important part in respiration. For nearly half a century the concept that these glands secreted a fluid which moistened the gills crept into almost every text-book dealing with the subject of respiration in woodlice. Great, therefore, was the surprise of Gorvett (1950), who has made a special study of the glands of woodlice, to find that 'Weber's glands' do not in fact exist either in the animals or in the publications of their supposed discoverer. Gorvett traced the myth to an 'inaugural dissertation' on respiration in woodlice published in 1909, in which glands described by Weber were confused with certain structures in the abdomen that had been described, also incorrectly, by Němec in 1895–6. Apparently the accounts of Weber and Němec had never been compared, or it would at once have been realised that the two authors were dealing with entirely different and totally unrelated structures.

At least five kinds of tegumental glands do, however, occur in woodlice, of which the rosette and lobed glands have so far been investigated by Gorvett. Some of the latter discharge an acid secretion smelling of butyric acid, but others possess an odourless, neutral solution. The glands vary in number and size in different species, but their variation appears to be independent of habitat or evolutionary position: in fact their function is probably to act as a deterrent to enemies, principally hunting-spiders, since they do not seem to prevent excess eva-

poration as has sometimes been suggested. They are thus analogous to the repugnatorial glands of millipedes, harvest-spiders and many insects (Gorvett, 1956). An unusual case of
mimicry has recently been noted by Levy (1965) in which
the pill bug *A. klugii* of Dalmatia mimics the poisonous spider
Latrodectes mactans, presumably as a deterrent to predatory
lizards.

Woodlice do not seem to be attacked to any great extent by
parasitoidal insects. Thompson (1934) made a detailed study of
their Tachinid parasites during which he dissected 1737 specimens of *Porcellio scaber* and *Oniscus asellus* collected from
various localities in England and France but only 9·1% were
parasitised, and the average parasitism of *O. asellus* was only
3·1%. He concluded, therefore, that Dipterous parasites are
not factors of major importance in the control of woodlice:
certain species are scarcely parasitised at all and in the case of
others, starvation and cannibalism come into play as density-
dependent factors[†] controlling the size of populations before
parasites can increase sufficiently to become of ecological importance. These conclusions have recently been confirmed
by Paris (1963), who found that only weather had any profound
effect on the mortality of *A. vulgare* in California. During the
rainy season the animals live in or near the soil surface but
during drought they seek refuge from desiccation by descending
deeply into soil fissures.

Reproduction and life cycle

Like other Crustacea, woodlice carry their eggs in a thoracic
brood pouch or marsupium and a whole family of newly

[†] See discussion of density-dependent and density-independent factors
on p. 176.

hatched young may be found huddled up on the underside of the mother. The number of eggs varies from seven per brood in *Trichoniscus* to 100–200 or more in *Armadillidium*.

The newly hatched larvae have a distinct head and eyes, segmented body and short, stumpy limbs. They are incapable of movement for the first three days as their appendages are tightly doubled against the body. At this stage they are kept very moist, but as their size increases the fluid in the brood pouch decreases. The young emerge over a period of two or three days and the first moult occurs within 24 hours of liberation. The period between the first and second moult is the most critical in their lives, because if the soil is dry at this time they die, while if it is too moist they are usually killed by fungi. Later they are more resistant and their life may be quite a long one, for they seldom breed until they are two years old.

The life cycle of *Ligia oceanica* lasts for three years according to Nicholls (1931). At least five broods of young are produced, and the average number of young per brood is 80. The time taken for the development of the young varies from 40 days in summer to 90 in winter, and although the greatest number of animals with brood pouches is found in spring, breeding occurs throughout the year. The greatest interval between moults occurs in full-grown males in winter, the shortest in young specimens during the summer. The growth rate was observed in a young specimen to average 1·3 mm increase in length and 0·5 mm in width per month. Copulation occurs after the appearance of the mature brood plates in the female. The ova are spawned about two days after the completion of the moult and, if unfertilised, remain viable for at least three days subsequent to their appearance in the brood pouch. Heeley (1941) found that the respective durations of the successive stages in the breeding processes, especially the embryonic and larval periods, whilst varying in different species are more or less constant for each particular species. These periods range from an average of 21½ days embryonic and 3 days larval period in *Philoscia muscorum* to an average of 64½ days embryonic (in first brood) and 9 days larval period in *Porcellio dilatatus*. In these species the breeding phase ranges from an average of 36 days in *Ph. muscorum* to 84 days in *P. dilatatus*. The average ratios of the larval period to the embryonic period of development in the brood pouch, in different species, increases approximately in proportion to the average numerical size of the broods.

The gravidity period for *Armadillidium vulgare* in Michigan averages 43 days at normal temperatures, according to Hatchett (1947). For *Cylisticus convexus* it varies from 44 to 62 days and averages 53 days, while *Porcellio scaber* carries its brood for an average of 44 days. Females of *P. (Tracheoniscus) rathkei* are gravid on an average for 39 days. Many females of *A. vulgare*, *C. convexus* and *P. scaber* have at least two broods per year, while *P. rathkei* usually reproduces only once. The size of the brood in *C. convexus* ranges from 10 to 70 with an average of 33 and the number of young in broods raised in the laboratory was 24. Under similar conditions *A. vulgare* raised 28, *P. scaber* 24 and *P. rathkei* 17 young.

In contrast in Dallas, Texas, *A. vulgare* has been found to produce from 29 to 79 young, whilst in Scotland, Collinge (1915) reported that individuals raised in captivity had broods of 50 to 150 with a maximum in one instance of 267. In France the number varies from 48 to 156.

When the young are ready to leave the brood pouch they become rather active and crawl about until they are released through an opening between the plates of which the pouch is composed. During their departure, the mother usually remains quiet or moves very slowly, keeping the first pair of legs immobile: the young emerge head first and climb down her first or second pair of legs. The majority of the young, after leaving their parent, are not very active and remain together in a group. Towards the end of the emergence period the female moves away, this time using all her legs, and their motion forces the few remaining young from the marsupium. If she is disturbed while carrying young in her brood pouch the female may, by rhythmical contraction of her body, force apart the pairs of plates forming the marsupium and release all her brood at once. A full brood pouch makes it necessary for the female to move around rather slowly and in a humped position: after the release of the brood she assumes her normal position and moves about more quickly.

BIBLIOGRAPHY

Identification

EDNEY, E. B. (1953) The woodlice of Great Britain and Ireland. A concise systematic monograph. *Proc. Linn. Soc. Lond.*, **164**, 49–98.

——(1954) *Synopses of the British Fauna, No. 9. British Woodlice*. London: Linn. Soc.

SARS, G. O. (1896–9) *An Account of the Crustacea of Norway*, **2**, (*Isopoda*). Bergen.

VAN NAME, W. G. (1936) The American land and freshwater Isopod Crustacea. *Bull. Amer. Mus. Nat. Hist.*, **71**, 1–535.

WEBB, W. M. and SILLEM, C. (1906) *The British Woodlice*. London.

Biology

BOER, P. J. DEN (1961) The ecological significance of activity patterns in the woodlouse *Porcellio scaber* Latr. (Isopoda). *Arch. Néerl. Zool.*, **14**, 283–409.

BRERETON, J. LE G. (1957) The distribution of woodland Isopods. *Oikos*, **8**, 85–106.

CLOUDSLEY-THOMPSON, J. L. (1952) Studies in diurnal rhythms, II. Changes in the physiological responses of the woodlouse *Oniscus asellus* to environmental stimuli. *J. Exp. Biol.*, **29**, 295–303.

——(1955) The biology of woodlice. *Discovery*, **16**, 248–51.

——(1956) Studies in diurnal rhythms, VII. Humidity responses and nocturnal activity in woodlice (Isopoda). *J. Exp. Biol.*, **33**, 576–82.

CLOUDSLEY-THOMPSON, J. L. (1958) The effect of wind upon the nocturnal emergence of woodlice and other terrestrial Arthropods. *Ent. Mon. Mag.*, **94**, 106–8, 184–5, 283–4.

CLOUDSLEY-THOMPSON, J. L. and GUPTA, M. (1959) *Ibid.*, **95**, 167–8.

COLLINGE, W. E. (1915) Some observations on the life history and habits of Isopoda (woodlice). *Scot. Nat.*, **24**, 299–307.

——(1935) Woodlice, their folklore and local names. *North W. Nat.*, **10**, 19–21.

EDNEY, E. B. (1954) Woodlice and the land habitat. *Biol. Rev.*, **29**, 185–219.

——(1954) *Idem. New Biology*, **17**, 41–57.

GORVETT, H. (1950) 'Weber's glands' and respiration in woodlice. *Nature, Lond.*, **166**, 115.

——(1956) Tegumental glands and terrestrial life in woodlice. *Proc. Zool. Soc. Lond.*, **126**, 291–314.

GUPTA, M. (1963) Seasonal variation in the humidity reaction of woodlice, *Oniscus asellus* L. and *Porcellio scaber* Latr. (Crustacea: Isopoda). *Proc. Nat. Inst. Sci. India*, **29**, 203–6.

HATCHETT, S. P. (1947) Biology of the Isopoda of Michigan. *Ecol. Monogr.*, **17**, 47–79.

HEELEY, W. (1941) Observations on the life-histories of some terrestrial Isopods. *Proc. Zool. Soc. Lond.* (B), **111**, 79–149.

HEWITT, C. G. (1907) Ligia. *L.M.B.C. Memoirs*, XIV, 1–37.

KUENEN, D. J. (1959) Excretion and waterbalance in some land-Isopods. *Ent. Exp. & Appl.*, **2**, 287–94.

KUENEN, D. J. and NOOTEBOOM, H. P. (1963) Olfactory orientation in some land-isopods (Oniscoidea, Crustacea). *Ibid.*, **6**, 113–42.

LEVI, H. W. (1965) An unusual case of mimicry. *Evolution*, **19**, 261–2.

NICHOLLS, A. G. (1931) Studies on *Ligia oceanica*, 1. A. Habitat and effect of change of environment on respiration. B. Observation on moulting and breeding. *J. Mar. Biol. Ass. U.K.*, **17**, 655–74.

PARIS, O. H. (1963) The ecology of *Armadillidium vulgare* (Isopoda: Oniscoidea) in California grassland: food, enemies and weather. *Ecol. Monogr.*, **33**, 1–22.

PERTTUNEN, V. (1961) Réactions de *Ligia italica* F. à la lumière et à l'humidité de l'air. *Vie et Milieu*, **12**, 219–59.

THOMPSON, W. R. (1934) The Tachinid parasites of woodlice. *Parasitology*, **26**, 378–448.

VANDEL, A. (1943) Essai sur l'origine, l'évolution et la classification des Oniscoidea (Isopodes terrestres). *Bull. biol.*, **30**, 1–136.

CHAPTER II

MILLIPEDES

Classification and distribution

The Diplopoda, commonly called millipedes, were formerly associated with the Chilopoda, Pauropoda and Symphyla in a class, the 'Myriapoda', which contained all the terrestrial Ar-

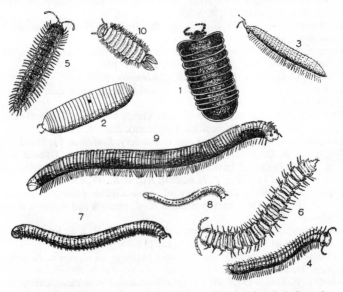

FIG. 5. Examples of millipede families: 1. Glomeridae, 2. Polyzoniidae, 3. Chordeumidae, 4. Craspedosomidae, 5. Polydesmidae, 6. Strongylosomidae, 7. Iulidae, 8. Blaniulidae, 9. Spirobolidae, 10. Polyxenidae. (Drawings not to scale.) (After various authors.)

thropods that were not Crustacea, Arachnida or Insecta, but they are now treated as a separate class. The name Diplopoda, which means 'double-footed', was given to them because in these animals most of the segments of the body are provided with two pairs of limbs, a condition arising from the confluence of two adjacent tergal plates. As in the Pauropoda and Symphyla, the reproductive organs have their apertures on the ventral side of the fore part of the body near the head, whereas in the Chilopoda these open on the last abdominal somite as they do in insects. Millipedes have a distinct head bearing a pair of short, unbranched antennae, at least two pairs of jaws and usually eyes. Spiracles leading into tubular tracheae open above the coxae of the legs and the dorsal plates of the segments are greatly developed as compared with the ventral.

The majority of the Diplopoda are included in the sub-class Chilognatha and their integument is hard and horny. Each double segment is composed typically of a vaulted or nearly circular tergum, one or two small pleural plates, two sternites and two pairs of legs. The tergites, pleurites and sternites may

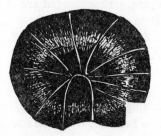

FIG. 6. The pill-millipede *Glomeris marginata*. (After Cloudsley-Thompson, 1956.)

all be movable, or they may coalesce into a solid ring, the significance of which will be considered later. There are only two pairs of mouthparts; the first are biting mandibles composed of two or three segments; the second pair is fused to form a broad plate or gnathochilarium. In the males one pair of legs is modified for mating purposes and its structure is a diagnostic character in many species.

The order Oniscomorpha contains millipedes whose body is short, broad, strongly convex above and flat below, and capable of being rolled into a ball as in some woodlice. There are from 11 to 13 tergal plates of which the second is enormously expanded at the sides while the last forms a rounded shield which fits against it and conceals the head when the animals are coiled up. In the males the last, or last two pairs of legs form claspers and the basal segments of the last pair are modified as sperm carriers. The family Glomeridae contains the common British pill-millipede, and a number of other small species found in Europe, America and Asia; while the Sphaerotheriidae have a southern distribution and occur in South Africa, Madagascar, southern Asia and Australasia. Some of them are of large size, surpassing a golf ball when rolled up.

The millipedes of the order Limacomorpha resemble the Oniscomorpha in general structure but are of small size, measuring not more than about one-quarter of an inch in length. The two families Glomeridesmidae and Zephroniodesmidae inhabit tropical America and tropical Asia respectively: nothing is known of their biology.

The third order, Colobognatha, and those that follow differ from the two preceding in that the last tergal plate encircles the anus which is closed below by a sternite and laterally by a pair of valves. The last pair of legs is unmodified in the male. The body is long, spirally coiled when at rest and contains a large and variable number of tergal plates which carry repugnatorial glands usually opening on tubercles or larger keel-like outgrowths. This order is found in all the warmer countries of the world where it is represented by several families, such as the

Pseudodesmidae, Platydesmidae, Polyzoniidae and Siphono-
phoridae, which exhibit a progressive reduction of the mandibles. In *Siphonophora* spp. the mouth opens at the tip of a
long, pointed, sucking and piercing beak formed by the labrum
and gnathochilarium, the mandibles within it being greatly
reduced. The only British member of the Colobognatha is
Polyzonium germanicum which has been found on the chalk
downs of Kent and Surrey. It is a bizarre form with semi-
suctorial mouthparts and can be readily identified in collec-
tions from the fact that when preserved in alcohol it is convex
dorsally and flat or concave ventrally.

The members of the order Ascospermophora have 26 to 32
segments. The tergal plates coalesce with the pleura, but the
sternites are free. In this feature they contrast with all other
Chilognatha except the Oniscomorpha. The tergites are provided with three pairs of symmetrically placed bristles and are
usually keel-shaped or carinate at the sides, but have no stink
glands. There is a pair of spinning papillae on the last tergal
plate. The order is represented by several families, of which the
Chordeumidae, Brachychaeteumidae and Craspedosomidae
are found typically in Europe and North America in the northern hemisphere, while the Heterochordeumidae range from
tropical Asia to New Zealand in the southern hemisphere.
The British forms are small, pale animals and include species
of *Brachychaeteuma*, *Microchordeuma*, *Craspedosoma rawlinsi*
which is more richly coloured and has lateral tergal expansions
like those of the Polydesmidae, and *Polymicrodon polydesmoides*, which usually inhabits the leafy floor of deciduous woodlands.

The flat-backed millipedes of the order Proterospermophora
have 19 or 20 tergal plates welded with the pleura and sternites
to form solid rings usually provided with lateral shelf-like
carinae. In this, they differ from other flat-backed forms

(Brachychaetumidae). There are no eyes, no spinning papillae on the last tergal plate, and the pores of the repugnatorial glands when these are present are borne on the lateral carinae. The members of this order belong to several families such as the Polydesmidae, Cryptodesmidae and Strongylosomidae, and are referred to a vast number of genera and species found in all the countries of the world. Some of the tropical species are large reaching a length of about six inches, and may be brightly coloured. The British fauna includes a number of species of Polydesmidae of which *Polydesmus angustus* is the most common, a doubtful record of *Eumastigonodesmus bonci* (family Mastigonodesmidae) and some representatives of the family Strongylosomidae. These include *Macrosternodesmus palicola*, the smallest British Diplopod, *Ophiodesmus albonanus* and *Oxidus* [*Paradesmus*] *gracilis* which is found in greenhouses all over the country.

The Lysiopetalidae, which are usually regarded as a separate sub-order from the previous families which are grouped together in the sub-order Polydesmoidea, are not represented in the British faunal list. These animals are found in Europe, Asia Minor and North Africa and have a great and variable number of tergal plates, most of which are provided with repugnatorial glands. The anterior pair of legs of the seventh segment is again modified, as sperm carriers however, and the seminal ducts perforate the basal segments of the second pair. Some species of *Lysiopetalum* may reach four or five inches in length.

The last order of Chilognatha is the Opisthospermophora, the members of which have a large and variable number of cylindrical tergal plates all of which, except for a few at the anterior end, are provided with repugnatorial glands. In number of species, genera and families, the order surpasses all other orders of the Chilognatha. The families are usually grouped into three sub-orders, the first of which includes the Stemmiulidae which are found in the tropics of Asia, Africa and America. The second contains the families Iulidae, Blaniulidae, which are represented in Britain by many species and genera, and the Spirostreptidae, which is abundant in the tropics and contains some of the largest millipedes in the world. The third sub-order includes the Spirobolidae which are also widely distributed in tropical regions and are represented by numerous genera and species, some of which rival the largest species of *Spirostreptus* in size.

The sub-class Pselaphognatha contains a single widely distributed order, Penicillata, comprising the family Polyxenidae and two genera *Polyxenus* and *Lophoproctus*. These are minute millipedes having a soft integument without horny plates but richly provided with rows and tufts of peculiarly shaped bristles. The mouthparts are complicated and appear to consist of four pairs. The body is composed of eleven somites of which the first four carry a single pair of legs, the next four two pairs and the ninth one pair, the last two segments being legless. Of the thirteen pairs of legs none is modified as gonopods. One species, *Polyxenus lagurus*, occurs in Great Britain.

General behaviour

From a study of the locomotory mechanisms and associated structures of a series of millipedes representing the major subdivisions of the Diplopoda, Manton (1954) has shown that the evolution of the class has been related to the development of a marked ability to push by the motive force of the legs. By this means the animals achieve either head-on burrowing into leaf mould, or push with the dorsal surface of the back into splits in wood, spaces under bark and other specialised habitats. The habit of curling the body into a protective spiral has been a second factor of major evolutionary importance. The necessary power for this pushing is achieved by the use of gaits in which the backstroke of the limbs is of very much longer duration than the forward stroke. These gaits require the presence of very many legs to each metachronal wave and this has been achieved by the evolution of numerous diplo-segments. Although moderate fleetness has been evolved many times, particularly in the Colobognatha and Polydesmoidea, fast gaits usually appear to be of lesser significance to millipedes than the slow, powerful gaits. Some species of Iulidae can on occasion make use of an unusual escape reaction. Instead of curling up, they writhe the body in a series of undulating flexions, wriggling rapidly through the grass or vegetation without using their feet at all (Fryer, 1957, etc.).

This habit appears to be an incidental accomplishment, however, and has not been of evolutionary significance. More important is the ability to climb smooth rock surfaces at any angle, found in *Polyzonium germanicum* and among the other Colobognatha, which are also adapted for pushing in stony places. This climbing habit necessitates a powerful grip by the opposite legs of a pair and possibly the use of adhesive coxal sacs when the animal is at rest. Various specialisations exist for strengthening the skeleton and for resisting telescoping at the inter-ring joints (Manton, 1954). This may well be the explanation for the unusual solidity of the millipede cuticle which is hardened not only by phenolic tanning as in insects and Arachnids, but also by the deposition of calcium as in the Crustacea (Cloudsley-Thompson, 1950b).

From a physiological point of view dependence upon moist and humid surroundings is one of the most important factors in the lives of millipedes, as of woodlice, centipedes and other myriapods. For example, it has been shown that *Oxidus* [*Paradesmus*] *gracilis*, a tropical species widely distributed in glasshouses in temperate regions, and the 'spotted snake millipede'

Blaniulus guttulatus, are stimulated by drought and come to rest only in moist places (Cloudsley-Thompson, 1951c). Under the influence of desiccation the animals show positive geotaxis and move deeper into the soil. Although the reactions of millipedes to moisture are far more marked than are their responses to the humidity of the atmosphere, Shelford (1913) has shown that *Fontaria corrugata* is repelled by dry air and more recently Perttunen (1953) has found that whereas *O. gracilis* is very sensitive to differences at the higher end of the humidity range, *Schizophyllum sabulosum*, which has a much lower rate of water-loss, particularly in summer, tends initially to move towards dry air and the reaction is gradually reversed to moist as desiccation proceeds. Orientation is entirely 'kinetic' or non-directional, speed is greater in dry air than in moist, and in an experimental chamber in which a choice of humidities is provided, both the time spent and the distance covered are greater on the moist side. In this species females that are just about to start egglaying show a reversal of their humidity reaction and there is then a clear and intense response to moisture (Perttunen, 1955). In a similar way, during the summer, *Polyzonium germanicum* walks on the under surface of smooth chalk boulders, where it may remain for hours or days hanging on 'in a chiton-like manner with neither head, antennae or legs exposed', but during the winter it penetrates into damp and compact vegetable matter and leaf mould, frequently deep in moss, where it remains curled up for weeks without moving. It is then difficult to find despite its bright orange colour (Manton, 1954).

The response of millipedes to moisture has some economic importance for, under conditions of drought, they may be forced to attack growing crops for the sake of water. After some years' research on the physiology and ecology of these animals, the writer concluded that outbreaks of the 'spotted snake millipede' tend to be stimulated by a dry spell following a period suitable to the reproduction of the species when the soil is damp, undisturbed and rich in humus. It was shown experimentally that humus and rotting substances have a texture which is preferred by millipedes to that of living plant tissues, and that the animals are attracted to dilute concentrations of sugars.

No doubt a moist season combined with the use of farmyard manure or the growing of some crop producing a considerable amount of humus will engender a great increase in the numbers of millipedes in the soil, particularly if the ground is not disturbed by ploughing, etc. They may be beneficial at this stage in aiding the breakdown of the humus, but if the following season is dry, even for a short spell, they may be compelled to attack crops for the sake of moisture. Once an attack has been initiated, a return to their normal diet of humus and decomposing matter is most unlikely, due to the attraction of sugars in the plant sap. It is unlikely that damage by millipedes to crops with tough exteriors such as potatoes and mangolds can ever be primary, for not only do their weak mouthparts prevent them from gaining access, but in addition they are not attracted to unbroken skins of potatoes, only to cut surfaces. Once an entrance has been achieved, however, through mechanical damage or the bites of wire-worms and other pests, the millipedes will eat out the entire centre of a potato and the damage they cause is often followed by fungal attack (Cloudsley-Thompson, 1950a). Furthermore, the fact that single potatoes have been found containing over a hundred *Blaniulus guttulatus* of all ages while the remainder of the crop was unharmed shows that they must have been attracted to a damaged tuber and could not have bred there.

Millipedes tend to avoid the light, but with the exception of a directed response or 'taxis' away from light in those forms that possess eyes and a response to gravity (which of course cannot be other than directed since the stimulus is constant) the behaviour reactions of millipedes are entirely non-directional. *Oxidus gracilis* and *Blaniulus guttulatus* are without eyes but they

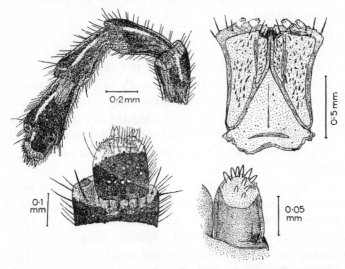

FIG. 7. Sense organs of the millipede *Oxidus gracilis*. Left, antenna and, below, the seventh and eighth segments more highly enlarged to show peg and cone sensillae. Right, gnathochilarium or lower lip with one of the palps more highly magnified to show peg-organs. (After Cloudsley-Thompson, 1951.)

possess a dermal light sense. When illuminated they crawl around until by chance they find themselves in darkness where they come to rest. Their temperature reactions fall into three categories. There is a general metabolic effect upon the speed of locomotion and duration of the spiral reflex and a kinetic 'preference' for temperatures about 15° C, while sudden drops of temperature engender intense locomotory activity. Airborne odours are apparently not detected, but millipedes respond to sugars by means of taste sense organs on their antennae and mouthparts (Cloudsley-Thompson, 1951c). As they walk about, millipedes steadily tap the surface over which they are moving with the tips of their antennae and no doubt constantly test its nature by means of the sensory hairs and chemo-receptive sensillae referred to.

Although to millipedes, as to woodlice and to the other myriapods, humidity is the most important factor of the environment, these animals are not able to find their way directly to damp places: instead, they are merely repelled by drought. Nevertheless, this stereotyped and curiously negative behaviour is surprisingly effective in preventing them from wandering away from their normal habitats: but it does raise the problem of how dispersal can take place and new habitats become colonised.

There are a number of cases on record of millipedes, sometimes accompanied by centipedes, and woodlice migrating in vast armies. Occasionally they have crossed railways and been squashed in such numbers that locomotives have been impeded and sand has had to be strewn on the lines before their driving wheels would grip. At other times cattle have refused to graze on invaded pastures, wells have been filled with drowned corpses and workmen cultivating the fields have become nauseated and dizzy from the odour of millipedes crushed by their hoes. However, such mass migrations are of rare occurrence and local in extent, so that their net effect on distribution is probably negligible.

The subject of migration in myriapods has been reviewed by Cloudsley-Thompson (1949b; 1951a) and it has been suggested that although certain aspects of the phenomenon are still not explained, the evidence lends support to the hypothesis that mass migration is merely an extreme case of the more familiar sudden attacks on crops due to extremely favourable local conditions, followed by drought and possibly accompanied by abnormal physiological conditions of reproduction.

An explanation of the problem of how dispersal can take place has been suggested as a result of recent work in which it has been shown that millipedes are markedly nocturnal and show a diurnal cycle of rhythmic activity. In *O. gracilis* and *B. guttulatus* this is primarily a response to light and darkness, but is also correlated with the stimulus of falling temperature in the evening. Aktograph experiments on two large West African species of millipedes have demonstrated an endogenous diurnal rhythm independent of fluctuating light and temperature and persisting in *Ophistreptus* spp. up to nineteen days. Locomotory activity is stimulated by increases or decreases of temperature, and it is probable that in tropical forms temperature fluctuations are of primary importance in the initiation of diurnal rhythms. Perhaps in their natural gloomy habitat in tropical forests, light is an insignificant environmental factor (Cloudsley-Thompson, 1951b). Thus it is at night that millipedes, like other myriapods and woodlice, are able to disperse themselves and overcome the restrictions inherent in the physiology of their integuments.

Blower (*in* Kevan, 1955)* has suggested that millipedes are distributed at various depths in the soil according to their water-relations and body forms. Nematophora and Polydesmoidea which are most susceptible to desiccation and wetting tend to inhabit thick leaf-litter which is proof against flood and drought, while many of the Iulidae and Blaniulidae penetrate deeply into the soil. He also makes the interesting suggestion that calcium ions in the soil water may exert a beneficial effect by limiting the permeability of the epidermis.

Some other aspects of the biology of the Diplopoda are worthy of mention. Millipedes not infrequently occur as guests in the nests of ants and termites. In Britain three species,

Blaniulus guttulatus, Proteroiulus fuscus and *Polyxenus lagurus*, are frequently myrmecophilous (Donisthorpe, 1927)* and in the tropics several species have been seen accompanying columns of army ants on the march. A number of species are cavernicolous and have become adapted in varying degrees to

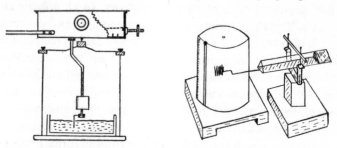

FIG. 8. Two types of aktograph apparatus suitable for use with millipedes, each consisting of an arena or box pivoted on a knife-edge along its median transverse axis. Any movement of an animal along the longitudinal axis tips the arena and is recorded by a lever balanced by an adjustable counterpoise and writing on a revolving smoked drum. (After Gunn and Kennedy, 1937, and D'Aguillar, 1952.)

a troglodytic existence. There is extensive literature on the subject.

Reports of luminous millipedes are few. One of the most striking examples is *Luminodesmus sequoiae,* a large and handsome species measuring some 40 mm in length, that inhabits the Sequoia National Forest in California. Luminescence first appears on hatching. It is continuous, under no voluntary control. Its source apparently lies in the deeper layers of the integument. Attempts to demonstrate the classical 'luciferin-luciferase' activity in this species have been unsuccessful (Davenport, Wootton and Cushing, 1952).

Finally there are a number of cases on record of pseudoparasitism by millipedes in the alimentary tract of man (p. 60).

Food and feeding habits

Millipedes are vegetarian and feed on a wide range of plant substances, although on account of their weak mouthparts many species tend to prefer soft or decomposing tissues (Brade-Birks, 1930). They have also been recorded as eating dead worms, molluscs, insects and vertebrates. As already mentioned, a number of species are well-known agricultural and glasshouse pests. Of these, without doubt the worst offender in temperate climates is the 'spotted snake millipede', *Blaniulus guttulatus*, which has long been regarded as a pest of sugar beet, potatoes, mangolds, oats, wheat, strawberries and other agricultural crops and fruit. It has been shown that outbreaks of this species often tend to be stimulated by a dry spell following a period suitable to the reproduction of the species, when the soil is damp, undisturbed and rich in humus. They usually occur on medium or heavy soil and are inhibited or destroyed by extreme drought. Breeding is probably inhibited by moderately dry weather. The species may be beneficial in aiding the breakdown of humus, but is a potential danger to growing crops and may even attack potatoes and mangolds if wireworms and other agricultural pests are present to make an initial entry (Cloudsley-Thompson, 1950a). Schubart (1942) has given a comprehensive bibliography of the myriapods and their relation to agriculture, and this has been supplemented by Remy (1950a), while Brade-Birks (1930) has studied the economic status of the British Diplopoda.

Although it has long been assumed that myriapods possess powers of taste and various antennary and gnathochilarial structures have been regarded as gustatory sense organs, the ability of millipedes to react to contact chemical stimuli has only once or twice been tested experimentally. In 1943, Lyford published an interesting account of his experiments on the palatability of various forest leaves to *Cylindroiulus londinensis*. It was found that the palatability of leaves from the same tree and from adjacent trees of the same species showed some variability but not enough to mask the difference in palatability between species. In general, the most palatable leaves had a high calcium content while the unpalatable leaves had not. More recently it has been found that *Iulus* and *Cylindroiulus* spp. eat quantities of newly fallen leaves from the surface of a mixed beech forest floor, and even more of the leaves that are a year older. *Iulus* spp. eat more oak than of any other type of leaf, *Cylindroiulus* spp. more pine. It has also been shown that *Oxidus gracilis* and *Blaniulus guttulatus* are attracted to glucose and sucrose with a threshold of about 0·5 gm/litre, but there is no attraction to asparagine or starch. As already mentioned, the antennal and gnathochilarial basiconic sensillae are the sensory receptors for taste stimuli; millipedes do not respond to airborne odours (Cloudsley-Thompson, 1951c).

Enemies

Millipedes, on occasion, are eaten by a wide range of predatory animals. These include spiders, some species of which will feed reluctantly on the common black *Tachypodoiulus niger*, *Oxidus gracilis* and other small forms; ants, fishes, amphibians, reptiles, mammals and birds (Cloudsley-Thompson, 1949). Of these, only toads and birds feed on millipedes to an appreciable degree. Millipedes form a constant article of diet of the American toad *Bufo lentiginosus*, as many as seventy-seven having been found in one stomach, and 10% by bulk of the food of this species is composed of millipedes. The British *B. vulgaris*, which will eat almost anything it can catch, will readily devour millipedes, which are also eaten by frogs and salamanders. Millipedes comprise a proportion of the food of

many species of birds, but as far as is known, none equals the
starling in their destruction. In America millipedes average up
to 11·71 % of this bird's yearly diet. In April they form 54·69 %,
in May 42·19 % and in June 23·66 %. After a falling off in the
later summer months they again rise to 7·64 % in October. The
fact that in April 119 of 132 adult birds examined, in May 133
of 140 and in June 146 of 215, had eaten millipedes, gives an
idea of the persistence with which starlings must search for
such food. Fifteen of the birds taken in April were found to
have eaten nothing else, and nine tenths of the food of fourteen others was composed of millipedes.

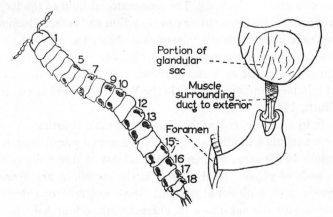

FIG. 9. Distribution of repugnatorial glands on the segments of
a millipede, *Oxidus gracilis*. Right, section of an individual gland.
(After Weber, 1882.)

To most animals, however, millipedes are rendered somewhat unpalatable on account of their tough integument and by
the irritant exudates secreted by the repugnatorial glands of
the Colobognatha, Proterospermophora and Opisthospermophora. The structure of these glands is very similar in all three
orders. They are sac-like in shape and each discharges into a

lumen which in turn leads to the foramen or opening. Though the glands themselves cannot be compressed, their openings can be regulated by special muscles, while other muscles nearby exert considerable pressure when the animal moves suddenly. In most cases the secretion is exuded fairly slowly from the pores of the glands but in some of the larger tropical forms it can be discharged to a considerable distance in the form of a fine jet or spray.

The maximum recorded achievement was a double salvo from a *Rhinocricus lethifer* in Haiti which sent its discharge 28 inches on one side and 33 on the other, the droplets falling fanwise around the body. The repugnatorial fluid of the large tropical species has a strong caustic action and causes blackening on contact with the human skin. Later the affected part peels, leaving a wound which heals only very slowly. It is dangerous to the eyes and is responsible for numerous cases of blindness among chickens in the West Indies and elsewhere (Burtt, 1947).

In its smell and colour the secretion of most Opisthospermophora resembles iodine and stains the fingers a purplish-brown colour in the same manner as this substance. The chief compounds of physiological interest in the secretions are hydrocyanic acid, iodine and quinine. Small amounts of chlorine which give the substance its characteristic odour have been determined experimentally. It has been suggested that the disinfecting properties of the chlorine and hydrocyanic acid may assist in keeping the animal free from bacteria and other micro-organisms.

In contrast the Proterospermophora rarely secrete visible quantities of odoriferous substance, although if a number of Polydesmid millipedes be gathered together, a distinct almond-like smell becomes discernible. The natives of central Mexico grind up *Polydesmus ricinus* with various plants to make a poison for their arrows and the large *Lysiopetalum foetidissimum* takes its name from the obnoxious smell of the secretion from its stink glands. Many of the tropical species exhibit patterns of strongly contrasted warning colours which are clearly associated with their poisonous nature. The majority of the Colobognatha do not appear to secrete repugnatorial fluids, but species of *Polyzonium* produce a whitish substance that may have an odour of camphor and is probably again a deterrent to predatory enemies.

The Oniscomorpha and Limacomorpha curl up into a ball when disturbed and members of the other orders form a more or less compact spiral. These defensive reactions not only render the animals less vulnerable to their enemies, but also are effective in reducing water-loss by evaporation when the millipedes are in dry surroundings (Toye, 1966). They have been a factor of major evolutionary importance (Manton, 1954).

The minute Pselaphognatha are covered with tufts of peculiar hairs like small pin-cushions which resemble the urticating hairs of some Lepidopterous caterpillars. Like them they are hollow, very easily detached from the body and bear a number of retroverted barbs or processes near their tips and along their axes. These and the small size of the animals constitute their only means of defence.

The commonest parasites of millipedes are Gregarinidea. Thus, it has been found that of 165 *Iulus* and *Paraiulus* spp. examined, 158 were parasitised by Gregarines, 26 out of 32 *Polydesmus* sp. and 6 out of 16 *Lysiopetalum* sp. The parasites had no seasonal cycle and all stages were found together. No doubt the Iulidae were so persistently parasitised on account of their gregarious habits and diet of rotting wood and vegetable matter. *Lysiopetalum* spp. which live under stones in drier places and are somewhat solitary are far less parasitised. After Gregarinidea, Coccidia and Flagellates are the most numerous parasites of myriapods. It is probable that a high degree of tolerance has been reached between parasite and host, and unlikely that the former do any harm. Most of the millipedes from the Amazon basin are infested with nematodes and these parasites are by no means uncommon elsewhere; several Diplopoda are intermediate hosts of Cestodes of the related families Dilipididae and Hymenolipididae (Remy, 1950b). No doubt phytophagous animals which consume a certain amount of soil with their food are especially liable to infection by these animals.

Numerous mites of two ecologically separate and systematically unrelated groups are found on millipedes. In the first, which includes Mesostigmata and Acaridae, the myriapods are used merely for transport (phoresy)[†] while the second group, all Mesostigmata, includes more or less intermittent commensals which live freely, not attached to their host and feed on detritus. Evans (1955) has reviewed the Laelaptidae parasitic on myriapods. Sometimes the body of a sick millipede may become covered with a multitude of little mites but usually these parasites are confined to the head, front legs and gonopods whence they cannot easily be removed. The adults of one species of mite found on Iulidae in Natal and Zululand feed upon the liquid secreted by the repugnatorial glands of their host.

An interesting case of aggressive parasitism of a millipede by a fly of the family Phoridae which battled with a huge black *Iulus* sp. for several hours has been recorded, and larvae of another species of Phoridae, *Megaselia juli*, have been found in a number of species of *Iulus* and *Spirobolus*. Planidium larvae of parasitic Hymenoptera have been found on *Gymnostreptus parasitarius* in Brazil and a larval Lampyrid beetle introduces itself through the anus into the posterior intestine

† See discussion of phoresy on p. 129.

of *Pachyiulus* spp. (Remy, 1950b). It is probable that parasites play a negligible part in controlling the density of millipede populations.[†] Only three classes parasitise them to an appreciable degree: Acari, which are little more than commensals, Sporozoa and Nematoda which probably cause little inconvenience to their host.

Reproduction and life cycle

There is a Malay belief that if the vertebra of a fish is kept under a mattress for some time it becomes a centipede, and that the strands which are found between the pulp and the rind of a plantain become millipedes if they are securely bottled up and kept in a dark corner!

The paired genital openings of millipedes are situated on the third segment just behind, or on the second pair of legs. In the female, the orifice is surrounded by two sclerotised pieces, one forming the bursa, arranged like the two shells of a mussel with the hinge directed posteriorly and the second, the operculum, covering the gape of the two valves of the bursa. The whole ensemble is termed the vulva and is of diagnostic value. In the male the genital openings may or may not be developed into paired or single penes. The accessory genitalia consist of one or both appendages of the seventh segment which are modified to form intromittent organs called gonopods, except in the Oniscomorpha and Limacomorpha where the hindermost legs serve this function. These organs are the only criteria for accurate diagnosis: in some species they are retracted within the cavity of the seventh segment. Before copulation takes place the male, by flexing his anterior segments, 'charges' his gonopods from the opening on the third body segment.

[†] See discussion of density-dependent and density-independent factors on p. 176.

From the gonopods the spermatic fluid is transferred to the vulvae of the female; fertilisation is internal.

During copulation the positions assumed by the male and female are somewhat similar in all species. The following description applies to *Oxidus gracilis* in particular. The ventral surface of the posterior 13 or 14 body somites of the male is parallel and dorsal to the anterior 10 or 11 body somites of the female and the legs of the male on these somites are bent closely

FIG. 10. Millipedes of the family Polydesmidae in copulation. The male is below. (After Seifert, 1932.)

around the female. In the region of the eighth, ninth and tenth somites the body of the male is twisted half around the female so that his gonopods are in contact with her vulvae which open on the third body somite. The head and thorax of the male are directed anteriorly and bent over the head of the female which is held by his seven anterior pairs of legs. Bright light or handling usually causes a pair to separate, but if undisturbed copulation may occur several times and last for several hours (Causey, 1943).

The male *Polydesmus angustus* approaches the female from behind and runs along her back until her head is reached. Suddenly turning round towards her ventral surface, he seizes her gnathochilarium with his mandibles, retaining this hold until her body is for the most part of its length embraced in his broader grasp. It is interesting to note that a fertilised female, when touched on the anal segment by a male, immediately darts forward and refuses to be caught. The fertilised females in a collection can be readily recognised by touching lightly on the anal segment with a camelhair brush (Evans, 1910). In *Glomeris marginata* the male is much smaller than the female and copulation takes place by apposition of the pair in the head to tail position. In contrast to the Proterospermophora, copulation in the Oniscomorpha is brief, which may be correlated with the fact that egg-laying is an interrupted process and the female lays her eggs in small groups in several places, usually buried in loose soil and always under cover of moss or dead leaves. The British Opisthospermophora begin their breeding rather later in the year than do the Polydesmids.

In some species of millipedes the eggs are coated with earth and excrement and then left in crevices in the soil; in others a nest is constructed of soil particles that have been moistened with saliva. When completed, the nest has the shape of a hollow sphere. The inside is lined with dried excrement and is smooth and even, whereas the outside is rough and irregular. Sometimes the female does not leave the nest immediately, but remains for several days curled round it so tightly that she is difficult to remove (Foye, 1967).

When the female *Glomeris marginata* is about to lay she rolls over on her back and the little egg is passed backwards from segment to segment until it arrives at the end of the body. There it is held immediately over the anal region and the rectum is everted to a considerable extent so as to form a mobile pad holding a small quantity of very fluid excrement which is carefully plastered over the egg. When dry this forms a spherical chamber in which the egg lies freely. Occasionally two or three eggs are enclosed in one mass, but always in separate

compartments. In *Polydesmus angustus* and other Proterospermophora and Colobognatha, all the eggs are enclosed in a
common covering. The nest is like a thin-walled, dome-shaped
tent surmounted by a narrow tubular chimney. It is built on
some firm substratum—a stone, a leaf, the inside of an acorn
cup, or the inner surface of a piece of bark—and is constructed
with the mobile surface of the extroverted rectum. The female
first gnaws a small cavity on the surface on which she intends
to lay. Then she bends herself into a circle and walks round
and round, leaving a rapidly drying blob of excrement as she
goes, until the concave spot is surrounded by a rampart, the
circumference of which is slightly greater than the length of
her body. When the nest has reached about two-thirds its full
height the eggs are laid. The female lies across her nest and the
eggs drop in one after the other, sticking together as they fall.
The nest is then roofed over and the chimney completed with
the aid of the everted rectum and the supra-anal process which
possesses six tactile hairs. When the nest is finished the female
does not leave it immediately but remains coiled around it for
about a week. She covers it with bits of leaves and wisps of
grass and will replace them over and over again if they are
removed (Evans, 1910). *Oxidus gracilis* females, however, deposit their eggs in small rough cavities from 3 to 15 mm below
the surface of the soil, but do not construct brooding chambers
nor remain with them during the incubation period.

In contrast, most of the Opisthospermophora construct a
very crude nest which is mainly built from the inside, only the
top being laid on from the outside. The female burrows into
loose soil until she comes to a firm foundation, usually a stone,
where she proceeds to make a dome-shaped clearing, the shap-
ing being done by her jaws. This space is then plastered from
the inside with liquid excrement by means of the everted rectum, the animal meanwhile having to assume some very awk-

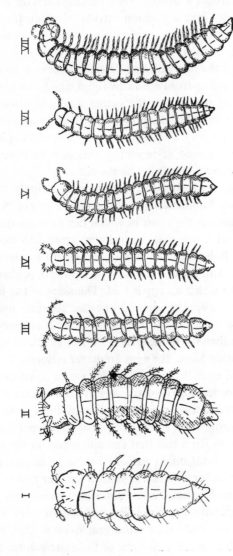

Fig. 11. Stages in the development of a millipede of the family Strongylosomidae. (After Seifert, 1932.)

ward positions during the process. On emerging from the recess she pushes her way into a position astride the open top and lays her eggs. After closing the hole she pays no further attention to her nest (Evans, 1910).

The function of the nest building described above is to protect the eggs and young from attack by fungi which are an ever present menace, as they are to the young stages of woodlice, and also from the cannibalistic proclivities of the males of the species. In a similar way, *Polymicrodon polydesmoides* spins a silk tent for the purpose of moulting and also to cover its cluster of eggs. After a moult it eats the silk.

The Blaniulidae lay their large, elongated eggs singly, however. The Spirobolid millipede *Arctobolus marginatus* of North America manufactures the cases in which her eggs are individually enclosed with material regurgitated from her mouth. The moist lump is held by the legs of the eighth to eleventh pairs and shaped with the convex front of the head. A shallow bowl is made into which an egg is laid. The sides of the bowl are then drawn up over the egg and kneaded together until a perfect sphere is produced. The completed pellet is dropped by the mother, who then starts the next (Loomis, 1933). In many species, on the other hand, the eggs are never covered.

The number of eggs laid by millipedes varies considerably among different orders and also among different species of the same order. There is a tendency for the size of the egg to decrease in direct proportion as the number of young per brood increases. It follows from this that the differences in the total amount of yolk contained in various broods, whether they contain a large number of small eggs or a smaller number of large eggs tends to be evened out. *Polyxenus lagurus* only lays from 10 to 20 eggs with 4 to 8 per nest, but species of *Polydesmus* lay between 100 and 200, *Oxidus gracilis* up to 300, *Iulus* spp. lay 60 to 100 or more, and some of the Spirobolidae may also lay up to 300 eggs. The maximum recorded clutch of *Arctobolus marginatus* in Washington was 261.

Incubation of the eggs may take several weeks before hatching occurs. This process is assisted by a strong conical egg-tooth situated, in the Opisthospermophora, on the middle of the head.

Glomeris marginata seeks no special protection during moulting, but does so in some loose earth or on the surface under moss or dead leaves. The case of both Proterospermophora and Opisthospermophora is very different. The millipedes of these orders build moulting chambers which are essentially similar to their nests. If the moulting chamber is damaged so that other millipedes can enter, the helpless animal that has just shed its skin is almost invariably eaten by the invaders. After moulting it is customary for millipedes to eat their cast exuvium, thereby restoring lost supplies of calcium: further development does not proceed normally unless they do so.

All Diplopoda are anamorphic and the larvae pass through a number of moults during each of which the number of legs and post-cephalic somites is increased. Additional legs and somites are added in the embryonic region between the anal somite and the one that was last formed. Colobognatha, Ascospermophora and Proterospermophora pass through seven larval stadia, in each of which the number of leg pairs and somites is constant for the species or the group. The Opisthospermophora also normally pass through seven larval stadia but after the first or second the number of legs and somites is not constant for the species. In the Oniscomorpha, development is hemianamorphic: a series of anamorphic moults is followed by three moults which are unaccompanied by increases in the number of legs and somites (Verhoeff, 1928). The youngest larvae have three pairs of legs, the next stage usually seven, and at each subsequent moult some four more segments each with eight pairs of legs are added on. The time required for moulting increases with each succeeding ecdysis from a few hours for the first to several weeks for the last.

Verhoeff (1933b, 1939) has shown that in some species of Iulid millipedes that live in cold climates the mature males may regress to an interpolated intercalary form lacking the highly differentiated gonopods of the mature animal. In the life of an individual there may be as many as four periods of sexual maturity alternating with three interpolated stages. During the interpolated period, growth continues with an increase in the number of segmental glands. This cycle is related to season, functional males appearing in late winter and the interpolated forms in summer. It is a method of prolonging life through dry or cold seasons, and enables adult males to live for two or more years. The activity of the testis automatically declines at the onset of the moult which initiates the interpolated stage and this appears to be correlated with the fact that the complicated gonopods are moulted only with great difficulty. The post-embryonic development of millipedes in a Devon oak wood has been described recently by Blower and Gabbutt (1964).

BIBLIOGRAPHY

Identification

ATTEMS, G. (1937) Myriapoda 3, Polydesmoidea 1. *Das Tierreich*, **68**, 1–300.
——(1938) *Idem.* 2, *Ibid.*, **69**, 1–487.
——(1940) *Idem.* 3, *Ibid.*, **70**, 1–577.
BLOWER, G. (1952) British millipedes with special reference to Yorkshire species. *Naturalist*, **1952**, 145–57.
BROLEMANN, H. W. (1935) Myriapodes. Diplopodes-Chilognathes 1. *Faune de France*, No. 29, 1–369, Paris.

CHAMBERLIN, R. V. (1943) On Mexican millipedes. *Bull. Univ. Utah.*, **34**, (7), 1–103.

LANG, J. (1954) Mnohonožky—Diplopoda. *Fauna Č.S.R.*, **2**, 1–183.

LATZEL, R. (1884) *Die Myriopoden der Oesterreichs-Ungarischen Monarchie, II. Die Symphylen Pauropoden und Diplopoden.* Wien.

LOHMANDER, H. (1925) Sveriges Diplopoder. *Göteb. Kongl. Vet. Handl.*, **30**, (2), 1–115.

SCHUBART, O. (1934) Tausendfüssler oder Myriapoda, 1. Diplopoda. *Tierw. Dents.*, **28**, 1–318

VERHOEFF, K. W. (1926–31) Diplopoda *in* H. G. BRONN'S *Klass. Ordn. Tierreichs*, **5**, II (2), 1–1072.

(*See also references under Chilopoda, Chap. III*)

Biology

BLOWER, J. G. and GABBUTT, P. D. (1964) Studies on the millipedes of a Devon oak wood. *Proc. Zool. Soc. Lond.*, **143**, 143–76.

BRADE-BIRKS, S. G. (1930) Notes on Myriapods, XXXIII. The economic status of Diplopoda Chilopoda and their allies. *J. S-E. Agric. Coll. Wye*, No. 27. 103–46.

BURTT, E. (1947) Exudate from millipedes, with particular reference to its injurious effects. *Trop. Dis. Bull.*, **44**, 7–12.

CAUSEY, N. B. (1943) Studies on the life history and the ecology of the hothouse millipede, *Orthomorpha gracilis* (C. L. Koch, 1847). *Amer. Midl. Nat.*, **29**, 670–82.

CLOUDSLEY-THOMPSON, J. L. (1949a) The enemies of Myriapods. *Naturalist*, **1949**, 137–41.

—— (1949b) The significance of migration in Myriapods. *Ann. Mag. Nat. Hist.*, (12), **2**, 947–62.

—— (1950a) Economics of the 'spotted snake millipede' *Blaniulus guttulatus* (Bosc.). *Ibid.*, (12), **3**, 1047–57.

—— (1950b) The water relations and cuticle of *Paradesmus gracilis* (Diplopoda: Strongylosomidae). *Quart. J. Micr. Sci.*, **91**, 453–64.

—— (1951a) Supplementary notes on Myriapoda. *Naturalist*, **1951**, 16–17.

—— (1951b) Studies in diurnal rhythms–1. Rhythmic behaviour in millipedes. *J. Exp. Biol.*, **28**, 165–72.

—— (1951c) On the responses to environmental stimuli, and the sensory physiology of millipedes (Diplopoda). *Proc. Zool. Soc. Lond.*, **121**, 253–77.

—— (1954) Problems of dispersal in some terrestrial Arthropods. *Advanc. Sci.*, **11**, 73–5.

DAVENPORT, D., WOOTTON, D. M. and CUSHING, J. E. (1952) The biology of the Sierra luminous millipede *Luminodesmus sequoiae* Loomis and Davenport. *Biol. Bull.*, **102**, 100–10.

EATON, T. H. Jr., (1943) Biology of a mull-forming millipede, *Apheloria coriacea* (Koch). *Amer. Midl. Nat.*, **29**, 713–23.

EVANS, G. O. (1955) A review of the Laelaptid paraphages of the Myriapoda with descriptions of three new species (Acarina: Laelaptidae). *Parasitology*, **45**, 352–68.

EVANS, T. J. (1910) Bionomical observations on some British millipedes. *Ann. Mag. Nat. Hist.*, (8), **6**, 284–91.

FRYER, G. (1957) Observations on some African millipedes. *Ann. Mag. Nat. Hist.*, (12), **10**, 47–51.

LOOMIS, H. F. (1933) Egg-laying and larval stages of a millipede. *Arctobolus marginatus* (Say) Cook, native at Washington. *J. Wash. Acad. Sci.*, **23**, 100–9.

LYFORD, W. H., Jr. (1943) The palatability of freshly fallen forest leaves to millipedes. *Ecology*, **24**, 252–61.

MANTON, S. M. (1954) The evolution of Arthropodan locomotory mechanisms—Part 4. The structure, habits and evolution of the Diplopoda. *J. Linn. Soc. (Zool.)*, **42**, 299–368.

PALMÉN, E. (1949) The Diplopoda of Eastern Fennoscandia. *Ann. Soc. Zool. Fenn. Vanamo*, **13**, (6), 1–54.

PERTTUNEN, V. (1953) Reactions of Diplopods to the relative humidity of the air. Investigations on *Orthomorpha gracilis*, *Iulus terrestris* and *Schizophyllum sabulosum*. *Ibid.*, **16**, (4), 1–69.

REMY, P. (1950a) Les myriapodes et les plantes cultivées (Bibliographie). *Bull. Soc. Linn. Lyon.*, **19**, 232–4.

—— (1950b) On the enemies of Myriapods. *Naturalist*, **1950**, 103–8.

SCHUBART, O. (1942) Os myriápodes e suas relações com a agricultua. Com uma bibliografia completa sobre o assunto. *Pap. Avul. Dep. Zool. S. Paulo*, **2**, 205–34.

SHELFORD, V. E. (1913) The reactions of certain animals to gradients of evaporating power of air. A study in experimental biology. *Biol. Bull.*, **25**, 79–120.

TOYE, S. A. (1966) Effect of desiccation on the behaviour of three species of Nigerian millipedes. *Ent. Exp. & Appl.*, **9**, 378-84.

—— (1967) Observations on the biology of three species of Nigerian millipedes. *J. Zool., Lond.*, **152**, 67-78.

VERHOEFF, K. W. (1930) Zur Geographie, Ökologie und Systematik sudalpenlandischer Chilognathen (116. Diplopoden—Aufsatz). *Z. Morph. Ökol. Tiere*, **18**, 575–668.

—— (1933a) Revolution bei Diplopoden. *Zool. Anz.*, **104**, 59–64.

—— (1933b) Wachstum und Lebensverlängerung bei Blaniuliden und über die Periodomorphose. *Z. Morph. Ökol. Tiere*, **27**, 732–49.

—— (1935) Zur Biologie der Spirostreptiden. *Zool. Anz.*, **109**, 288–92.

—— (1939) Wachstum und Lebensverlängerung bei Blaniuliden und über die Periodomorphose. II. Teil. *Z. Morph. Ökol. Tiere*, **36**, 21–40.

CHAPTER III

CENTIPEDES

Classification and distribution

Although the Chilopoda are a widely dispersed class, the biology of centipedes has attracted comparatively little attention from zoologists, who have tended to confine their attentions to the systematics of the group. In these animals, the body is divided into a variable number of somites, each of which is provided with a pair of limbs used for locomotion. The head bears a pair of multi-segmented antennae and three pairs of mouth-parts. The first of these post-oral appendages are toothed mandibles, the second are foliaceous maxillae, while the third are leg-like palps. Behind the head is the first segment of the body, known as the basilar segment. Its appendages are the maxillipedes or taxocognaths. These are poison-claws with which the prey is captured and killed. At the tips of their strong, piercing terminal segments are the orifices of the ducts of the paired venom-glands. Where present, the eyes are in the form of clusters of ocelli, except in the Scutigeromorpha which have compound eyes (see below). The number of legs varies from fifteen to over a hundred pairs, but however many there may be, the number is always odd. Each somite of the body is flattened when seen in cross-section and is composed externally of a dorsal plate or tergite and a ventral sternite united by pleural membranes with which the legs articulate

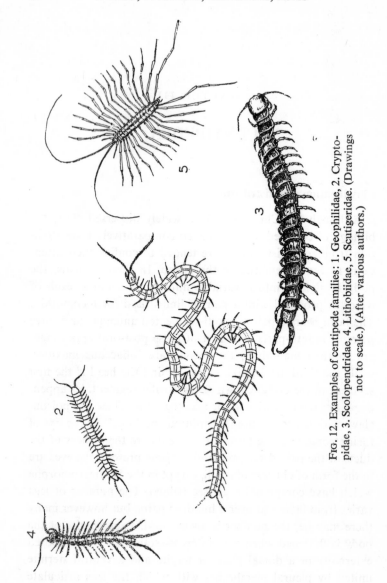

FIG. 12. Examples of centipede families: 1. Geophilidae, 2. Cryptopidae, 3. Scolopendridae, 4. Lithobiidae, 5. Scutigeridae. (Drawings not to scale.) (After various authors.)

and upon which the spiracles leading into the trachea usually open.

The class Chilopoda is sub-divided into five orders. The first of these, the Geophilomorpha, includes the long, worm-like centipedes with the pairs of legs varying in number from 31 to 177. The fore part of each somite is marked off from the hinder part by a distinct joint, there is a pair of spiracles on each

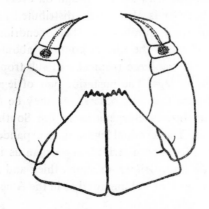

Fig. 13. Poison claws of a centipede showing position of poison glands and their ducts.

segment except the first and last, and the antennae are always composed of fourteen segments. There are a very large number of families in this order which has a wide distribution in all the warm and temperate countries of the world. Most of them are subterranean but a few are found under stones and seaweed below tide marks. The largest species, like the North African *Orya barbarica*, measure about six or seven inches in length, but most are only an inch or two long. The writer has recently discovered a smaller species of *Orya*, *O. almohadensis*, in central Tunisia which measures just over two inches when extended and is scarcely longer than the common British *Haplophilus subterraneus*.

The centipedes of the order Scolopendromorpha differ from the Geophilomorpha in never having more than 23 pairs of legs, while the segments of the antennae vary in number from 17 to 30. The somites are not markedly divided and the tergal plate of the basilar segment is fused with that of the first leg-bearing somite. Spiracles are not found on every segment of the body. This order is also widely distributed and includes two most important families, the Scolopendridae and the Cryptopidae, of which the former contains about 16 genera, including most of the large tropical and sub-tropical species having 21 pairs of legs. The posterior pair of legs is usually longer and stouter than the others, but may be modified as antenniform tactile sense-organs as in the South American genus *Newportia*. The terminal legs may be expanded and leaf-like at the end, forming a stridulating organ as in the large tropical African genus *Alipes*, or short, thick and armed with a piercing claw used for holding food as in the American genus *Theatops*.

Some of the tropical species of *Scolopendra* are commonly six or eight inches in length, while the largest, *S. gigantea* from tropical America, measures as much as a foot. Many of these are attractively coloured in the living state. For example, the South African *Rhysida afra* is a deep and striking shade of blue or blue with a greenish tinge, *S. morsitans* has green crossbars on a yellow background, while *S. cingulata* is a beautiful olive green. This species is distributed widely throughout the Mediterranean regions of Europe, North Africa and the Middle East, but varies considerably in size in different localities. African and Asiatic specimens may reach a length of 18 cm when fully extended and have a yellow body and blue hind legs. Unfortunately they all tend to fade to a uniform dull brown colour when preserved. *S. morsitans* and *S. subspinipes* have been transported all over the tropics by commerce, but are unable to establish themselves in temperate latitudes. Related genera are *Ethmostigmus*, which is abundant in Africa, and *Cormocephalus* which is equally abundant in both the Ethiopian and Indo-Australasian regions. Only three representatives of the order occur in the British Isles, namely *Cryptops hortensis, C. anomalans* and *C. parisi*. Of these, the most common is the orange-coloured *C. hortensis* frequently found in potting sheds and under the bark of trees, etc.

The order Craterostigmomorpha has been established for the centipedes of the genus *Craterostigmus* which is intermediate in many points between the Scolopendromorpha and the Lithobiomorpha, and, like many ancient and annectant types, occurs in Australasia. There are only 15 pairs of legs and sterna and the spiracles are reduced to seven pairs as in the Lithobiomorpha, but there are 21 tergal plates representing the somites of the leg-bearing segments of the Scolopendromorpha. Unfortunately nothing is known of the biology of these animals.

The Lithobiomorpha are distinguished from the Scolopendromorpha by having a body composed of 15 leg-bearing somites, of which only six or seven possess spiracles, the terga of those without spiracles being greatly reduced in size. The basal segments of the legs are somewhat enlarged and the antennal segments number from 20 to 50. The centipedes of this order are referred to three families: Lithobiidae, Henicopidae and Cermatobiidae. They are mostly of small size, the largest being the continental *Lithobius fasciatus*. Several species of *Lithobius* are common in England, the best known being the large *L. forficatus*. Nearly as large is *L. variegatus* which is easily recognised by its attractive variegated colour pattern. This species is of interest because it is found only in the Channel Islands and Britain, where it occurs mostly in damp woodlands. We also have one species of Henicopidae, *Lamyctes fulvicornis*, a small form distinguishable from *Lithobius* spp. by the presence of a single pair of ocelli instead of many, and by the presence of spiracles on the first leg-bearing somite. The Cermatobiidae resemble the Henicopidae in many characters and are noteworthy on account of the absence of pores on the last pair of legs and the long, thin, many-segmented antennae. These characters tend to link them with the Scutigeromorpha. The genus *Cermatobius* is found in the Moluccas.

The remaining order, the Scutigeromorpha, is sometimes placed in a separate sub-class, the Anartiostigma, represented by a single family, the Scutigeridae. Its representatives are remarkable for the extraordinary length of their limbs and for their extreme agility. They are medium-sized centipedes having fifteen pairs of legs and sternal plates, but only eight tergal plates. Their eyes are compound and bulging, the antennae widely separated at the base and exceedingly long. The spiracles leading into sacular, tufted tracheae are unpaired and open dorsally upon the first seven tergites. These animals are found in all warm tropical and temperate countries, the largest, *Scutigera longicornis* and *S. clunifera*, occurring in India and southern China and reaching two or three inches in length of head and body. There are no indigenous British species, but *S. coleoptrata*, common in southern Europe, was once introduced into a paper-mill in Aberdeen where it succeeded in establishing itself.

General behaviour

Centipedes are nocturnal creatures and lack an impervious cuticular wax-layer (Cloudsley-Thompson, 1954). Their locomotion has long fascinated biologists, but only recently has its mechanics been analysed in detail by means of high-speed photography, showing it to be of evolutionary and functional significance. Ray Lankester, who studied this matter in 1889, reached the conclusion that if the animals had to settle the question themselves they would not get on at all! He ended a letter to *Nature* with the following well-known rhyme:

> A centipede was happy quite
> Until a toad in fun
> Said, 'Pray which leg moves after which?'
> This raised her doubts to such a pitch,
> She fell exhausted in the ditch,
> Not knowing how to run.

However, Manton (1952, 1953) has recently shown that the long Geophilomorpha have become specialised in the ability to choose and vary their footholds so that they may or may not show a regular repetition of the locomotory pattern all along the body. At the same time they are adapted to burrowing 'by the earthworm-like method of becoming 'fat', the active pressing on the soil being done by longitudinal contraction and widening of a segment'. The legs serve as anchoring points, like the chetae of the worm, and when used for walking execute large angles of swing to compensate for their shortness. An increase in burrowing capacity is correlated with the presence of large numbers of leg-bearing segments and the burrowing habit explains many of the morphological characters of these animals. The head end of a contracted animal can be thrust forward more rapidly by the contraction of the musculature and telescoping of the segments than by walking. A combination of walking movements in some regions of the body with muscular contractions and expansions in others results in a thrust or a pull being exerted on parts of the body in which the legs are not used. This provides an efficient method of moving across gaps or places where footholds are discontinuous or shifting and must also be of major importance in widening crevices in the soil.

In contrast, the evolution of the Scolopendromorpha appears to have been associated with acquiring increased speed. Fast gaits are possible as the relative duration of the backstroke of the limbs is shorter than in most other Arthropoda. The body may momentarily be supported by only two or three legs on each side, but excessive sagging of the body between these widely separated supports is countered by the body musculature. At the same time, alternate-sized tergites appear to contribute an anti-undulation mechanism which becomes necessary as the legs increase in length and the gait becomes faster. These achievements have been made at the expense of the primitive flexibility of locomotory movements as are found in the Onychophora and which have been exploited in relation to the burrowing habit of the Geophilomorpha. Thus, the gaits of the Scolopendromorpha are performed with greater regularity than those of the Geophilomorpha, but little choice of footholds is possible.

The legs of the Lithobiomorpha and Scutigeromorpha are longer than those of the orders so far considered. The gaits in these two groups are essentially similar. Only a small range is possible, and movements must be executed with great precision because the fields of up to four successive legs may overlap. Undulations of the body at faster speeds are partially controlled in *Lithobius* by the alternate-sized tergites, and more completely by a reduction in tergite number in *Scutigera* in which the legs are of differential length, the fourteenth pair being almost double the length of the first. With the great fleetness of the Scutigeromorpha are associated several structural advances beyond the conditions seen in other Chilopoda. The long legs require a firm grip on the ground to prevent them from slipping, and instead of the single or double digitigrade spine present in other centipedes, the leg of *Scutigera* ends in a multi-articulate plantigrade foot, each joint possessing numerous gripping hairs. Fast running indicates a high metabolic rate correlated with greater complexity of the maxillary excretory gland, a unique respiratory system and the presence of an efficient respiratory carrier in the blood.

The mechanism of breathing and blood circulation is similar to that of spiders and scorpions since in the Arachnida the blood must traverse the interlamellar spaces before returning to the heart. In *S. coleoptrata* the lungs are dorsal and situated in the pericardial cavity where aspiration due to systole is strongest. They are bathed by blood in the ventro-lateral lacunae which are connected with the pericardial cavity by pulmonary veins. Thus an active mode of life, somewhat analagous to that of the wolf spiders which hunt their prey in the open, is associated with analagous morphological structures. At the same time the presence of compound eyes in *Scutigera*, in contrast to the simple ocelli of the other Chilopoda, may be associated with fast running after flies and other insects.

Of course the Geophilomorpha do not always burrow, particularly the shorter-bodied species which often seek shelter under stones, nor do the members of the other orders run fast all the time: on the contrary they sprint only occasionally and with reluctance. Nevertheless locomotion appears to be the habit with which their evolution has been chiefly associated (Manton, 1952, 1953).

Centipedes always live in damp, dark and obscure places under stones, fallen leaves, logs, under bark and in crevices of the soil, from which, like woodlice and millipedes, they issue forth at night. Sinclair (1895) claimed that in Malta *Scutigera* darts about in the hot sunshine after its prey, but in India it is said to exhibit a strong 'dislike' of daylight and hides during the daytime in dark places. Its most common habitat is under matting covering the floors of bungalows or on walls in dark corners and under stones out of doors. In Italy too *S. coleo-*

ptrata appears to be photo-negative (Cloudsley-Thompson, 1949).

With the exception of their eyes which usually do not seem to be of much importance, the sense organs of centipedes take the form of hairs connected with nerve fibres; the animals find their prey by means of these hairs which are sensitive to touch. They are also very sensitive to moisture and contact stimuli. The whole subject has been reviewed by Cloudsley-Thompson (1952b). According to Bauer (1953) *Lithobius forficatus* shows a 'preference' for high humidities and a ground temperature of about 12° C.

Auerbach (1951) has found that the distribution of *Bothropolys multidentatus*, *Lithobius forficatus* and *Neolithobius voracior* in the Chicago area of North America does not follow a uniform pattern. The first reaches a peak of abundance in wet forest communities, the second in dry forest, while *N. voracior* is plentiful in those localities in which floor moisture conditions are intermediate: and this distribution is related to the different times of survival of the three species when placed in dry air. It is of course true that certain centipedes such as *Scutigera*, *Scolopendra* and *Dignathodon* spp., and in our own country *Lithobius calcaratus*, tend to inhabit dry places, but it is probable that this phenomenon is analagous to that found in woodlice and that the different species vary merely in the length of time that they can survive away from dampness. Recently Palmén and Rantala (1954) have suggested that the orientation of the Geophilid centipede *Pachymerium ferrugineum* in its natural habitats, is chiefly guided by reactions to air humidity and moisture and, to a lesser degree, to temperature. When the relative humidity of the air decreases in a niche inhabited by this species, the result will be an increase in locomotory activity and orientation towards moisture. If high temperature is combined with unusually low atmospheric humidity, the increased desiccation caused will intensify the responses of the animal to moisture.

Many species of centipedes are cave-dwellers and a few of the Geophilomorpha are marine. Two British species are found on the seashore under stones and seaweed at low tide level. The smaller, *Scolioplanes maritimus*, was first discovered by Leach in 1817, who wrote somewhat optimistically, 'Habitat in Britannia inter scopulos ad littora maris vulgissime.' It was rediscovered some fifty years later at Plymouth and has since turned up in the Isle of Man, Somerset, Cornwall, Sussex, Co. Dublin and on the coast of Galway. It is evidently fairly widely distributed on the North Sea coast of France, Denmark, Sweden and Germany. The second species, *Hydroschendyla submarina*, is very much less common. It has nevertheless been found in Cornwall, Jersey, Pembrokeshire and Yorkshire, as well as on the coasts of France, Italy, Scandinavia, North Africa and Bermuda, where it lives in muddy situations around the edges of eroded flat stones, and in isolated honey-combed blocks of limestone about nine inches below mean high water (Chamberlin, 1920). *Pectinunguis americanus* occurs under seaweed, driftwood etc. on the coasts of Mexico, including Florida and the coasts of lower California, and other marine centipedes have been collected from the Cape Verde Islands and the Galapagos. In the former case they inhabit crevices in the crust of worm tubes which cover all rocks at low tide inside bays, and in the latter large empty barnacle shells also at low tide level. Bonnell (1930) obtained a number of *Mixophilus indicus* from under stones and soft moist soil along with various Polychaete worms in the bed of the Cooum River, Madras. As a result of experiments on their resistance to submersion he concluded that little air is required by this species; the tracheae store enough for 24 hours and in addition air is entangled by a loop of the posterior end of the body and in chitinous channels in the coxae of the last legs. In this latter respect they appear to differ from *H. submarina* and *S. maritimus*, both of which, however, can survive several days immersion in sea water without any ill effects. The literature on marine myriapods has been reviewed by Cloudsley-Thompson (1948, 1951). See also Lewis (1961, 1962).

The idea of centipedes living in water has persisted from classical times, for Pliny wrote of a marine 'Scolopendra' as a very poisonous animal, but there is little doubt that he was referring to one of the marine worms. The German naturalist Gesner gave an account in 1569 of a similar 'marine Scolopendra' which, soaked in oil or pounded up with honey, was believed to cause the hair to fall. Charles Owen, in his *Essay towards a Natural History of Serpents* (1752) wrote: 'The Scolopendra is a little venomous worm and amphibious. When it wounds any, there follows a blueness about the affected part and an itch all over the body like that caused by nettles. Its weapons of mischief are much the same with those of the spider only larger; its bite is very tormenting, and produces not only pruriginous pain in the flesh, but very often distraction of the mind. These little creatures make but a mean figure in the ranks of animals, yet have been terrible in their exploits, particularly in driving people out of their country. Thus the people of Rhytium, a city of Crete, were constrained to leave their quarters for them (Aelian, lib. XV., cap. 26).' This is the only recorded instance of a mass migration of centipedes although they have accompanied migrating armies of millipedes.

A number of cases of pseudoparasitism have been recorded in which both centipedes and millipedes have been found living in the nasal sinus or the alimentary canal of man, into which they have become accidentally introduced. On occasions they have been vomited up in numbers by patients who alleged that the animals were breeding inside them. There is a considerable literature on the subject but its biological importance is slight. The explanation probably lies in the fact that centipedes seem to exert a weird fascination on the morbid appetites of the hysterical and insane (Jackson, 1914; Shipley, 1914).

Food and feeding habits

Centipedes are primarily carnivorous but certain of the Geophilomorpha will on occasion feed upon plant tissues and may even be positively injurious to crops if present in sufficient numbers. They also feed upon worms, and the marine *Hydroschendyla submarina* in the Bermuda Islands is said to eat Leodicids, biting them, licking up their juices and carrying off the fragments into which the worms autotomise (Chamberlin, 1920). Geophilids are not easy to maintain in captivity and do not readily take food under laboratory conditions. Consequently our knowledge of their feeding habits is somewhat scanty, but probably they devour a variety of small soil-inhabiting Arthropoda (Brade-Birks, 1929).

The Lithobiomorpha will occasionally feed on worms and slugs too, but insects probably form their staple diet: *Lithobius forficatus* readily accepts flies in captivity. This species has been observed on a wall at night carrying off a woodlouse in its jaws. It has also been known to resort to entomologists' sugar patches for the purpose of capturing the luckless insects which come for the sweets. Small moths have no chance of escape, but the larger Noctuids sometimes succeed in tearing themselves away although it is surprising how tenaciously the centipedes hold on. The Scutigeromorpha are probably entirely insectivorous, but study of the literature shows that the Scolopendromorpha have a wide range of diet, although in many cases the precise identification of species is dubious. A particularly large specimen of *S. gigas* (possibly *S. gigantea*) from

Trinidad kept for over a year in the Insect House of the Zoological Society of London, fed principally on small mice which it devoured with alacrity. Scolopendras have been known, in India, to kill and eat small birds, while one voracious centipede (*S. gigantea*) was found devouring the side of a living toad. On the other hand, specimens of *S. morsitans* from Texas refused to bite toads. More recently, Lawrence (1953) has seen *S. morsitans* speedily kill small geckoes of the genus *Pachydactylus* by biting them in the neck. One large unidentified Scolopendra was discovered on the floor of a house at Kokine, a suburb of Rangoon, with a small snake writhing in its clutches, from the tail of which the skin and flesh for about two inches had been completely removed.

Under laboratory conditions *S. heros* feeds freely upon the agriculturally noxious insects provided: it prefers to remain underground on warm days but is restless on the surface in cloudy and wet weather. *S. viridis* refuses woodlice and earthworms but is partial to flies; the prey, of which the hard parts are rejected, is held firmly to the mouth by the poison claws whilst the mandibles and maxillae tear it to pieces. Lawrence (1934) observed a large *S. subspinipes* feeding on a slug (*Veronicella leydigi*), but in captivity the same species from Borneo does not touch raw meat, worms or various insects. *S. subspinipes* is abundant in the vicinity of the town of Tarragona in the Philippine Islands, and Remington (1950) wrote: 'Almost every night the writer saw one or two of the great chilopods feeding voraciously on the winged insects which swarmed into his pyramidal laboratory tent, attracted by the electric light. The centipedes climbed the walls of the tent easily, fastened their powerful anal legs near the ventilator hole of the tent peak and swung their bodies quickly to one side or the other to seize insects which alighted nearby.'

The present writer kept a female *S. cingulata* found near

Marseilles for several months in a crystallising dish covered with a sheet of glass. She was fed on medium-sized nymphal cockroaches of which on the average she ate about one per week throughout the summer. Adult cockroaches had to be disabled before she would tackle them. She fed also on spiders, flies, moths and other insects and chewed up some worms which she did not finish. She even ate bees and wasps which she caught in mid-air, rearing up the fore part of her body to snatch them with her poison claws as they flew past. These she dropped quickly and waited until her poison had had time to take effect (Cloudsley-Thompson, 1955).

During warm weather she was given water daily which she drank, sometimes for periods of several minutes, and the lapping movements of her mandibles and maxillae could readily be observed through the glass of her container. In contrast, *S. clavipes* from central Tunisia were pale, soft and comparatively weak creatures without the robust appetite of *S. cingulata* (Cloudsley-Thompson, 1955, 1961).

The smaller Cryptopidae feed upon worms, soft-skinned insects or any animal small enough to be killed by them.

Enemies

Centipedes are carnivorous and will eat one another if an opportunity presents itself. *Lithobius forficatus* must not be overcrowded in captivity, or cannibalism will result, particularly if one of the animals is smaller than the others or has been injured. It has been suggested too that Geophilids form part of the natural food of the Cryptopidae. Centipedes are probably distasteful and it does not appear likely that they are eaten to any degree by spiders and other predatory animals unless other food is scarce. Scorpions have been known to kill and eat *S. morsitans* but the big *Scolopendra* often gets the better of its adversary. The Scutigeromorpha readily autotomise their legs if attacked, and in some species the detached limbs continue to stridulate, thereby attracting a predator's attention while its former possessor makes its escape.

The West African *Rhysida nuda* exhibits a similar defence mechanism, which is also found in some other Scolopendromorpha. If the centipede is disturbed, one of the anal legs may be autotomised and lie stridulating on the ground (Cloudsley-Thompson, 1961). The South African species *Alipes crotalus* rapidly vibrates its posterior legs with their large, leaf-like tarsi when threatened, and this produces a rustling, fluttering sound (Lawrence, 1953)*.

On account of their retiring habits, centipedes tend to escape notice and their poison also protects them from enemies. There are numerous scattered accounts in the literature of the effects of the bite of the larger centipedes, but in many the animal has not been adequately identified and in the remainder the conclusions drawn by the authors are often much at variance. Thus *Scolopendra cingulata* is said to cause painful oedema and real discomfort to humans, but *S. heros* and *S. viridis* produce, at most, only temporary sharp pain. The large *S. subspinipes* of Brazil produces intense pain, blistering, swelling, local inflammation, bubos and subcutaneous haemorrhage. This species may reach a length of 25 cm and Remington (1950) who was bitten by one while on the island of Leyte in the Philippines wrote that it caused a fiery pain which at first was almost unbearable and did not diminish for about twenty minutes. A swollen, tender and mildly painful condition persisted for about three weeks. The only authentic case recorded in the literature in which a centipede bite was fatal to a human is that of a seven-year-old child in the Philippines who was bitten on the head and died twenty-nine hours later. Bucherl (1946) has published the results of experiments with the five commonest and largest Brazilian Chilopods and has included a morphological and histological study of the poison apparatus. Having experimented with mice, guinea-pigs and pigeons injected with solutions of the venom at varying concentrations, he reached the conclusion that the poison of even the largest of the Brazilian species was too feeble ever to endanger the life of man or even young children.

Nevertheless, giant centipedes which are so abundant in tropical regions are dreaded by the human inhabitants. In 1798 the renowned natural historian Donovan wrote of *Scolopendra morsitans*: 'Travellers agree that the temperate parts of Asia would be a terrestrial paradise, were it not for the multitude of troublesome insects and reptiles with which they are infested. In a well cultivated country, like China, many of these creatures can scarcely find shelter; but such as harbour in the walls or furniture of human dwellings are as abundant in that, as in any other country that lies within or near the tropics. Amongst the latter, none produce more terrible effects than the centipede, whose poison is as venomous as that of the scorpion, which also is a native of China.' A small specimen only 85 mm long was found by a zoology student of Exeter University College under a boulder at Cassis, near Marseilles, in 1949. It bit him on the second finger of his right hand as he caught it. After about a quarter of an hour the base of the finger had swollen considerably and the pain was similar to that of a hornet sting. Within an hour the whole hand had swollen to twice its normal size but was not painful to touch. The effects had quite gone three days later (Turk, 1951).

The refrain of a Trinidad calypso runs: 'Man centipede bad, bad; woman centipede worse than bad.' Nevertheless, Indian children have been seen to drag huge centipedes out of the earth and eat them. The African Arabs devour Scolopendras alive, often in company with scorpions, broken glass, leaves of prickly pear and other unpleasant things under the influence of religious excitement. In Siam centipedes are roasted and given to children suffering from 'thinness and swollen belly' (malaria or hookworm), and roasted centipedes powdered and soaked in alcohol and the juice of borapet are used medicinally as a stimulant.

Few temperate species are big enough to be able to penetrate the human skin with their poison-claws. *Lithobius forficatus* causes a sharp pain that is noticeable for some time, but signs of injury are insignificant. The long-legged *Scutigera forceps* has been recorded as giving a bite that is followed by intense local pain.

On the whole, although Buffon, in a contemporary English translation, wrote: 'Of these hideous and angry insects we know little except the figure and the noxious qualities', centipedes are for the most part comparatively innocuous members of the community of animals. Even the large Scolopendras do not bite unless molested and will always try to escape rather than fight.

Many of the Geophilomorpha, including the common British *Geophilus electricus*, *G. carpophagus*, *Necrophlaeophagus longicornis* and *Scolioplanes crassipes*, exude a phosphorescent fluid when disturbed. The phosphorescence may be excited at any time of year by mechanical stimulation and by immersion in water: it also occurs when the centipedes are attacked by ants and similar enemies. In autumn, at the time of sexual maturity, centipedes tend to leave their burrows and for this reason an abundance of luminous specimens is found at that time of year. The luminescence is simply a protective reaction and is not related to sexual behaviour as has sometimes been suggested, for these animals are eyeless.

In southern California the large greenish *Scolopendra heros* is greatly feared, not only on account of its poisonous bite but because it also produces a reddish streak where it has crawled upon the body. Like many other tropical and subtropical Scolopendromorpha, it makes tiny incisions with its numerous feet. In themselves these are trifling, but when alarmed the centipede drops into each incision some kind of venom that causes intense irritation so that the affected part becomes inflamed and the two rows of punctures show white against the flesh. No doubt the poisonous and phosphorescent fluids secreted near the coxae of the legs are additional protective devices that render centipedes dangerous and distasteful to their enemies.

With regard to parasites, the carnivorous Chilopoda afford a sharp contrast to the vegetarian Diplopoda since few parasitic Nematoda have been recorded from them although they are sometimes infested by Mermithidae. Other parasites that have occasionally been found include bacteria and fungi, Protozoa and Nematomorpha (Remy, 1950). Thompson (1939) dissected some 300 specimens of *Lithobius forficatus* and found no parasite other than two species of Tachinid flies. The average parasitism was only 7·5%, and almost half the parasitised centipedes contained more than one larva: in most cases both parasite larvae died. On one occasion, however, some larvae of the Proctotrupid wasp *Cryptoserphus ater* were seen issuing from the body of a *Lithobius forficatus* which had succumbed to their attacks.

Reproduction and life cycle

Details of reproduction in centipedes have not often been closely studied, but it appears that many species show a remarkable degree of parental care. In temperate regions, egg-laying usually takes place throughout the spring and summer. In many tropical species there seems to be no regular annual breeding season. The sexes are very similar and can often be distinguished only by microscopic examination. In the Lithobiomorpha and Scutigeromorpha the segmental organs at the posterior end of the body are differently formed in the two sexes, that of the female being used for holding the egg. Male centipedes produce spermatophores which are picked up by the females. This was first observed by J. H. Fabre a century ago in Geophilomorpha. Demange (1956) has recently shown that in *Lithobius piceus* the male centipede deposits a spermatophore on a small web and this is afterwards taken up by the female. The same occurs in Scolopendromorpha and Scutigeromorpha (Klingel, 1960). The young of all the orders leave the egg-shell with the full number of legs with the exception of the Lithobiomorpha and Scutigeromorpha, which hatch with seven pairs of legs including the poison claws.

The Geophilomorpha and Cryptopidae usually lay 15 to 35 eggs in a loose mass which is often merely left in the soil. In the Geophilid *Pachymerium ferrugineum*, which has a wide geographical range in Europe, Asia, Africa and America, fertilisation takes place in the spring in southern Finland, but may also occur before hibernation. The main period of egg-laying extends from the last week of May to the middle of July and the number of eggs per brood varies between 20 and 55, and is usually 25 to 45. When disturbed during brooding, the female either eats her eggs and young, or else abandons them, but adolescent young do not seem to be attacked. If the relative humidity drops only 1–3 % below saturation, the eggs begin to shrink, owing to desiccation. If they are separated from the mother they become infected with fungi within a few days: it is probable that when mouthing and touching the eggs the female coats them with some fungicidal secretion that prevents spores from developing. The maximum size of the young at the end of their first summer is 16 mm: some of the individuals become mature during their second summer, others not until their third. As the size of the mature females varies considerably the largest individuals are probably at least four years old (Palmén and Rantala, 1954).

In the Lithobiomorpha the eggs are laid individually in the soil after being covered with earth by the female, but in the Scolopendromorpha the young are usually guarded by their mother until they are able to shift for themselves. Often a roughly hollowed-out cavity is made in soft or rotting wood by the body of the mother before the eggs are laid. The parent centipede then curls herself around her eggs and young so that as she lies on her side they are enclosed in a basket-like framework formed by the ventral surface of her body and the inwardly pointing legs. The eggs or young are thus safeguarded

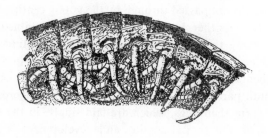

FIG. 14. Parental care in a *Scolopendra*.

from contact with the soil, and the mother centipede maintains this position for several weeks until the departure of the adolescent young (Cornwell, 1934; Lawrence, 1947, 1953*). In the case of *S. dalmatica* it appears that the earth of the 'nest' is stuck together by some viscous fluid. Early wrters such as Gervais and Lucas believed that Scolopendras iwere ovoviviparous but this error was later corrected by Silvestri who suggested that the mistake arose as an erroneous inference from the way in which *S. cingulata* assiduously guards its eggs and young ones.

Little exact knowledge of the breeding habits of Scolopendromorph centipedes is available, and this is partly due to the fact that if the incubating mothers are disturbed they react either by devouring the eggs and embryos or by deserting their brood which is then attacked by fungi (Lawrence, 1947). Thus, when a specimen of *S. angulata* was sent with her brood from Trinidad to the London Zoo in 1894, on arrival only one young and the adult were found, and both of them were dead. Parent centipedes feed quite casually on their young and, at times, even greedily when kept without food.

Unlike that of the Diplopoda the development of centipedes proceeds mainly by epimorphosis. It is not known exactly how many moults are passed through by the young centipedes after leaving their mother, but there must be a considerable number. After leaving the brood chamber growth is continuous and gradual and is chiefly concerned with increase in size and strengthening of the chitinous epidermal structures, especially the mouth parts. The Lithobiomorpha and Scutigeromorpha at first carry their eggs, which are laid singly, in the claspers situated on the genital somite, and development is initially anamorphic and later epimorphic. The first seven-legged stage of the Lithobiomorpha lasts only a few hours, after which there are four ecdyses at the last of which the young centipede has twelve pairs of legs. This completes the anamorphic stage. The epimorphic phase consists of four stages, in all of which there are fifteen pairs of legs, and the sexually mature adult emerges from the last one. The size of *Lithobius forficatus* after leaving the egg may increase from 3 to 24 mm and the number of antennal segments and teeth on the maxillipedes also increases. The time taken to complete the various stages differs considerably, the second being 10 to 14 days, the third 80 to 84 days. The whole development from egg to mature centipede requires about three years, so that larval and immature centipedes are usually found together with sexually mature forms. In *Scutigera coleoptrata* the larvae hatch with four pairs of legs and there are five more larval stages with 5, 7, 9, 11 and 13 pairs of legs respectively. This anamorphic stage is succeeded by an epimorphic one of four adolescent stages each with fifteen pairs of legs. The first three larval stages require about three weeks for their completion. Centipedes are long-lived creatures and specimens of *Lithobius forficatus* have been known to live for up to 5 to 6 years (Verhoeff, 1937a, b).

BIBLIOGRAPHY

Identification

ATTEMS, C. G. (1926) Progoneata, Chilopoda *in* KÜKENTHAL, W. & KRUMBACH, T. *Handbuch der Zoologie*, Berlin, **4**, (1–4), 1–402.
——(1928) The Myriapoda of South Africa. *Ann. S. Afr. Mus.*, **26**, 1–431.
——(1929) Myriapoda, Geophilomorpha. *Das Tierreich*, **52**, 1–388.
——(1930) Chilopoda, Scolopendromorpha. *Ibid.*, **54**, 1–308.
BLOWER, G. (1955) Yorkshire centipedes. *Naturalist*, **1955**, 137–46.
BRADE-BIRKS, S. G. (1939) Notes on Myriapoda XXXVI. Sources for description and illustration of the British fauna. *J. S-E. Agric. Coll. Wye*, No. 44, 156–79.
BRÖLEMANN, W. H. (1932) Chilopodes. *Faune de France*, **25**, 1–405.
CHAMBERLIN, R. V. (1920) The Myriapoda of the Australian region. *Bull. Mus. Comp. Zool.*, **64**, 1–269.
CLOUDSLEY-THOMPSON, J. L. (1952) Collecting centipedes and millipedes. *Bull. Amat. Ent. Soc.*, **11**, 5–8.
EASON, E. H. (1965) *Centipedes of the British Isles*. London.
LATZEL, R. (1880) *Die Myriopoden der Oesterreichish–Ungarischen Monarchie. 1. Die Chilopoden*. Wien.
VERHOEFF, K. W. (1902–28) Chilopoda *in* H. G. BRONN's *Klass. Ordn. Tierreichs*, **5**, II (1), 1–725.
WANG, Y. M. (1951) The Myriapoda of the Philippine Islands. *Serica* **1**, 1–80.

Biology

AUERBACH, S. I. (1951) The centipedes of the Chicago area with special reference to their ecology. *Ecol. Monogr.*, **21**, 97–124.

BAUER, K. (1955) Sinnesökologische Untersuchungen an *Lithobius forficatus*. *Zool. Jahrb.* (*Zool.*), **65**, 267–300.

BONNELL, B. (1930) Geophilid centipedes from the bed of the Cooum River (Madras). *J. Asiat. Soc. Bengal*, (N.S.), **25**, 181–4.

BUCHERL, W. (1946) Ação do veneno dos Escolopendromorfos do Brasil sóbre alguns animais de laboratorio. *Mem. Inst. Butanan. S. Paulo*, **19**, 181–97.

CLOUDSLEY-THOMPSON, J. L. (1945) Behaviour of the common centipede, *Lithobius forficatus*. *Nature, Lond.*, **156**, 537–8.

——(1948) *Hydroschendyla submarina* (Grube) in Yorkshire: with an historical review of the marine Myriapoda. *Naturalist*, **1948**, 149–52.

——(1949) A note on the Myriapods and Arachnids of northern Italy. *Ent. Mon. Mag.*, **85**, 285.

——(1951) Supplementary notes on Myriapoda. *Naturalist*, **1951**, 16–17.

——(1952a) The biology of centipedes and millipedes. *Discovery*, **13**, 18–21.

——(1952b) The behaviour of centipedes and millipedes–1. Responses to environmental stimuli. *Ann. Mag. Nat. Hist.*, (12), **5**, 417–34.

——(1954) The ecological significance of diurnal rhythms in terrestrial Arthropoda. *Sci. Prog.*, **42**, 46–52.

——(1955) Some aspects of the biology of centipedes and scorpions. *Naturalist*, **1955**, 147–53.

——(1961) A new sound-producing mechanism in centipedes. *Ent. Mon. Mag.*, **96**, 110–13.

CORNWELL, W. S. (1934) Notes on the egg-laying and nesting habits of certain species of North Carolina myriapods and various phases of their life histories. *J. Elisha Mitchell Sci. Soc.*, **149**, 289–91.

DEMANGE, J.-M. (1956) Contribution à l'étude de la biologie, en captivité, de *Lithobius piceus gracilitarsis* Bröl. (Myriapode-Chilpode). *Bull. Mus. Hist. nat. Paris*, (2), **28**, 388–93.

JACKSON, A. R. (1914) A preliminary list of the Myriapods of the Chester district. *Lancs. Nat.*, **6**, 450–8.

KLINGEL, H. (1960) Vergleichende Verhaltensbiologie der Chilopoden *Scutigera coleoptrata* L. ("Spinnenassel") und *Scolopendra cingulata* Latreille (Skolopender). *Z. Tierpsychol.*, **17**, 10–30.

LAWRENCE, R. F. (1947) Some observations on the post-embryonic development of the Natal forest centipede *Cormocephalus multispinus* (Kraep.). *Ann. Natal. Mus.*, **11**, 139–56.

LAWRENCE, T. C. (1934) Notes on the feeding habits of *Scolopendra subspinipes* Leach (Myriapoda). *Proc. Hawaii Ent. Soc.*, **8**, 497–8.

LEWIS, J. G. E. (1961) The life history and ecology of the littoral centipede *Strigamia* (= *Scolioplanes*) *maritima* (Leach). *Proc. Zool. Soc. Lond.*, **137**, 221–48.

——(1962) The ecology, distribution and taxonomy of the centipedes found on the shore in the Plymouth area. *J. Mar. Biol. Ass. U.K.*, **42**, 655–64.

——(1965) The food and reproductive cycles of the centipedes *Lithobius variegatus* and *Lithobius forficatus* in a Yorkshire woodland. *Proc. Zool. Soc. Lond.*, **144**, 269–83.

MANTON, S. M. (1952) The evolution of Arthropodan locomotory mechanisms—Part 3. The locomotion of the Chilopoda and Pauropoda. *J. Linn. Soc. (Zool.)*, **42**, 118–67.

——(1953) Locomotory habits and the evolution of the larger Arthropodan groups *in* Evolution. *Symp. Soc. Exp. Biol.*, **7**, 339–76.

PALMÉN, E. (1949) The Chilopoda of Eastern Fennoscandia. *Ann. Soc. Zool. Fenn. Vanamo*, **13**, (4), 1–45.

PALMÉN, E. and RANTALA, M. (1954) On the life-history and ecology of *Pachymerium ferrugineum* (C. L. Koch) (Chilopoda, Geophilidae). *Ibid.*, **16**, (3), 1–44.

REMINGTON, C. L. (1950) The bite and habits of a giant centipede (*Scolopendra subspinipes*) in the Philippine Is. *Amer. J. Trop. Med.*, **30**, 453–5.

REMY, P. A. (1950) On the enemies of Myriapods. *Naturalist*, **1950**, 103–8.

SCHUBART, O. (1955) Tausendfüsser als Nahrung im Tierreich. *Nach. Nat. Mus. Aschaffenburg*, **49**, 1–29.

SHIPLEY, A. E. (1914) Pseudoparasitism. *Parasitology*, **6**, 351–2.

SINCLAIR, F. G. (1895) Myriapods: *in* HARMER, S. F. and SHIPLEY, A. E. *The Cambridge Natural History*, **5**, 29–80.

TURK, F. A. (1951) Myriapodological Notes, III. The iatro-zoology, biology and systematics of some tropical 'Myriapods'. *Ann. Mag. Nat. Hist.*, (12), **4**, 35–48.

VERHOEFF, K. W. (1937a) Zur Kenntnis der Lithobiiden. *Arch. Naturgesch.* (N.F.), **6**, 171–257.

——(1937b) Zur Biologie der *Scutigera coleoptrata*, und über die jüngeren Larvenstadien. *Z. wiss. Zool.*, **150**, 262–82.

CHAPTER IV

OTHER 'MYRIAPODS'

IT HAS already been pointed out that the Diplopoda and Chilopoda were formerly associated with the less familiar Pauropoda and Symphyla and regarded as orders of a class 'Myriapoda', composed of Arthropoda possessing bodies formed of many similar somites each provided with at least one pair of legs. It is now realised, however, that the 'Myriapoda' included an

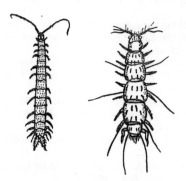

FIG. 15. Pauropoda and Symphyla. Left, *Scutigerella* sp. (body length 4 mm); right, *Pauropus* sp. (body length 1·5 mm).

unnatural assemblage of superficially similar but unrelated groups which are now considered as separate classes, having no more relationship to one another than to the Crustacea, Insecta and Arachnida. Indeed, there is strong reason to suspect that the modern Symphyla are closely allied to the extinct ancestors of insects.

Class PAUROPODA

The Pauropoda resemble the Diplopoda in having the orifice of the reproductive organs on the fore part of the body, that is to say in the third somite behind the head, and in the fusion of the two adjoining tergites to represent a single somite; but differ from them in the structure of the two pairs of jaws, in having the end of the antennae branched and in the possession of only twelve somites and ten pairs of limbs of which nine have a locomotory function, the first pair being reduced to mere buds. In addition the legs are very widely spaced, tracheae are absent and five pairs of long tactile bristles are attached to the sides of the body.

Pauropods are minute Arthropoda measuring only about one-twentieth of an inch in length. The first was discovered by Lubbock in 1886. They have since been found in Europe, Asia and America where they inhabit damp situations beneath decaying leaves, logs and so on. In some (*Pauropus* spp.) which are more active in their movements, the body is narrow, compared with its length; but in the more sluggish forms (*Eurypauropus* spp.) it is very wide, its sides and front being produced so as to conceal the legs and head. At the present time six families are known to science, but little information is available about their ecology and distribution other than that they are believed to be generally distributed except in the arctic, antarctic and desert regions of the world. Indeed, owing to their concealed habits they are sometimes believed to be rare, but Starling (1944) estimated an annual average of 1,672,704 per acre (to a depth of 5 inches) in oak stands on clay soil and 2,178,000 in pine stands on sandy loam in the Duke Forest,

North Carolina. Five times as many Pauropods were found in oak humus on clay soil as in the same level under pine stands on sandy soil, and his observations suggested that moisture and temperature are the two main factors that affect the distribution of these animals. The greatest number was collected from sandy soil when the moisture percentage of the oven-dry weight was 11–20%. In clay soil Pauropods appeared to prefer 21–30% of moisture. The optimum range of temperature based on activity and mortality rate when Pauropoda were placed in constant temperature cabinets was found to be 16–20° C: the optimum, based on field observations, 17–23° C. Summer appears to be the most favourable season for development and activity, and eggs were obtained in June and July. A correlation appears to exist between optimum temperature for fungal growth and a high incidence in Pauropod distribution which may be related to their feeding habits.

Little is known concerning the food of Pauropods. Speculations have been made that the slowly moving species feed on decaying plant and animal material, whereas the more agile types may consume microscopic animals (Latzel, 1884). A species of *Pauropus* has been seen feeding on dead flies floating in a puddle. No doubt most species feed either on fresh sap or the semi-liquid products of decaying wood. Harrison (1914) observed Pauropods browsing 'on particles of soil in which nothing in the way of food could be distinguished', and concluded that they were humus-feeders, while Starling (1944) observed that *P. carolinensis* ate the mycelia of moulds growing on decaying leaf particles but did not appear to feed on dead animal material such as Collembola, Diptera and other Pauropoda that were placed at their disposal.

According to Tiegs (1947), Pauropoda are preyed upon by carnivorous mites and false-scorpions which frequently take toll of larvae and even of adults. Nematodes have never been found in Pauropoda and nothing else appears to be known of their enemies.

The eggs are deposited singly or in clumps in secluded crevices of damp and decomposing vegetation. Like Diplopoda, the young of Pauropods hatch with three pairs of legs, after which they pass through four successive larval stages before attaining the nine-legged adult condition. The newly hatched *Pauropus huxleyi* is one seventy-second of an inch in length and has six legs, three large dorsal plates and two lateral hairs. Development proceeds slowly and resembles that of the Diplopoda in being anamorphic. In *P. silvaticus* the egg hatches after 12–13 days, rupture being assisted by stout cutting setae of the embryological cuticle. A quiescent 'pupoid' stage with two pairs of rudimentary limbs emerges which lasts only 3–4 days and is followed by four successive larval stages which have 3, 5, 6 and 8 pairs of legs and require approximately 2, 4, 5 and 3 weeks respectively to develop. The period from egg to adult in this species is thus about fourteen weeks in duration, and the dults do not moult again (Tiegs, 1947).

a The life histories of *Pauropus carolinensis*, *P. amicus* and *Eurypauropus spinosus* appear to be similar. The eggs are laid in groups of from 3 to 12, each egg being perfectly spherical, pearly white and 0·17 mm in diameter. The outer membrane, which is opaque, is covered with minute pustulations. On the twelfth day the outer membrane breaks and the embryo partially emerges: its anterior end becomes free while the posterior end is still enclosed in the membrane. The embryo is covered by one embryonic membrane which bears outgrowths that cover the antennae and three pairs of legs are visible inside. The embryo remains motionless in this condition for three days and then, by dorsal splitting of the second cuticle, issues out ʒ an actively moving hexapod larva with two tactile setae Harrison, 1914). The remaining instars have 5, 6, 8 and 9 legs

respectively and the number of tactile bristles are 3, 4, 4 and 5.
Before moulting the animals become somewhat rigid but remain upright throughout the process. The head and antennae
are bent ventrally and when the process, which takes only
about twenty-five minutes, is almost complete, vigorous pro-
pulsions, which first free the head, enable the white, moist and
weak animal to drag itself from its old cuticle.

Class SYMPHYLA

The reproductive organs of the Symphyla, like those of the
Pauropoda, open upon the third somite behind the head, but
otherwise the two classes are very dissimilar. In the Symphyla
the antennae are very long and many jointed, there are four
pairs of peculiarly modified jaws and the head bears a pair of
tracheal spiracles. There are twelve pairs of walking legs, but
the number of tergal plates, namely fifteen, the first being very
small, is greater than the number of legs and not less as in the
Diplopoda and Pauropoda. The basal segments of the legs of
the third to twelfth leg-bearing segments are provided with a
protrusible sac thought to have a respiratory function, whereas
in Pauropods there is but a single pair on the floor of the
collum or first post-cephalic segment. With the last somite
articulates a pair of tail-like processes upon which spinning
glands open, and just in front of them is a papilla carrying a
tactile hair. Symphyla are small, pallid arthropods resembling
tiny centipedes in appearance and activity, that live in damp
places under stones, dead leaves, etc. Two families are known,
Scutigerellidae and Scolopendrellidae, both of which are represented in the British fauna.

The class Symphyla has held the interest of many naturalists
since about the middle of the eighteenth century and numerous
articles have been published which deal with its members.

Nearly all of these are concerned principally with the taxonomy, anatomy and phylogenetic relationships of the group while a few of the later papers consider its ecological and economic aspects. The first species was described in 1763 as *Scolopendra nivea* by Scopuli, who evidently little realised that the organism possessed characters so distinct from those of the Chilopoda that eventually it would be placed in a class by itself. In 1839 Gervais named the second species, which he collected near Paris, *Scolopendrella notacantha* and in 1847 he placed this genus in the Geophilidae: but Menge in 1851 suggested that *Scolopendrella* should be considered as transitional between the Scolopendridae and the Lepismidae! The best-known species, *Scutigerella immaculata*, occurs on both sides of the Atlantic, and in America has risen to the rank of a serious economic pest (Michelbacher, 1938). Since 1920, numerous important papers have been published on this subject.

S. immaculata is widely distributed in the Northern Hemisphere but is known to occur only in a single locality, Buenos Aires, south of the equator. It does not appear to be widespread in Africa but has been reported from several localities in Algeria and Tunisia, and has been found in the Alps at a height of 9842 ft. There are no definite records of it from Asia or Australia. Nothing can be said of its southern limits, but it probably extends well into the tropics since the climate of the Hawaiian Islands seems well suited to its development. Other species of Symphyla are found widespread throughout the world: their northern distribution seems to be limited by expected minimum temperatures of about 26° C. Under experimental conditions *Scutigerella immaculata* can withstand a temperature of 20° C for long periods but seems unable to survive freezing for any length of time if previously held at room temperature. If kept at 4·5° C first, however, it may withstand 0° C for months (Michelbacher, 1938).

Many species are well distributed in the tropics and although none has yet been recorded from China or Siberia, they probably occur there too.

Symphyla are negatively phototactic but the response is not very strongly developed for they appear to come to the surface of the soil to feed without hesitation at any hour of the day. It is not uncommon to find them lying perfectly motionless on the surface of the ground where they are fully exposed to the sunlight. When in motion the antennae are kept constantly moving, but while feeding they are, as a rule, held backwards. Symphyla can run very rapidly when disturbed and quickly retreat into the soil. If their antennae are touched with a camel's hair brush or other instrument they reverse their course with lightning speed. In turning round the posterior end of the body is held still and acts as a pivot (Verhoeff, 1934). The very young, however, never come to the surface of the soil and apparently do not feed until they have moulted a second time. Symphyla are not restricted to any particular level of the soil, and may be found from the surface to a depth of four feet or more. Moisture is the most important factor determining their vertical distribution, but temperature, soil texture, structure and vegetation also influence them.

They exhibit complex seasonal vertical migrations in the soil in response to its moisture content and cannot survive when soil air is less than 100% relative humidity. The zone of optimum temperature of *S. immaculata* is 15°–21° C (Edwards, 1961).

Symphyla appear to be vegetarians and to prefer decaying and succulent materials although they will feed on many kinds of lower plant life. Newport in 1845 thought that they must be carnivorous, preying perhaps on the microscopic Poduridae to be found in the same places, but Duboscq, some years later, noted the absence of a poison gland in *Scolopendrella. Scuti-*

gerella immaculata normally feeds upon decaying vegetable matter but may attack living plants, often doing very much damage to field and glass-house crops such as young seedlings, asparagus, lima beans, peas, tomatoes and cultivated flowers. It has conical taste sensillae at the apex of the second maxillae (considered to be homologous with the gnathochilarium of Diplopoda), but these are simpler in structure and considerably fewer in number than those of millipedes. Population studies in the field and greenhouses show that Symphyla may be present in large numbers, sometimes as many as 22 million per acre out of doors, and 90 million per acre in glass-houses. Suitable methods for checking damage in greenhouses consist of using raised benches, steam treatment, insecticides and soil fumigation (Michelbacher, 1938).

As in the case of the Pauropoda, little is known of the predators of these creatures, but Chilopods are said to be among the most important of their natural enemies. A large Gamasid mite has been observed to seize a Symphylid with its jaws and carry it rapidly away: various gregarines have been found in *Scutigerella immaculata*, *Hanseniella hova* and *H. agilis* and there is a single record of a nematode in the first named species (Remy, 1950).

Many Symphyla lay a clump of eggs in a crevice or hollow of the soil, attaching them to its wall by a short stalk so that the eggs are free from contact with the sides or floor of the shelter thereby obtaining some protection from fungi and other enemies. In *Scutigerella immaculata*, 4–25 eggs are laid (Filinger, 1931): in *Hanseniella agilis* 3–8. The young hatch with six or seven pairs of legs after an average period of about eleven days: there are five further stages each having one more pair of legs than the last, up to the number of eleven. From this eleven-legged larva, the adult emerges after a final moult. According to Filinger (1931) the first moult occurs within one to four days, usually after 24–36 hours, the succeeding ones at intervals of about eight days. Sexual maturity is reached after 40–60 days. During moulting a split occurs between the head and the first body segment, but as the whole cuticle is soft it is not usually cast in one piece as in most other myriapods, but is moulted irregularly in strips and tattered fragments at various points of the body.

Michelbacher (1938) found that *S. immaculata* moults from time to time during its entire life, and since it may live for a period of four years or more, the maximum number of moults probably exceeds fifty. The moulting characteristics of different individuals vary greatly: a sex factor is present and some evidence has been obtained which indicates that a genetic factor may also be involved. Other factors which influence moulting are: type of food, temperature, humidity and mutilation. Above and below 28° C the moulting rate decreases. The earliest that egg-laying was observed to begin was between the seventh and eighth moults which would indicate that this is about the time of sexual maturity.

In most cases, however, eggs are not produced until a much later date. Oviposition occurs a short time before moulting. At birth, the species of *Scutigerella* so far investigated have been found to have six pairs of legs and six antennal segments, whereas *Hanseniella* spp. have seven pairs of legs and six antennal segments (Tiegs, 1945). It is surprising to find these differences in so homogeneous a group as the Symphyla. The larva slowly and laboriously works its way out of the egg through the cut made in the blastodermic cuticle and chorion by the two pairs of sharp spines at the bases of the antennae. These spines are part of the embryonic cuticle and are rejected with the latter at eclosion. During the first few hours of freedom the larva enlarges, evidently by ingestion of fluid from without. For the first day it crawls sluggishly over the decaying

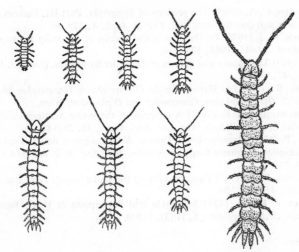

FIG. 16. Stages in the development of *Scutigerella immaculata*.
(After Michelbacher, 1938.)

vegetation on which it feeds, but thereafter becomes more
active. After 7–12 days it retreats to the shelter of some secluded crevice and there moults. With the sixth moult the organism receives all its morphological parts, but complete diffe-
rentiation does not occur until a much later period, the life-
history being rather complex. After each moult more segments
are usually added to the antennae and broken antennae are regenerated. This has been observed in individuals nearly three
years old. As already mentioned, the total life span may exceed
four years.

BIBLIOGRAPHY

Identification

ATTEMS, C. G. (1926) Progoneata, Chilopoda *in* KÜKENTHAL, W. and
KRUMBACH, T. *Handbuch der Zoologie*, Berlin, **4**, (1–4), 1–402.

BAGNALL, R. S. (1914) A synopsis of the British Symphyla, with descriptions of new species. *Trans. Nat. Hist. Soc. Northumb.*, (NS), **4**, 17–41.

EDWARDS, C. A. (1961) The ecology of Symphyla, Part III. Factors controlling soil distributions. *Ent. Exp. & Appl.*, **4**, 239–56.

HANSEN, H. J. (1902) On the genera and species of the order Pauropoda. *Vidensk. Medd.*, **1902**, 323–424.

——(1903) The genera and species of the order Symphyla. *Quart. J. Micr. Sci.*, **47**, 1–101.

LATZEL, R. (1884) *Die Myriapoden der Osterreichisch–Ungarischen Monarchie*. 2. *Die Symphylen, Pauropoden und Diplopoden*. Wien.

MICHELBACHER, A. E. (1942) A synopsis of the genus *Scutigerella* (Symphyla: Scutigerellidae). *Ann. Ent. Soc. Amer.*, **35**, 267–88.

REMY, P. (1938) Pauropodes de France, d'Allemagne et des Balkans avec description de quatre formes nouvelles. *Bull. Soc. Hist. nat. Metz.*, **35**, 153–78.

STARLING, J. H. (1943) Pauropoda from the Duke forest. *Proc. Ent. Soc. Wash.*, 45, 183–200.

VERHOEFF, K. W. (1934) Symphyla und Pauropoda *in* H. G. BRONN'S *Klass. Ordn. Tierreichs*, **5**, II (3), 1–200.

Biology

FILINGER, G. A. (1928) Observations on the habit and control of the garden centipede, *Scutigerella immaculata* Newport, a pest of greenhouses. *J. Econ. Ent.*, **21**, 357–60.

——(1931) The garden centipede, *Scutigerella immaculata* Newport. *Bull. Ohio Agr. Exp. Sta.*, No. 486, 1–33.

HARRISON, L. (1914) On some Pauropoda from New South Wales. *Proc. Linn. Soc. N.S.W.*, **39**, 615–34.

KENYON, F. C. (1895) The morphology and classification of the Pauropoda, with notes on the morphology of the Diplopoda. *Tufts Coll. Stud.* No. 4, 77–146.

MICHELBACHER, A. E. (1938) The biology of the garden centipede, *Scutigerella immaculata*. *Hilgardia*, **11**, 55–148.

RAVOUX, P. (1962) Étude sur la segmentation des Symphyles. *Ann. Nat. Zool.*, (12), **4**, 141–472.

STARLING, J. H. (1944) Ecological studies of the Pauropoda of the Duke forest. *Ecol. Monogr.*, **14**, 291–310.

TIEGS, O. W. (1945) The post-embryonic development of *Hanseniella agilis* (Symphyla). *Quart. J. Micr. Sci.*, **85**, 191–328.

——(1947) The development and affinities of the Pauropoda, based on a study of *Pauropus silvaticus*. *Ibid.*, **88**, 165–267, 275–336.

WILLIAMS, S. R. (1907) Habits and structure of *Scutigerella immaculata* (Newport). *Proc. Boston Nat. Hist. Soc.*, **33**, 461–85.

CHAPTER V

SCORPIONS

Classification and distribution

Although different in size, all scorpions are more or less alike in general appearance and are easily distinguished from other Arachnida by a combination of characters that are always

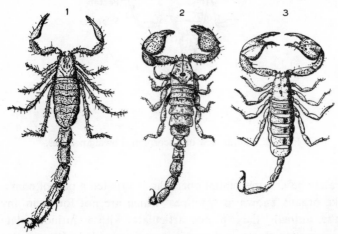

FIG. 17. Examples of scorpion families: 1. Buthidae, 2. Scorpionidae, 3. Chactidae. (Drawings not to scale.) (After various authors.)

present. Their most striking features are the large pedipalps furnished with stout chelae or claws and the division of the abdomen into two portions: a broad pre-abdomen consisting

of seven segments which are as wide or wider than the cephalothorax or prosoma, and a slender tail-like post-abdomen. At
the end of the tail is a sting, somewhat curved and pointed. Its
base is enlarged and contains a pair of poison glands which
open near the tip. On the ventral side of the abdomen, imme-

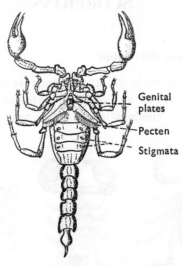

Genital
plates

Pecten

Stigmata

FIG. 18. Ventral view of a scorpion showing pectines.

diately behind the genital opercula, is situated a pair of comb-
like organs known as 'pectines' which are not found in any
other animals. Each pecten articulates with a chitinous plate
representing the second sternite and is provided with complex
musculature. Its components form three longitudinal series.
Of these the back is composed of three parts, the proximal
being the longest, while the lamellae or teeth comprise the third
series and are inserted between the constituents of the median
row. These lamellae vary in number from three to more than

forty depending upon the sex and species of the scorpion, and are richly supplied with nerves.

The dorsal surface of the prosoma is covered by a compact and unsegmented shield or carapace which bears a pair of median and from three to five pairs of lateral simple eyes. The mouth is ventral in position and is situated between an anterior and a posterior lip. In front and above the base of the pedipalps are a pair of short chelate chelicerae used for mashing and shredding the food, while the first two of the four pairs of walking legs have maxillary plates and harbour glands that secrete digestive enzymes.

Scorpions live in hot and tropical countries. In Europe several species are found in Greece, Italy, Spain and the Balkans and at least one has a range extending into southern Germany. On the American continent they are found from Patagonia to the more southern of the United States. Their geographical distribution has been made the subject of several studies and is interesting because scorpions are a very ancient group, are not readily dispersed to new localities and consequently are of great importance in biogeographical research. They are absent from many islands, including New Zealand.

The order is divided into six families, of which the most important is the Buthidae with more than 600 species including *Buthus occitanus*, the common yellow scorpion of France and the Mediterranean region, and *Androctonus australis* the fat-tailed scorpion of North Africa, while the species of *Centrurus* and *Tityus* are Neotropical. The Diplocentridae are found in the Palaearctic region, the isle of Sokotra in the Gulf of Aden and Mexico, the Scorpionidae in Africa, Madagascar, Asia and Australia, while the Vejovidae occur mostly in Asia and America. The Chactidae have a somewhat similar distribution and include the small black *Euscorpius* spp. of southern Europe and the Mediterranean, while the Bothriuridae live in Australia,

Most species have a very limited range, excepting *Isometrus maculatus*, which is ubiquitous in the warmer parts of the globe, and *Scorpio maurus* which extends from the Atlantic to India. Few are found at high altitudes, but *S. maurus* and *Buthus occitanus* occur in the Atlas Mountains and *Euscorpius germanus* in the Tyrol. On morphological grounds the Buthidae can be separated from the remaining families of scorpions, and it is believed that the two groups may have evolved independently, perhaps even since the Silurian epoch.

General behaviour

Scorpions resemble other Arachnida and insects in having an impervious integument and efficient powers of water retention. (Cloudsley-Thompson, 1956). They are markedly nocturnal but this habit cannot be dictated primarily by the need to avoid dry air. Indeed, Sergent (1947) has shown that the negative reactions to light of *Androctonus australis*, *Buthus occitanus* and *Scorpio maurus* are less marked than are their positively thigmotactic responses, so it is probable that their nocturnal behaviour has an ecological rather than a physiological significance. Scorpions are essentially inhabitants of warm climates and become sluggish in cold weather, although they can withstand freezing for several weeks (Vachon, 1953).

Their lives are comparatively simple: not even the most primitive forms of animal association are known and all species lead strictly individual lives and usually either avoid each other or fight to the death. The fact that aggregations are sometimes found in certain areas is not due to social instincts—these are conspicuously absent—but to the fact that the young do not scatter far from their place of birth. Fabre's (1907) claim that when two are found beneath the same stone they are either mating or else one is devouring the other may be an exaggerated generalisation, but is probably not entirely without foundation.

Some scorpions (e.g. *Euscorpius* spp.) normally frequent damp places, others (e.g. *Pandinus*, *Palamnaeus* spp.) are forest dwellers whilst perhaps the best known (e.g. *Scorpio*, *Buthus*, *Androctonus* spp.) are inhabitants of dry and desert regions. Most scorpions do not drink, but moisture loving species such as *Euscorpius italicus* are sensitive both to drought and to excessive moisture (Bott, 1951; Cloudsley-Thompson, 1951). Schultze (1927), however, found that the large Philippine forest scorpion *Palamnaeus longimanus* had to be given a certain amount of water every day, and it was astonishing what large amounts of water this creature would drink. The scorpion would take up drops of water from grooves in bark, drops scattered on its body or sip with its mandibles water that had accumulated between the chelae—that is, it would move the latter close to the mandibles 'in the way a man holds a glass in his hand and brings it towards his mouth'. At the same time, Sergent (1946) has shown that although *A. australis* is a species particularly adapted to a dry climate, it does not avoid water and can resist prolonged immersion (31 % survived 24 hours), while *S. maurus* can survive immersion for up to 48 hours (67 %). Probably all species will drink if desiccated.

From his interesting studies Vachon (1952, 1953) has recently suggested that since modern scorpions represent the remains of an ancient fauna, they originally lived under quite different conditions of temperature and humidity. They are very responsive to microclimatic variations and each species seems to have to live and reproduce itself within strictly limited and characteristic ecological conditions. Nevertheless, scorpions have managed to survive in conditions of heat and drought largely on account of their nocturnal habits and subterranean habitats. Thus the Buthidae are usually found in shallow scrapes under rocks which they dig with their chelae and legs (Lankester, 1883). According to Pocock (1893) *Parabuthus capensis* stands on its first and fourth pairs of legs using the tips of the chelae as props while it kicks sand backwards with its disengaged legs. *Euscorpius* spp. do not dig, but hang upside down under pieces of wood, etc. or hide under rocks, while *Palamnaeus* and *Scorpio* spp. dig deep holes (up to 75 cm in the case of *S. maurus* whose enlarged pedipalps are probably specially adapted for this purpose). Scorpions of the genus *Hadrurus* in Arizona frequently dig down two or three feet in sandy wastes and river banks. Here they remain even though the burrow has collapsed 'apparently finding no difficulty in breathing' (Strahnke, 1945). However, Millot and Paulian (1943) have shown that *A. australis* can withstand the blocking of seven of its eight lungs for many months without much ill effect, and it is evident that scorpions have considerable respiratory reserves. The South African *Opisthophthalmus latimanus* often comes to the mouth of its burrow during the day. In this species 'stilting', or elevation of the abdomen, occurs as an adaptation to temperature stress (Alexander and Ewer, 1958).

Food and feeding habits

No doubt the ability to survive for long periods without food is of great service to scorpions living under the hazardous conditions of desert regions. Thus a well-fed *Hadrurus* sp. may remain buried for four or five months, and in experiments specimens have lived for nine months without food or water (Strahnke, 1945), while according to Waterman (1950) the West Indian *Tityus trinitatis* can survive three or four months without food provided that water is available. *A. australis* can survive six months' starvation and *B. occitanus* has lived for up to 368 days without feeding. Fabre (1907) remarked that the appetite of *B. occitanus* was very slight and Lankester (1883) found great difficulty in feeding *A. australis*. On the other hand the writer has found that the same species in captivity feeds readily on cockroaches, eating at least one per week during the summer months, although they do not touch hard beetles such as *Blaps* spp. and *Akis spinosa* unless starved (Cloudsley-Thompson, 1955a).

More segmental appendages have been brought into service as mouth parts in scorpions than in other Arachnids. There is the usual association of the chelicerae, labrum and pedipalp coxae, and in addition the under lip is composed of endite lobes of the coxae of both the first and second pairs of legs. The prey is picked to pieces by alternate movements of the chelicerae and the juices and soft tissues are drawn into the tiny mouth by the pumping action of the pharynx. In consequence feeding is slow and takes several hours.

The food of scorpions consists chiefly of spiders, harvest-men, flies, cockroaches, grasshoppers, crickets, mantids, butterflies, ants, beetles (adult and larvae), myriapods and even small mice. According to Strahnke (1945) *Hadrurus* sp. will eat readily of soft-bodied insects but rejects woodlice and harvest-men (when hungry they will even tackle hard beetles and small lizards), whereas *Euscorpius germanus* eats bluebottles, flies, small cockroaches, woodlice, spiders and centipedes (Pocock, 1893).

Schultze (1927) found that various species of Blattidae seem-ed to be favoured by *Palamnaeus longimanus* but that crickets, earwigs and certain larvae of Coleoptera were also taken at times. This species is usually found in old or virgin forest under loose bark of dead standing trees, under decaying trunks of trees and logs, or in cavities of rotten stumps located in the jungle, mostly in rather humid and damp places, where such insects abound.

According to Vachon (1953) it is not entirely clear how the scorpion first detects its prey. The eyes are too crude to be of much assistance and in any case the scorpion is a nocturnal animal, for which visual impressions can be of no great significance. Other sense organs must therefore be concerned, notably the sensory hairs or trichobothria found only on the pedipalps. 'These are richly supplied with nerves, and can detect minute air currents such as those caused by movements of the prey. They are, in fact like tiny receiving sets, pointing in all directions and spread out along the pedipalpi, which when extended act as huge antennae.' When hungry, the animal moves slowly forward supported by its hind legs with claws open and extended and tail raised and pointing forwards. 'Often the scorpion will then hesitate and the final act of capture seems almost accidental: an act of defence rather than of attack. If the prey is active, the scorpion may even withdraw for a time, but it waits patiently and finally achieves its aim.'

Scorpions probably do not usually go to seek their food. Instead, they wait for the insects that come to their lairs to hide. Some scorpions such as *E. italicus* and *P. longimanus* appear seldom, if ever, to use poison to kill their prey (Cloudsley-Thompson, 1951; Schultze, 1927) and the sting is used only as a defensive weapon. On the other hand, *S. maurus*, *B. occitanus* and *A. australis* will lash out with their sting at the slightest provocation, although if the prey is comparatively quiet it may be devoured alive.

Enemies

The greatest threats to the scorpion's existence are probably food shortage, drought and human activities. From ancient times man has feared, maligned and hated the animals on account of their poison. Nevertheless, there are other enemies which also destroy them. In the tropical rain forests of Africa and America scorpions are sometimes caught by raiding armies of driver ants. Although many times the size of their tormentors, the scorpions rapidly succumb to their attacks, are overpowered and dismembered. Various centipedes, spiders, Solifugae, lizards, snakes and birds have been recorded as predators and African baboons have been observed catching large scorpions, tearing off the tail and greedily devouring the rest of the body. It has also been reported that certain natives of Africa enjoy eating live scorpions! In addition many scorpions are inveterate cannibals. Among the few parasites known are various mites and nematode worms which are unlikely to be very harmful.

The pectines already mentioned are known to represent the modified appendages of the ninth somite of the body (= third mesosomal segment) but their function has long remained problematical. They have been regarded as external respiratory organs and external genitalia, and it has been claimed that the lamellae of the male and female scorpion become interlocked and serve to hold the two sexes together during mating. An alternative suggestion has been made that their function is to clean the extremities of the pedipalps, legs and tail. In 1883 Lankester made experiments on the tactile sense of the pectiniform appendages, and wrote: 'They appeared to me to possess no special sensitiveness. When they were pinched with forceps, the scorpions showed no sign of discomfort. It is quite possible that they may acquire a heightened sensibility at the breeding season, and serve as guides to the male and female in effecting copulation.' A few years later, nerve terminations were discovered in the lamellae of the pectines of scorpions by Gaubert, who wrote: 'Il est incontestable que leur richesse en nerfs en fait des organes sensitifs.'

Pocock (1893) suggested that the pectines were tactile organs of some importance. He pointed out that their situation near the genital aperture, their larger size in males and the modification of their basal portion in females of the same species indicated some sexual function. Apart from this he considered that it was highly probable that they were useful organs of touch in other aspects of life, enabling their possessor to learn the nature of the surface over which it was walking. He added: 'In favour of this view may be adduced the fact that these animals have been seen to touch the ground with their combs. Moreover, it is a very noticeable circumstance that scorpions which, like *Euscorpius*, creep along with their bellies close to the ground, have very short combs while in others which, like *Parabuthus*, stand high upon their legs, the combs are exceedingly long. I once noticed a *Parabuthus* marching over a piece of dead cockroach. When she had half crossed it, instead of going straight ahead as was expected, she halted abruptly, backed a little and stooping down started to devour the fragment. From the height at which the body was being carried, I am persuaded that no portion of the lower surface, except the combs, could have come into contact with the piece of food; so there can be little doubt that its presence was detected by the organs in question.'

Shortly afterwards it was suggested that the pectines of scorpions, like the special sense organs of *Limulus*, and of *Galeodes* and other Arachnids were probably to be accredited with the functions of equilibration and audition, but Warburton (*in* Harmer and Shipley, 1909)* supported Pocock's (1893) view.

From a detailed histological study of the pectines, Schröder concluded that they were chemotactic organs and had a double function as receptors for taste and smell and were perhaps also used during mating as a stimulatory organ (*Wollustorgane*) in the recognition of the sexes. With still more imagination,

Ubisch attributed to them an auxiliary role in respiration. She suggested that with their complex musculature, the pectines could be used as fans to blow fresh air across the lung-books while the scorpion was in its stuffy retreat, and that they served to ventilate the lung-books when the animal rested on the ground by lifting the pre-abdomen and thus permitting air to pass freely beneath the body.

On the other hand, Schultze (1927) observed in the case of the large Philippine forest scorpion *Palamnaeus longimanus* that while giving birth to young the pectines of the mother scorpion 'were carried in a vertical position pointing downwards, seemingly to serve as holders or bracers'.

Finally, Lawrence (1953)* wrote: 'The pectines of scorpions have been interpreted either as tactile or stimulatory organs during courtship, or as organs of smell. The latter seems to be the more likely explanation except that their position is peculiar in the arthropoda, where these organs are generally located on the antennae or legs.' After reviewing some of the functions that have been attributed to the pectines, Millot and Vachon (*in* Grassé, 1949)* concluded with justifiable caution: 'Toutes ces hypothèses ne font que masquer notre complète ignorance.'

As a result of experiments carried out on *Buthus occitanus*, *Androctonus australis* and *Euscorpius germanus*, in which it was found that the response of the scorpions to a vibrating tuning fork decreased markedly after the pectines had been painted over, it has recently been suggested that the function of these organs lies in the perception of ground vibrations (Cloudsley-Thompson, 1955b). Probably they are used more as a warning of danger than in the detection of prey. (See also p. 101.)

It is a well-known fact that a number of the larger species such as the greenish-black *Palamnaeus swammerdami* of southern India will frequently emit audible sounds under the stimulus of fear or of anger. The sound is said to be almost as loud as, and very similar to, that made by briskly and continuously drawing the tip of the index finger backwards and forwards in a direction transverse to its coarse edges over the ends of the teeth of a very fine-toothed comb. The stridulatory apparatus consists of a scraper on the flat outer face of the basal segment of the pedipalps and a rasp on the equally flat inner face of the corresponding segment of the first pair of legs. The scraper is tolerably thickly, but regularly, beset with stout conical sharp spinules like a tiger's canine, only more curved towards the points, some of which terminate in a long, limp hair, while the rasp is studded with minute tubercles shaped like the tops of mushrooms.

In the genus *Heterometrus*, the sounds are made by the movement of a 'keyboard' of flattened bristles on the pedipalp coxa against a rasp of finely striated cuticle on the coxa of the walking leg (Alexander, 1958), while in *Pandinus* the positions of the two are reversed. Alexander (1960) has explained this by suggesting that the factor which was decisive in determining which type of mechanism evolved was a difference in the behaviour of the two species. In threat situations, the response of *Heterometrus* was originally mainly aggressive and clutching movements of the pedipalps predominated, whereas in *Pandinus* the principal movements were defensive. These differences then conferred selective advantages on the elaboration of devices increasing the noise produced by friction.

There is no evidence that scorpions or large spiders can hear the sounds that their own stridulating organs produce, and Pocock (1896) points out that many poisonous animals including wasps and snakes are frequently rendered conspicuous by bright and staring colours or by sound-producing organs which, when in action, serve as a danger signal to meddlesome intruders, warning them to beware of hostile interference. In this way the poisonous forms are not destroyed by carnivorous creatures in mistake for other harmless and edible species. The existence of stridulatory organs implies the existence of an auditory sense, not necessarily in the performers themselves, but only in the enemies that might otherwise destroy them. The fact that monkeys, which are partial to a diet of scorpions and skilful enough to handle them without damage, pay no heed to the hissing when searching for these animals beneath stones does not detract from the theory. Despite their warning

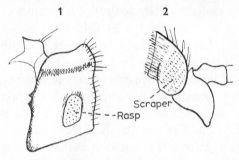

FIG. 19. Stridulatory apparatus of a scorpion. 1. Coxa of claw with rasp. 2. Coxa of first leg with scraper. (After Pocock, 1896.)

colours, bees are devoured by frogs and toads and the cobra is killed by the mongoose—indeed, few species are devoid of predatory enemies. Nevertheless, the existence of poison, coupled with the presence of aposematic sound production, will deter many potential enemies, thereby imparting an evolutionary advantage to their possessors.

Poison

The poison of scorpions has attracted attention since earliest times and observations as to its effects on man and other vertebrates have often been made. Unfortunately these have been somewhat conflicting and scientifically accurate data has been obtained only comparatively recently. One source of error has been lack of knowledge of the physiological state of the animal on which the observation was made, of the quantity of poison injected by the scorpion into the wound and its relation to the total weight of the victim. Another has been inaccurate and uncertain determinations of the species of scorpion, for it is known that different species vary greatly in the degree of virulence and type of their poison. Exact knowledge can be obtained only under carefully controlled laboratory experiments which may be supplemented by field observations provided that the scorpion is identified by an expert. Such observations have led to the conclusion that at least two types of poison exist. One of these is local in effect and comparatively harmless to man: it is exemplified by the European *Euscorpius italicus* and the American *Centruroides vittatus*. The other type is neurotoxic resembling some kinds of snake venom and can be extremely dangerous. It is found in *Buthus occitanus* and *Androctonus australis* in North Africa and in *Centruroides sculpturatus* and *C. gertschi* in North America. Poison for experiments may be obtained in pure form without injury to the scorpion by electrical stimulation. It has been found that *B. occitanus* of southern France produces at one time about 8 mg of fluid poison: curiously enough the same species from North Africa is said to be much more dangerous, while the sting of *A. australis* has been known to kill a man in about four hours, a dog in seven minutes and has a toxicity almost equal to that of a cobra.

The symptoms caused by scorpion poison of the less virulent type consist mostly of sudden sharp pain followed by numbness of the limb and local swelling: these pass away within an hour or two. Certain scorpions have reduced poison glands and their venom may have no effect whatsoever. Not so with species whose poison is neurotoxic. Here the symptoms resemble poisoning with strychnine. In the case of the American *C. sculpturatus* the venom does not produce a swelling or discoloration at the site of the sting. First, a feeling of tightness develops in the throat so that the victim tries to clear his throat of an imaginary phlegm. The tongue develops a feeling of thickness and speech becomes difficult. The victim next becomes restless and there may be slight, involuntary twitching of the muscles. Small children at this stage will not be still: some attempt to climb up the wall or the sides of their cot. A series of sneezing spasms is accompanied by a continuous flow of fluid from nose and mouth which may form a copious froth. Occasionally the rate of heart-beat is considerably increased. Convulsions follow, the arms are flailed about and the extremities become quite blue before death occurs. This complex pattern of reactions may last from 45 minutes to 10 or 12 hours. In those adults and children who recover, the effects of the venom persist longest at the original site of the sting, which may be hypersensitive for several days, so that only a slight bump will send painful or tingling sensations throughout the immediate surrounding area.

The effect of scorpion poison on different animals varies a good deal. Hedgehogs, jerboas and fennec foxes are practically immune, but guinea-pigs and dogs are especially susceptible. Birds are quite sensitive, as are frogs and fishes. The poison has a haemolytic action destroying red blood corpuscles and also contains adenosine tri-phosphatase in large quantities. Anti-scorpion serums are produced in various centres including Algeria, Mexico, Brazil, Arizona and London.

Mating habits

In scorpions the two sexes are distinct and show slight but visible differences in the relative proportions of the body. The male is more slender and has a longer tail. It also has a pair of organs used in copulation, but visible only when the animal is turned on its back. In addition to the now thoroughly discredited legend of their suicidal tendencies, scorpions appear to

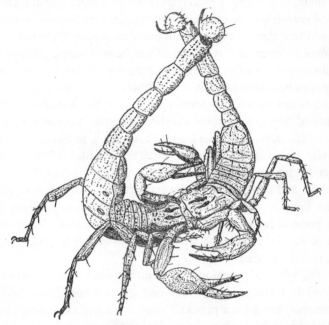

FIG. 20. Courtship dance of scorpions. (After Vachon, 1953.)

arouse popular interest for a number of reasons, not the least being their curious mating habits. Courtship takes the form of a dance ('promenade à deux') first observed by Maccary in 1810 and later described by Fabre (1907), Serfat and Vachon (1950) and Thornton (1956). On finding a female, the male grasps her pedipalpal claws with his and walks sideways or backwards while she follows, usually without reluctance. In *Buthotus alticola* the promenade is preceded by a manoeuvre during which the two animals face each other, forcibly straighten the back parts of their bodies and compress their abdomens to the ground, whilst their tails, extended upwards, are continuously entwined and then disengaged. The promenade which follows is somewhat less energetic and the tails of the two animals are raised but supple. The male directs operations while his mate follows placidly as he leads the dance. The process may last several hours and in the case of *Buthus occitanus* the tails may again be entwined but of course without hostile intent.

Spermatophore production occurs throughout the order Scorpiones and has been recorded in the Chactidae, Bothriuridae and Buthidae as well as in the Scorpionidae (Alexander, 1959; Angerman, 1957; Rosin and Shulov, 1963; Shulov and Amitai, 1958). Spermatophores are produced by Arachnida in which mating is delayed by courtship behaviour and their primary function is to prevent desiccation of the semen. Three behaviour patterns occur during the promenade: 'sand-sweeping', whose value seems to be the clearing of a space suitable for the deposition of a spermatophore; 'kissing', in which the mouth parts of the two animals are brought into close proximity; and 'juddering', during which the scorpion jerks its body rapidly forwards and backwards seven or eight times while its feet are held still. In *O. latimanus*, juddering occurs only at preliminary meeting ceremonies and may be of importance in sex recognition (Alexander, 1957, 1959). Selection of a suitable substrate for deposition of the spermatophore is achieved by means of special sense organs on the pectines (Carthy, 1966).

In the South African *Opisthopthalmus latimanus* the classical 'arbre droit' is either absent or only fleetingly present, while the 'promenade à deux' does not usually last longer than an hour. The male holds the chelicerae of the female and not, as in other species, her pedipalps. The promenade takes place in a limited area and if the ground is rough the male clears the soil particles from the space in which the pair are dancing. Shortly after the start, the genital operculum of the female opens and a little later that of the male also opens as the extrusion of a spermatophore begins. As soon as this is clear of the genital aperture of the male he moves back slightly so that it lies freely on the ground. He then jerks the female violently, drawing her over the spermatophore and half lifting her at the same time. She lowers her body over the capsule of the spermatophore, which becomes inserted in her genital aperture. (Alexander, 1956, 1957.) Experiments have shown that *Leiurus quinquestriatus* selects a substrate suitable for the deposition of spermatophores that has a firm, coarse and convex surface (Cloudsley-Thompson, 1961).

Reproduction and life cycle

The fertilised eggs develop inside the mother and the young are born alive. The course of development varies according to whether the eggs are rich in yolk, as in the Buthidae, or lacking in yolk, as in the Scorpionidae. In the first case the eggs pass quickly into the oviduct and develop there, the embryos consuming the yolk with which they are filled; in the second, the fertilised egg remains in place and becomes closely commingled with the maternal tissues. At the end of its development each embryo lies in a diverticulum which possesses a tubular extension like an umbilical cord along which pass nutrient fluids from the wall of the mother's intestine. These are transformed by glandular secretions and then led through the tube to the mouth of the embryo which has a well-developed pharynx with which it sucks the maternal fluid (Vachon, 1950a). The chelicerae of the embryo scorpion end in contractile vesicular organs which actually take hold of the teat and carry it to the mouth!

In many species the young are born during the night, sometimes in two batches separated by an interval of a day, but in *Buthotus alticola* birth has been observed from 7.0 to 9.0 a.m. (Serfat and Vachon, 1950). According to Fabre (1907) and

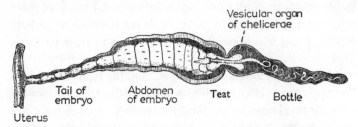

FIG. 21. Developing embryos of scorpion (family Scorpionidae) showing 'bottle and teat'. (After Vachon, 1953.)

Waterman (1950) the young, which are born enveloped in their chorion, are freed by their mother, but this unlikely hypothesis has been disproved in *B. occitanus*, and in *B. alticola* by Serfat and Vachon (1950) who state that the young free themselves without parental assistance, while in *Euscorpius flavicaudis* the young escape by lacerating the chorion with their stings (Cloudsley-Thompson, 1955a).

The process of mounting the mother's back may take up to two hours as the little scorpions are very plump and weak (Cloudsley-Thompson, 1951; Schultze, 1927). Here they remain until after their first moult. In *P. longimanus* this period lasts about ten days (Schultze, 1927). In *E. carpathicus* fourteen days (Berland, 1932)*, in *E. italicus* ten to twelve days (Cloudsley-Thompson, 1951), whilst in *E. germanus* it takes about sixteen days (Cloudsley-Thompson, 1955a). No doubt, however, the length of time depends much upon the season and temperature at which the animals are living. The mother scorpion carries her young around but does not feed them: they exist on the nourishment which they derive from digesting the embryonic yolk. Quite white and measuring only a few millimetres in length, they remain placidly on her back, often completely hiding her body from view so that only the appendages and tail remain visible. If they should happen to fall off, they make but feeble efforts to climb back and the stimulus for this is of short duration and inhibited by light. Their tarsi possess a specially modified pad which enables them to climb to their mother's back.

After the first moult the young acquire the typical scorpion-like appearance after which they remain with their mother for a day or two longer before finally scattering. Growth is accompanied by moulting as in all Arthropoda; the old skin cracks around the carapace and is shed completely, including the lining of the midgut and hindgut and of the four pairs of lung-books situated on the ventral side of the third to sixth pre-abdominal segments. The total number of moults of most species is not exactly known and may vary somewhat even in the same species, but it is believed that there are eight stadia in *Palamnaeus longimanus* and seven in *Androctonus australis*.

BIBLIOGRAPHY

Identification

GOUGH, L. H. and HIRST, S. (1927) Key to identification of Egyptian scorpions. *Min. Agr. Egypt Tech. Sci. Bull.*, No. 76, 1–8.
KRAEPELIN, K. (1899) Scorpiones und Pedipalpi. *Das Tierreich*, **8**, 1–265.
MELLO-LEITÃO (1945) Escorpiões Sul-Americanos. *Arq. Mus. Nac. Brasil*, **40**, 1–468.
POCOCK, R. I. (1900) *The Fauna of British India, including Ceylon and Burma. Arachnida.* London.

VACHON, M. (1952) *Études sur les Scorpions*. Alger.
WERNER, F. (1935) Scorpiones, *in* H. G. BRONN'S *Klass. Ordn. Tierreichs*, **5**, IV (4), 1–316.

Biology

ABUSHAMA, F. T. (1963) Bioclimate, diurnal rhythms and water-loss in the scorpion, *Leiurus quinquestriatus* (H. & E.). *Ent. Mon. Mag.*, **98**, 216–24.
——(1964) On the behaviour and sensory physiology of the scorpion *Leiurus quinquestriatus* (H. & E.). *Anim. Behav.*, **12**, 140–53.
ADAM, P. and WEISS, C. (1959) Scorpion venom. *Tropenmed. Parasitol.*, **10**, 334–8.
ALEXANDER, A. J. (1956) Mating in scorpions. *Nature, Lond.*, **178**, 867–8.
——(1957) The courtship and mating of the scorpion *Opisthophthalmus latimans. Proc. Zool. Soc. Lond.*, **128**, 529–44.
——(1958) On the stridulation of scorpions. *Behav.* **12**, 339–52.
——(1959) Courtship and mating in Buthid scorpions. *Proc. Zool. Soc. Lond.*, **133**, 145–69.
——(1960) A note on the evolution of stridulation within the family Scorpionidae. *Ibid.*, **133**, 391–9.
ALEXANDER, A. J. and EWER, D. W. (1958) Temperature adaptive behaviour in the scorpion, *Opisthophthalmus latimanus* Koch. *J. Exp. Biol.*, **35**, 349–59.
BERLAND, L. (1945) *Les Scorpions*. Paris.
BOTT, R. (1951) Beobachtungen am südeuropaischen Skorpion (*Euscorpius italicus*). *Natur. u. Volk.*, **81**, 290–3.
CARTHY, J. D. (1966) Fine structure and function of the sensory pegs of the scorpion pecten. *Experientia*, **22**, 89–91.
CLOUDSLEY-THOMPSON, J. L. (1951) Notes on Arachnida, 16.—The behaviour of a scorpion. *Ent. Mon. Mag.*, **86**, 105.
——(1955a) Some aspects of the biology of centipedes and scorpions. *Naturalist*, **1955**, 147–53.
——(1955b) On the function of the pectines of scorpions. *Ann. Mag. Nat. Hist.*, (12), **8**, 556–60.
——(1956) Studies in diurnal rhythms, VI. Bioclimatic observations in Tunisia and their significance in relation to the physiology of the fauna, especially woodlice, centipedes, scorpions and beetles. *Ann. Mag. Nat. Hist.*, (12), **9**, 305–29.
——(1961) Observations on the biology of the scorpion *Leiurus quinquestriatus* (H. & E.) in the Sudan. *Ent. Mon. Mag.*, **97**, 153–5.
——(1963) Some aspects of the physiology of *Buthotous minax* (Scorpiones: Buthidae) with remarks on other African scorpions. *Ibid.*, **98**, 243–6.
——(1965) The scorpion. *Sci. J.*, **1** (4) 35–41.
FABRE, J. H. (1907) *Souvenirs entomologiques*, Sér. 9, Paris.

106   SPIDERS, SCORPIONS, CENTIPEDES, MITES

LANKESTER, E. R. (1883) Notes on the habits of the scorpions *Androctonus funestris* Ehr. and *Euscorpius italicus* Roes. *J. Linn. Soc.* (*Zool.*), **16**, 455–62.

MCALISTER, W. H. (1965) The mating behaviour of *Centruroides vittatus* Say (Arachnida: Scorpionida). *Texas J. Sci.*, **17**, 307–12.

MILLOT, J. and PAULIAN, R. (1943) Valeur fonctionelle des poumons des scorpions. *Bull. Soc. zool. Fr.*, **58**, 97–8.

PETRUNKEVITCH, A. (1947) Scorpion. *Encyclopaedia Britannica*.

POCOCK, R. I. (1893) Notes upon the habits of some living scorpions. *Nature, Lond.*, **48**, 104–7.

——(1896) How and why scorpions hiss. *Nat. Sci.*, **9**, 17–25.

ROSIN, R. and SHULOV, A. (1963) Studies on the scorpion *Nebo hierochonticus*. *Proc. Zool. Soc. Lond.*, **140**, 547–75.

SCHULTZE, W. (1927) Biology of the large Philippine forest scorpion. *Philippine J. Sci.*, **32**, 375–89.

SERFAT, A. and VACHON, M. (1950) Quelques remarques sur la biologie d'un scorpion de l'Afghanistan: *Buthotus alticola* (Pocock). *Bull. Mus. Hist. Nat. Paris*, (2), **22**, 215–18.

SERGENT, E. (1946) Les scorpions et l'eau. *Arch. Inst. Pasteur d'Algérie*, **24**, 76–9; 304–5.

——(1947) Abris des scorpions. *Ibid.*, **25**, 206–9.

SHULOV, A. and AMITAI, P. (1958) On the mating habits of three scorpions: *Leiurus quinquestriatus* H. & E., *Buthotus judaicus* E. Sim. and *Nebo hierochonticus* E. Sim. *Arch. Inst. Pasteur d'Algérie*, **36**, 351–69.

STRAHNKE, H. L. (1945) Scorpions of the genus *Hadrurus* Thorell. *Amer. Mus. Nov.*, No. 1298, 1–9.

THORNTON, I. W. B. (1956) Notes on the biology of *Leiurus quinquestriatus* (H. E., 1929) (Scorpiones, Buthidae). *Brit. J. Anim. Behav.*, **4**, 92–3.

VACHON, M. (1950) Remarques préliminaires sur l'alimentation des organes chélicériens le biberon et la tétine de l'embryon du scorpion: *Ischnurus ochropus* C. L. Koch (Scorpionidae). *Arch. Zool. éxp. gén.*, **86**, 137–56.

——(1953) The biology of scorpions. *Endeavour*, **12**, 80–9.

WATERMAN, J. A. (1950) Scorpions in the West Indies with special reference to *Tityus trinitatis*. *Caribbean Med. J.*, **12**, 167–77.

CHAPTER VI

SOLIFUGAE

Classification and distribution

The Arachnids of the Order Solifugae or Solpugida, sometimes known as 'false-spiders' or 'wind-scorpions', are among the most formidable of the terrestrial invertebrates. A superficial resemblance to true spiders is belied by the segmented abdomen without spinnerets, whilst the legs of the fourth pair characteristically bear five 'malleoli' or 'racquet organs' whose function is unknown, although it has been suggested that they may serve to support the abdomen. It is more likely, however, that they are sense organs analogous with the pectines of scorpions. The hairy body is divided into two parts, a prosoma or cephalothorax and an opisthosoma or abdomen which are segmented and united to one another without a narrow pedicle as is found in spiders. The chelicerae are extremely well developed, forming two powerful pincers with which the prey is destroyed. Sometimes these are as long as the entire prosoma and they are possibly for their size the most formidable jaws in the animal world. The pedipalps have the normal six segments and end, not in a claw, but in a peculiar suctorial organ to be discussed below. The extreme speed and activity of these animals is probably correlated with their well-developed tracheal system.

The legs of the Solifugae are quite characteristic. The first pair are long and rather feeble. They are not used for walking but are carried stretched out in front and used as additional tactile organs, a habit found also in the 'whip-scorpions'. The remaining legs are true ambulatory limbs, those of the fourth pair, which are the strongest of all, bearing the malleoli. There

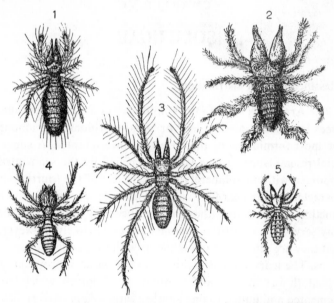

FIG. 22. Examples of Solifugid families: 1. Rhagodidae, 2. Hexisopodidae, 3. Galeodidae, 4. Eremobatidae, 5. Ammotrechidae. (Drawings not to scale.) (After various authors.)

are only three of these to each hind leg in the family Hexisopodidae, which includes the curious, short-legged *Chelypus* spp.

The size of the body varies from one to five centimetres in length, and the larger species such as *Galeodes arabs* and *G. araneoides* whose formidable appearance is enhanced by their unusual hairiness and bulk, can with their limbs span a width of five inches. Most species are uniformly yellow or brown in colour while those of the genera *Rhagodes* and *Dinorhax* are black. A few, however, have a pattern of longitudinal black stripes on a yellow background, or the reverse with occasional reddish tints.

Predominantly inhabitants of hot, dry and desert areas, the Solifugae are almost entirely confined to tropical and subtropical regions. In Europe only six species occur and these are found in warmer parts such as south-east Spain, Greece, the Balkans and the vicinity of the Black Sea. Ten families are known to science of which two, the Eremobatidae and Ammotrechidae, are uniquely Nearctic, while the remainder are restricted to the Old World. Of these the Ceromidae and Hexispodidae are found in Africa south of the Equator, the Solpugidae in Africa and Iraq, while the Daesiidae are distributed throughout Africa, Arabia, Asia Minor, Persia and southern Europe. The Rhagodidae and Galeodidae are restricted to an area north of the Equator ranging from Morocco to India and Turkestan: the remaining families, the Karschiidae and Melanoblossiidae, have a somewhat discontinuous distribution in Africa and Asia.

Solifugae are particularly abundant in Africa, but none are found in Madagascar and they are also absent from Australia and New Zealand.

General behaviour

These animals are lovers of warmth and are never found in cold or temperate countries, although one species, *Gylippus rickmersi*, inhabits the 10,000-foot plateau of the Pamir in Central Asia, north of the Hindu Kush Mountains. Even where they thrive, they hide away or hibernate throughout the winter season. They avoid fertile oases and seem to prefer utterly neglected regions where the soil is broken and bare, but this is not because they cannot exist in proximity with man.

On the contrary, they frequently enter the tents of travellers to catch flies and other insects. According to Aelian, an area of Ethiopia was deserted by its inhabitants on account of the appearance of an incredible number of scorpions and 'Phalangiums' but Pliny, in quoting the same story, replaced 'Phalangium' by 'Solfuga'. *Gluvia dorsalis* is said to be a familiar sight in the streets of Madrid and the species *Mummucia variegata* and *Pseudocleobis morsicans* often run about in the streets of Santiago where they are known as 'Arãnhas del Sol' (sunspiders). The majority of Solifugae, as their name indicates, are however, nocturnal and hide away under stones or in crevices of the soil during the daytime. It has been suggested that this habit may be correlated with a low temperature tolerance, but *Galeodes granti* can survive a temperature of 50° C (122° F) for 24 hours below 10% relative humidity which is a higher lethal temperature even than that of scorpions and desert beetles (Cloudsley-Thompson, 1962).

Hingston (1925) has described the process of burrowing in a Persian species of *Galeodes* (*G. arabs* or *G. araneoides*). No great skill is exhibited, and the procedure is laborious even in friable soil. Where the sand is loose, a furrow is ploughed with the pointed mandibles, the soil being raked back with the hairy legs. The animal faces its excavation with outstretched limbs; the long pedipalps are thrust forward to explore the way; the first pair of legs also is advanced, but it is the second pair that fulfils the purpose of rakes. These are pushed into the loose sand, their ends being turned inwards so as to gather it in armfuls. The rakings are repeated in such rapid succession that the sand comes spouting from beneath the abdomen in a rhythmical series of jets. From time to time the Solifugid reverses its positions, lowers itself into the excavation, thrusts its body into the place where it previously raked, and shovels up the débris with its broad head, especially any of the larger fragments which it cannot so easily dislodge with its rakes. Then it again turns about and resumes the scuffling with its second pair of legs. Sometimes the females merely cut a circle in the soil with their jaws and kick the loosened fragments away (Pocock, 1898). *Eremobates formicaria* constructs its burrow in the same manner as *Galeodes*, but instead of using a common burrow throughout the breeding season, a new one is constructed almost every night (Turner, 1916). A comparative study of the burrowing habits of North American Solifugae has demonstrated a broad similarity of behaviour in all species investigated (Muma, 1966c).

Food and feeding habits

Solifugae are exclusively predatory and carnivorous, having an extraordinary voracity. They will continue feeding until their abdomens are so distended that they can scarcely move. A young *Galeodes* scarcely 5 mm long has been seen to devour over 100 flies in 24 hours. Although insects, including even hard beetles, form their staple diet, Solifugae will kill and eat large spiders, scorpions and lizards. They have also been observed to kill mice and small birds. Several species such as *Solpuga sericea* and *S. lineata* burrow into the ground to catch termites while a Californian species of *Eremobates* kills bees, entering the hives in search of prey. The small nocturnal species *E. pallipes* from Colorado is said to hunt bed-bugs.

The prey is probably followed by sight in some species, for a blind *Galeodes* has difficulty in locating its victims, but the nocturnal South African *Solpugyla globicornis* searches at random with its pedipalps and first pair of legs stretched forward, and sight is not used. It is possible that the olfactory sense may also be used in orientation, as one specimen was observed trying to get hold of a snail that had retreated into its shell (Bolwig,

1952). The long-legged forms can run at great speed so that they resemble balls of yellow thistledown blown over the desert. Often when going at full speed, they stop abruptly and begin hunting about like a dog checked in mid-course by the scent of game. When gorged with food or when pregnant, however, they are fat and sluggish. Some species have been known to climb trees in search of insects and other prey. It is probable that the ability to move is the main attribute by which living prey is distinguished from non-living, for in captivity a dead insect will be attacked only if suitably moved (Turner, 1916).

Both tactile and visual responses are employed in the recognition of prey by *Galeodes granti*: males are more sensitive and less aggressive than females, which almost invariably kill them in combat (Cloudsley-Thompson, 1961a). Behaviour responses to enemies and prey have been classified as alertness, threat, high intensity threat (accompanied by stridulation) leading to attack or flight, often followed by displacement sand-digging (Cloudsley-Thompson, 1961b). Food-searching behaviour of North American Solifugae involves random running and congregating in areas of high prey density at night. The prey is located by orientation to tactile and visual stimuli and vibrations of the substrate. It is captured by chasing, ambushing and, occasionally, stalking (Muma, 1966d).

There has been much controversy as to the poisonous properties with which these creatures have been widely credited. Lichtenstein (1797) has endeavoured to show that the mice which plagued the Philistines (1 Sam. v. 6) when they captured the 'ark of the Covenant' may have been *Galeodes arabs*, and it is certainly true that their hairy bodies and rapid movements give to many species a mouse-like appearance. This author also suggested that the 'emerods' with which they were plagued referred to the sores caused by the bites of these animals, for Solifugae have been known to attack travellers asleep in the desert at night. Olivier (1807) disbelieved the awful reports of the Arabs, who were terrified at the sight of the wind-scorpions, which appeared in the tents at night, and who told yarns, each more horrible than the last, as to their dangerous bites. He did admit, however, that with *such* jaws the results would probably be most painful. People have been bitten accidentally by the animals getting under their clothes and the effect is sometimes severe. The inhabitants of Baku on the Caspian Sea believe that a local species is especially poisonous after its winter sleep, and they rub the wound with the carcass of the animal after first steeping it in boiling oil, in order to neutralise the effects of the venom. On the other hand, the Somalis do not regard them as noxious—indeed, they have no name in their language for anything so unimportant! Hutton (1843) records the case of a lizard bitten by a *Galeodes* which recovered in three days, and other authors have searched in vain for poison glands such as those in the jaws of spiders. Bernard (1897) suggested that poisoning might result from a simple exudation of toxic excretory matter through the setal pores which, he believed, could be traced along the tips of the jaws.

Phisalix (1922)* records a number of cases of Solifugae biting men and concludes that in view of the severity of the effects which may occasionally result in death, the possibility of poison cannot be entirely eliminated. Although the matter has not yet been fully tested experimentally, it is now generally assumed that Solifugae are not venomous since a number of people have allowed themselves to be bitten without any ill effects. On the few occasions that poisoning does occur, it is most probably due to infection of the wound.

In the silence of the night, the desert Solifugae race about, conduct their amours and glut themselves on innumerable insects to supply their requirements during the winter sleep.

The South African *Solpuga caffra* is a large species with

massive powerful jaws set in a very wide head-plate. The method of catching insects seems to depend on contact and within a certain critical distance the prey is seized with a short spring and lightning snap of the jaws. A cricket is seldom missed, but more active grasshoppers sometimes escape the first attempt to catch them. While being eaten the crackling sound of the harder parts of an insect's cuticle as they are crushed in the chelicerae can be heard from a distance of several feet! The pointed extremities of the jaws are often used to pierce the body of the prey (Lawrence, 1949) and I have observed the same when *Rhagodes* sp. feeds on large spiders.

The prey when caught is usually held cross-ways by both jaws. Mastication and maceration is a fairly complicated procedure since there are simultaneous movements of the jaws in two planes; first there is the opening and closing of the jaws alternately, a movement in the vertical plane; at the same time the prey is ground between the chelicerae, the left and right sides moving alternately backwards and forwards producing a horizontal movement. The prey is speedily reduced to a soft pulp and pressed against the mouth opening where most of it is absorbed in a semifluid condition. Even hard, chitinous parts, although usually rejected, may at times be devoured.

Most victims are overpowered with ease, but occasionally Solifugae encounter a more powerful adversary such as a centipede, scorpion or another Solifugid which will not submit without a stubborn fight. Hingston (1925) gives a graphic account of such combats in *Galeodes arabs* and *G. araneoides*. He believes that these species have not much faculty of vision, taste or hearing, but his experiments are open to the objection that he was testing the responses of the animals to unnatural stimuli which they do not encounter in their normal life. The chief sense is that of touch, which is located in the innumerable hairs with which the body is covered. The contest is usually more an exhibition of swiftness than of any particular strategical skill, the victim being quickly macerated by the jaws of its ferocious enemy.

Duels between rival Solifugids are usually more prolonged. The combatants rush at each other, their pedipalps taking the immediate shock and warding off the ponderous jaws. After this the contest becomes very variable. Sometimes the animals rock from side to side, their bodies kept apart by their projecting pedipalps like wrestlers at arm's length waiting for a chance to secure a grip. At others they come quickly in to closer apposition and their jaws interlock as they struggle to get a vital grip. Given the slightest opportunity one will drive its chelicerae into the soft parts of its opponent and the struggle ends. Not infrequently however the interlocking jaws are disengaged and the wrestlers spring apart only to charge again, when one may overwhelm the other.

Savory (1928)* writes that during the Great War Solifugae became familiar to the troops in Egypt and the Near East where *Galeodes arabs* is common. The soldiers named them 'jerrymanders' and admired them for their ferocity. At one time the men stationed at Aboukir kept pet Solifugae and matched them like fighting cocks. Each Company had its champion and bets were freely laid on the results of the fights. Size is not always a decisive factor and it sometimes happens that a smaller individual seizes its opponent between its too widely-opened jaws and conquers by holding on in a position in which the big creature is quite helpless. Combats with scorpions usually result in the death of the latter before they have time to use their stings. In 1942 in Libya, my troop corporal kept a short-legged, black *Rhagodes* in a biscuit tin on the back of his tank and fed it almost entirely on scorpions.

In addition to their use as buffers in the hour of battle, when they are of supreme importance, the pedipalps are used as implements of feeding. They are stretched forward like long arms to seize pieces of food with their terminal suckers. The morsels are then transferred to the jaws. When drinking, the tips are brought together, thrust into the fluid and then employed like a pair of hands to lift the liquid into the mouth (Hingston, 1925). The palpal organs were originally described by Lichtenstein (1797) as organs of scent, but later it was claimed that they were suckers. Towards the end of the last century, however, it was suggested on morphological grounds that the earlier view was the correct one and Heymons (1902) claimed that the male Solifugae recognised the females by the sense of smell, the receptor organs for which lay in the tarsi of the pedipalps. After amputation of these organs, males invariably fled when introduced into the presence of a female. It is not surprising, however, that the mating instinct should be destroyed by this crippling treatment.

Solifugae can climb up glass or out of a bucket by means of their pedipalps whose organs are undoubtedly suckers (Cloudsley-Thompson, 1954; Muma 1967).

Enemies

Little is known of the enemies of Solifugae, but Distant (1892) in the Transvaal saw a wagtail attack a *Solpuga hostilis* and Pocock (1898) suggests that they are probably eaten by insectivorous birds, small mammals and reptiles. They have recently been found in the stomach contents of an African Steppe Buzzard. Enemies also include large lizards, other reptiles and other Solifugae too, for cannibalism is by no means unknown.

The ninth somite of Solifugae is suppressed in the adult and the prosoma is joined to the opisthosoma across its whole width. Nevertheless, there is a great flexibility between the two parts of the body and the abdomen can be raised until it is almost vertical. This action is common in life and results in a scorpion-like appearance, particularly in the short-legged black Rhagodidae. It has been suggested (Cloudsley-Thomp-

FIG. 23. *Galeodes arabs* in defensive attitude. (After Millot and Vachon, 1949.)

son, 1949) that this behaviour may be a form of mimicry; at any rate, that raising the abdomen in this fashion may be an asset in deterring an attacker. At the same time this vulnerable member is kept away from danger and the foe is presented with a pair of gaping jaws surrounded by five pairs of strong limbs armed with long bristles, short spines and sharp claws.

Solifugae can stridulate and make grunting sounds by rubbing together a pair of horny ridges on the inner surface of the chelicerae. An enraged *Galeodes* has been said to 'screech' and this, like the hissing of scorpions and snakes, is probably a form of advertisement and a warning to enemies.

The only parasite of Solifugae so far recorded is the Indian Pompilid wasp *Salius sycophanta* which has been seen, after a prolonged struggle, to sting a *Galeodes* and drag it to a hole in which were afterwards found no less than five *Galeodes* all deprived of their legs and with a single egg attached to the hair on the underside of their stomachs. All were quite dead except for the last, which was still moving feebly.

Mating habits

Sexual differences in Solifugae are not striking. The male is smaller and of lighter build than the female, but his legs are longer. They probably stand him in good stead at mating time when the female is alleged to kill and devour her less powerful mate if she can! The jaws of the male are less bulky than those of the female which are used to dig burrows in which the eggs are laid. They are less strongly toothed and bear on their upper side a peculiar whiplike structure of unknown function known as the flagellum.

Mating takes place at dusk or during the night: it is rapid and brutal. According to Heymons (1902) who observed it in *Galeodes caspius* during a journey across the steppes of Turkestan, the male courts his mate by stroking her, thus reducing her to a state of lethargy. He then seizes her with his chelicerae, pedipalps and legs, usually without harming her, carries her for some little distance and lays her on her side. After massaging her ventral surface for some time with his jaws, he opens her genital orifice whose edges have become swollen from these attentions, lifts his abdomen and emits a mass of spermatozoa which falls to the ground. Gathering this with his chelicerae, he forces it into the vagina of the female, closes the sides and holds them shut for a while. Then he bounds off and flees before she can catch him. A male can effect several copulations in succession but after the first the spermatic mass is comparatively small and he dies shortly afterwards.

These actions are purely reflex, because if the animals are separated during copulation the male will continue his massaging movements against the hand of the observer, just as though the female were still there. Although the total act may last for several minutes, certain details are extremely rapid and it is difficult to see exactly what is occurring; for example, it is not quite clear how the mass of spermatozoa is gathered up and introduced into the genital orifice of the female.

Mating was not again witnessed until 1960 (Cloudsley-Thompson, 1961a) when I observed it in the large Sudanese species, *Galeodes granti*. The following year it was described in *G. sulfruripes* by Amitai, Levy and Shulov (1962). Although the procedure is essentially similar in all three species, minor differences occur. In *G. caspius* the male courts his mate by stroking her until she becomes lethargic; in *G. sulfuripes* the female becomes paralysed when the pedipalps of the two partners meet; in *G. granti*, the male merely touches the female with his pedipalps in reply to which she lifts her abdomen and allows him to grasp her with his jaws. In *G. sulfuripes* and *G. granti* the female awakens slowly, in *G. caspius* immediately after insemination has been completed. The most significant difference between mating in Solifugae and in scorpions and false-scorpions consists in the immediate transfer of the sperm ball which is not fixed to the ground. This may represent an evolutionary stage between the situation found in the scorpions and pseudo scorpions and that in spiders. More recently, mating has been observed in *Othoes saharae* by Junqua (1962) presumably in Algeria; and in three species of *Eremobates* from south-western U.S.A. by Muma (1966b). Sexual behaviour is quite distinct in the family Eremobatidae from that of the African and Asian family Galeodidae in that sperm is emitted directly from male to female genital opening. This suggests a transition from the usual indirect Arachnid method of sperm transmission to a direct one.

Reproduction and life cycle

After fertilisation the female develops an enormous appetite for two or three weeks. There follows a period of intense tunnelling operations during which a deep burrow is constructed, mostly at night. In *Solpuga caffra* egg-laying lasts for some $3\frac{1}{2}$–$4\frac{1}{2}$ hours (Lawrence, 1949), some 200 eggs being produced. In the smaller *S. hostilis* the number is under 100. During labour the female lies on her side rather listlessly while the eggs slip from her at regular intervals: she is limp and motionless except for rhythmic contractions of her body at a rate of approximately one per two seconds. The eggs of *Galeodes* may number more than 200. They are in the form of white and glistening spheres that reflect the sunlight with a beautiful metallic lustre as if made of mother-of-pearl: they adhere to one another in compact heaps. In *Solpuga caffra* the eggs are of a light, but dirty yellow colour, while in *S. hostilis* there are darker markings. Within a day or two after oviposition the female begins to take an interest in feeding. *Eremobates formicaria* lays more than one batch of small white spherical eggs per season, but closes the mouth of the burrow and leaves them to their fate. In Arizona and New Mexico, *E. durangonus* females deposit one to five batches averaging 64 eggs during August and September. They hatch within three or four weeks into an embryo-like, morphologically incomplete, inactive stadium (Muma, 1966a, e).

The appearance and detailed structure of the newly hatched

first larva appears to vary considerably in different genera. In *Galeodes* the young larvae emerge from the eggs within a day or two after they are laid. At first they are soft, white and helpless. They are unable to move, but after two or three weeks, during which they are closely guarded by their mother, the first moult takes place and from then on the young creatures rapidly become more active. Their integument hardens and progressively assumes the various external characters of the mature animal. Eventually they disperse. The number of moults and the length of time required to reach the adult condition is not known with certainty in any species of the order Solifugae.

BIBLIOGRAPHY

Identification

KRAEPELIN, K. (1901) Arachnoidea: Palpigradi und Solifugae. *Das Tierreich*, **12**, 1–159.
MUMA, M. H. (1951) The Arachnid Order Solpugida in the United States. *Bull. Amer. Mus. Nat. Hist.*, **97**, (2), 31–142.
ROEWER, C. F. (1934) Solifugae, *in* H. G. BRONN'S *Klass. Ordn. Tierreichs*, **5**, iv (4), 1–608.
——(1941) Solifugen 1934–46. *Veroff. deuts. Kolon.-Ubersee-Mus.*, **3**, 97–192.

Biology

AMITAI, P., LEVY, G. and SHULOV, A. (1962) Observations on mating in a Solifugid *Galeodes sulfruripes* Roewer. *Bull. Res. Counc. Israel*, **11** (B), 156–9.
BERNARD, A. (1897) 'Wind-scorpions', a brief account of the Galeodidae. *Sci. Prog.* (N.S.), **1**, 317–43.
BOLWIG, N. (1952) Observations on the behaviour and mode of orientation of hunting Solifugae. *J. Ent. Soc. S. Afr.*, **15**, 239–40.
CLOUDSLEY-THOMPSON, J. L. (1949) Notes on Arachnida, 9.—Do Solifugae mimic scorpions? *Ent. Mon. Mag.*, **85**, 47.

—— (1954) Notes on Arachnida, 22.–The function of the palpal organ of Solifugae. *Ibid.*, **90**, 236–7.

—— (1961a) Observations on the natural history of the camel-spiders *Galeodes arabs* C. L. Koch (Solifugae: Galeodidae) in the Sudan. *Ent. Mon. Mag.*, **97**, 145–52.

—— (1961b) Some aspects of the physiology and behaviour of *Galeodes arabs*. *Ent. Exp. & Appl.*, **4**, 257–63.

—— (1962) Lethal temperatures of some desert Arthropods and the mechanism of heat death. *Ibid.*, **5**, 270–80.

—— (1967) Reproduction in Solifugae. *Ent. Mon. Mag.*, **104**, 144.

DISTANT, W. L. (1892) Are the Solpugidae poisonous? *Nature, Lond.*, **46**, 247.

HEYMONS, R. (1902) Biologische Beobachtungen an asiatischen Solifugen. *Abh. preuss. Akad. Wiss.*, **190**, 1–65.

HINGSTON, R. W. (1925) *Nature at the Desert's Edge*. London. 192–261.

HUTTON, T. (1843) Observations on the habits of a large species of *Galeodes*. *Ann. Mag. Nat. Hist.*, **12**, 81–5.

JUNQUA, C. (1958) Observations préliminaires sur la mue et la croissance chez les Solifuges. *Bull. Soc. Zool. France*, **83**, 262–3.

——(1962) Donnes sur la reproduction d'un solifuge: *Othoes saharae* Panaoux. *C.R. Séane. Acad. Sci.*, **225**, 2673–5.

LAWRENCE, R. F. (1949) Observations on the habits of a female Solifuge, *Solpuga caffra* Pocock. *Ann. Transvaal Mus.*, **21**, 197–200.

—— (1965) Sun-spiders. *Animals*, **6**, 232–5.

LICHTENSTEIN, A. A. H. (1797) Gattungen Solpuga und Phalangium *in* HERBST, J. F. W. *Natursystem der ungeflügelten Insekten*, Berlin.

LONNBERG, E. (1899) Some biological observations on *Galeodes* and *Buthus*. *K. vetensk. Akad. Förh.* **56**, 977–83.

MUMA, M. H. (1966a) Egg disposition and incubation for Eremobatidae. (Arachnida: Solpugida). *Florida Ent.*, **49**, 23–31.

—— (1966b) Mating behaviour in the Solpugid genus *Eremo bates* Banks. *Anim. Behav.*, **14**, 346–50.

—— (1966c) Burrowing habits of North American Solpugida (Arachnida). *Psyche*, **73**, 251–60.

—— (1966d) Feeding behaviour of North American Solpugida. *Florida Ent.*, **49**, 199–216.

—— (1966e) Life cycle of *Eremobates durangonus* (Arachnida: Solpugida) *Ibid.* **49**, 233–42.

—— (1967) Basic behaviour of North American Solpugida. *Ibid.* **50**, 115–23.

OLIVIER, G. A. (1807) *Voyage dans l'Empire Ottoman, l'Egypte et la Perse*, **3**, Paris.

POCOCK, R. I. (1898) The nature and habits of Pliny's Solpuga. *Nature, Lond.*, **57**, 618–20.

TURNER, C. H. (1916) Notes on the feeding, behaviour and oviposition of a captive American false-spider *(Eremobates formicaria)*. *J. Anim. Behav.*, **6**, 160–8.

CHAPTER VII

FALSE-SCORPIONS

Classification and distribution

The order Pseudoscorpiones, Chelonethi or Chernetes comprises small Arachnids which resemble scorpions in the form of their pedipalps and of their body, except that the hind part of the abdomen is not narrow as is the post-abdomen or meta-

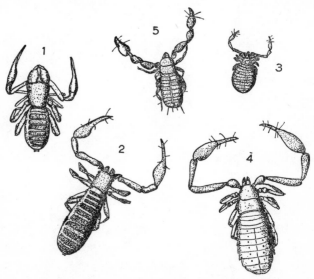

Fig. 24. Examples of False-scorpion families: 1. Chthoniidae, 2. Neobisiidae, 3. Cheiridiidae, 4. Chernetidae, 5. Cheliferidae. (After various authors.)

soma of scorpions and they have no caudal sting. The dorsal surface of the prosoma or cephalothorax is formed of a large sclerite bearing the eyes, when these are present, and six pairs of appendages: the chelicerae, pedipalps and four pairs of legs. The chelicerae are pre-oral in position and are composed of two segments. Their fingers bear a series of complicated structures known as the serrulae and laminae. The serrula exterior is keel-like, set with fine teeth and attached for varying degrees of its length to the movable finger while the serrula interior, attached to the base of the fixed finger, is even more variable in form. A flagellum, formed of setae whose number and shape are valuable taxonomic characters, is also attached to the fixed finger.

The mouth is situated between the basal segments of the six-segmented pedipalps. These are enormously developed and resemble the claws of scorpions. They serve as prehensible organs to capture and kill the prey and bear sensory hairs or setae. The immovable finger of the chelae has a row of cutting teeth along its inner edge, the last of which is considerably enlarged. Through this passes the duct of the elongated poison gland which itself is embedded in the substance of the finger. In certain families both fingers are equipped with poison glands. The coxae of the pedipalps are extended forward so as to form masticatory plates, or they may bear distinct endites with which the prey is held in front of the mouth during feeding. The four pairs of walking legs differ from those of other Arachnida in that the tibia is undivided so that there is no patella. At the same time in many species the femur is divided into two more or less distinct segments. The number of tarsal joints is of great systematic importance and is the chief character upon which the three sub-orders of the Pseudoscorpiones are differentiated.

The opisthosoma or abdomen is broadly attached to the

cephalothorax and consists of 12 segments, the last of which is small and forms a circumanal ring. The genital orifice is situated between the second and third sternites, the second forming an operculum while the first sternite is much reduced.

The order Pseudoscorpiones contains over 1500 species belonging to three sub-orders all of which are represented in the British fauna. False-scorpions are distributed all over the world with the exception of the arctic and antarctic regions. At present, nineteen families have been described, but the order is still by no means well known and others may yet be discovered. Some genera have a world-wide distribution, others are rare and local. As a rule they are sober-coloured animals, their livery consisting of various shades of yellow and brown.

A wide variety of habitats are colonised, the majority of species inhabiting soil and decaying vegetation while others live under stones and the bark of trees. None is parasitic: *Chelifer cancroides* has occasionally been recorded on man but it is probably merely phoretic (see below). This species, *Allochernes italicus, Cheiridium museorum*, etc., frequently live in human habitations. *Microbisium femoratum* lives exclusively in moss and members of the genus *Neobisium* are nearly always found in moss and humus: the species of *Chthonius* are nearly always found under stones while the genus *Chernes* includes bark-inhabiting forms. Species such as *Microbisium dumicola* and *Neobisium sylvaticum* that walk in the open on plants and bushes are extremely rare, but cavernicolous false-scorpions are relatively numerous, although they belong almost exclusively to the genera *Neobisium, Roncus* and *Chthonius*. Quite a number of species are myrmecophilous and live in the nests of ants: Donisthorpe (1927)* records the following amongst the British fauna, *Chthonius ischnocheles, Neobisium muscorum, Roncus lubricus, Microcreagris cambridgei, Pselaphochernes scorpioides* and *Allochernes wideri. Neobisium maritimum,*

Chthonius halberti and the large *Garypus beauvoisi* have a littoral distribution and are found in cracks in rocks between tidemarks on the sea shore while *Neobisium muscorum* and several other species occur in damp seaweed at the water's edge.

A number of species such as *Withius subruber*, *Cheiridium museorum* and *Toxochernes panzeri* are often associated with stored food products in warehouses, where they inhabit extremely dry environments: they also occur in birds' nests in hollow trees. In view of their small size it is obvious that their powers of water-retention must be extremely efficient. A number of other species are partial to heaps of manure and one or two cling to the legs of flies and other arthropods as a means of dispersal (see below). The well-known 'book-scorpion' *Cheiridium museorum*, already mentioned, has been known to live in human habitations since the time of Aristotle, for he wrote: 'In books other small animals are found, some of which are like scorpions without tails,' and in this country Hooke (1664) drew a picture possibly of the same species in his famous book *Micrographia*.

General behaviour

All false scorpions are of small size, seldom exceeding 7 or 8 mm in length. The giant *Garypus beauvoisi* of Corsica and the Mediterranean is only a quarter of an inch in length, and the largest British species, the handsome *Dendrochernes cyrneus*, is only 3·6 mm long. Because they are so small and have shy, retiring habits, pseudoscorpions are little known and seldom found unless specially sought. This is a pity, for they are interesting creatures and many aspects of their biology would provide suitable subjects for study by both amateur and professional zoologists.

Most pseudoscorpions are markedly photo-negative and do

not often venture into the open. They may be collected by hand from rotting leaves and from under the bark of trees, but this method tends to be laborious for they are by no means plentiful. The most effective method entails the use of the Berlese Funnel, but a simpler way is to scatter fallen leaves, moss and other vegetable débris onto a sheet of newspaper or a white table top. Despite their small size, the creatures can then be easily recognised by their squarish shape: they generally crouch motionless, their legs and chelae drawn in until they are touched, when they at once proclaim their nature by running backwards. False-scorpions walk slowly with an air of impressive dignity and calm deliberation which distinguishes them from most of the other small arthropods that inhabit the same type of locality, their enormous pedipalps spread out in front of them like the antennae of an insect. If, as they proceed, they happen to touch some other animal with the long setae on their extended palps, they dart sideways or backwards with surprising speed, looking rather like a startled crayfish. This sudden retreat is highly characteristic for not many animals can go backwards as easily as forwards, and very few more rapidly.

It has been pointed out that a few species inhabit a comparatively dry environment, but the majority are extremely susceptible to desiccation and must be provided with moisture if kept in captivity. Some species are light-shy, but in *Chelifer cancroides* no negative phototaxis has been observed although the animals tend to prefer a rough surface to walk on. Thanks to the arolium, a trumpet-shaped membranous sucker beneath the claws of the walking legs, false-scorpions are able to climb vertically and walk upside-down on the under surfaces of stones and logs. If they should happen to fall on their backs, however, they can only right themselves with difficulty by arching their bodies and rocking from side to side, or by grasping some nearby object with their claws.

The phenomenon of the utilisation of another animal for transport, to which the name 'phoresy' is commonly applied, is perhaps a particular type of commensalism. An example is afforded by *Limosina sacra*, a Borborid fly, numbers of which constantly ride on the backs of dung beetles in North Africa, apparently for the purpose of ovipositing in the particularly choice assemblage of faecal matter that the beetles collect and consolidate. In a similar way, bird-lice (Mallophaga) are frequently conveyed from one host to another by the Hippoboscid fly *Ornithomyia avicularia*. About twenty-five species of pseudoscorpions are known to obtain transport from one place to another on other animals such as Diptera, Hymenoptera, Coleoptera, Hemiptera, Orthoptera and other insects, harvestspiders and birds. Beier (1948) provides a useful summary of the extensive literature not only on phoresy but also on other types of association in which false-scorpions are concerned. He lists the species that have been found inhabiting the nests of birds and mammals, termites, ants and other Hymenoptera, and tabulates the Chernetes that have been recorded as attached to the extremities of the limbs and to the bodies of insects and other arthropods. The most important phoretic species in Europe is *Lamprochernes nodosus* which is not infrequently found attached to the legs of houseflies in summer and autumn although it also clings to hover-flies and other insects. False-scorpions occasionally ride on the backs of beetles, sheltering under their elytra. *Cordylochernes scorpioides* is a wellknown example frequently phoretic on the beetle *Acrocinus longimanus* in tropical America.

Various explanations of the phoretic habit have been suggested, but in most cases it seems that this behaviour is either accidental or motivated by hunger. Only female false-scorpions are phoretic, and the species involved are those that inhabit fallen leaves and débris, not those that live under stones and beneath bark (Vachon, 1947a).

The ability of false-scorpions to spin was denied by some of the earlier writers, but it is now known that they construct nests partly or wholly of silk from their own bodies. The animals usually enclose themselves in these nests for moulting, for brood purposes and, in some cases, for hibernation. Such nests are closed cells of spun tissue with or without an external cover of extraneous matter. They are roughly circular in shape and may be attached above and below to the solid surfaces of narrow crevices. When they are attached on one side only they have a free, convex roof and may be fixed here and there to surrounding objects. The external covering, if present, consists of earth or vegetable fibres which are not bound to the structure but are firmly attached to it, but the interior is smooth and always free from foreign matter. The spun tissue is thin and dense, composed of innumerable threads, crossed and recrossed and coalesced in irregular confusion without interspaces.

The silk is derived from glands in the cephalothorax whose ducts traverse the chelicerae to the apex of the movable finger. They open at the tips of the branches of the galea or on or near the margin of a tubercle which replaces that structure in some groups. The spinning is done with the chelicerae but the presence or absence of the galea does not appear to be associated with differences of method or in the tissue: the serrulae, etc. are not concerned. Nest building is carried out from within. The construction of an external framework is the first task, and where this has a coating of extraneous materials, the animal frequently goes out to collect them. They are picked up in the pedipalps, transferred to the chelicerae and attached to the nest by the application of silk to their inner surfaces. The silk is drawn from the galea or tubercle in several viscid and very fine threads which may remain separate or may coalesce, and the spinning is accompanied by continuous forward and backward movements of the body and by lateral movements of the chelicerae. At first, when attachments are being made from place to place, the threads usually do coalesce, but afterwards the animal settles down to long continued spinning and the silk is rapidly brushed onto the interior of the nest, first in one place, then in another. The animal continues at work gradually imprisoning itself, for days or even weeks until a dense tissue is produced over every part of the inside of its abode (Kew, 1914).

Food and feeding habits

Pseudoscorpions are exclusively carnivorous and feed on living or recently killed prey such as Collembola, Psocids, Thysanura, Diptera, other small insects, Symphyla and Arachnids. Unlike spiders, they are not usually cannibalistic if food is available but an injured or ailing individual has a poor chance of survival. It is doubtful if the prey is actively sought after, but rather that false-scorpions lie in wait, with their claws open, until some suitable animal accidentally brushes against their sensory hairs, when it is seized with extreme rapidity. It is said that some species of *Chthonius* can actually leap upon their prey. The rôle of the poison glands in the palps is not entirely clear. Sometimes the prey is paralysed immediately but not infrequently it is conveyed to the chelicerae whilst still struggling. Occasionally one false-scorpion has been observed to rob another of its food after a short struggle (Vachon *in* Grassé, 1949).*

The protonymph is the most active instar and is quite bold and fearless in its behaviour: it will even take food directly from a probe. The later stages do not feed so readily and adults may eat only once or twice a month. Levi (1948) found that in *Chelifer cancroides*, adults fed once a week in captivity seemed to be in better condition than those caught in the woods. During feeding the pedipalps may be vibrated, possibly by the action of the pharyngeal pump (Chamberlin, 1931).

The Argentine false-scorpion *Sphenochernes schulzi* recently described by Turk (1953) is very common in the nests of a leaf-cutting ant, *Acromyrmex lundi*. These pseudoscorpions live buried in the material of the nest and seemingly do not normally emerge except for their prey. They hold their pedipalps open almost continuously, catching at the legs of the ants as they run past, and holding fast until the ant dies from the effect of their poison. The attackers, and there are usually more than one, then probe their victim with their chelicerae, and proceed to suck the body fluids. It is a curious fact that these attacks take place only in daylight. If a vessel containing Chernetids and captured ants is darkened the ants are released, whereas in the light the hold of the Chernetids is so strong and persistent that they will not let go even when whirled about. The attacks of the pseudoscorpion are most clumsy, and this is thought to be the reason that the ant species continues to survive. The ants never succeed in freeing themselves from their attackers by biting. More recently Vachon (1954) has recorded an extraordinary association between *Ellingsenius hendrickxi* and bees in the Belgian Congo. This curiously ornamented and sculptured species is very common at Tshibinda and Katana where it passes its whole life cycle in bee hives. The false-scorpions often attach themselves to the legs of the bees and sometimes numbers combine to attack both workers and queens, which are killed and eaten like ordinary prey. The *Ellingsenius* forces its chelicerae into the articulations of the legs of the bee at intersegmental membranes and feeds upon it, holding on by its chelicerae only. If these become unfixed, however, the pedipalps are used to regain control.

After a meal a false-scorpion can often be seen to clean its mouth-parts and chelicerae. This habit it shares with spiders and harvestmen, which similarly pass their palps or legs through their jaws. Since the prey is digested externally by means of enzymes and then sucked in in solution, it is essential that the several channels and grooves in the mouth-parts should be

FIG. 25. *Ellingsenius hendrickxi.* (After Vachon, 1954.)

kept free from solid particles. In addition to this, however, false-scorpions are remarkable in that they also clean their chelicerae before a meal (Vachon, 1948). For example, when *Dactylochelifer latreillei* senses its prey it begins to clean its chelicerae with its pedipalps. On capture, the prey is grasped by the pedipalps. Often both are used, but the hold of one of them is soon relinquished and the prey is held aloft by the other. The free palp then continues to clean the mouthparts. After a few minutes the prey, which by now may well be inactive, is applied to the chelicerae which by their combined action make a small wound. The mouth-parts are inserted until the labrum appears to penetrate slightly into the wound. When fixation to the chelicerae is complete the pedipalps release their grip and take up a characteristic flexed attitude.

During feeding it can be seen that liquid is flowing both in and out of the prey. As sucking proceeds a soft-skinned insect becomes quite flaccid, only to become suddenly turgid due to the exudation from the false-scorpion of a liquid presumably containing digestive enzymes. The meal may last for an hour or more before the prey is finally discarded and the mouth-parts again cleaned (Gilbert, 1951).

The feeding behaviour of *Neobisium muscorum* and *N. maritimum* is similar, except that the food is actively kneaded by the chelicerae, which remain comparatively still in *D. latreillei*, and considerable use is made of the pedipalps in food capture. In *Chthonius ischnocheles*, however, the prey is disabled by the chelicerae. This may be correlated with the unusually large chelicerae and the absence of a palpal venom apparatus in the genus *Chthonius*. The chelicerae, by a chewing action, make a wound and this is quickly extended so that the prey becomes immobilised within two or three minutes. Feeding is accompanied by an incessant kneading of the prey, one chelicera being clenched in the wound while the other is closed round it, at the same time digging further inwards. This alternate insertion of each chelicera continues at intervals of about one second: at times the clenching of the chelicerae is not alternate, one of them opening and closing several times in succession. Chamberlin (1931) mentions that the modification of the serrulae seems to parallel the prehensile or nonprehensile functions of the chelicerae, and Gilbert (1951) suggests that there may be a correlation between genera in which the serrulae are fixed throughout their length to the cheliceral fingers and those whose chelicerae are inactive during feeding. At the same time it is possible that the possession of partially free serrulae in *Neobisium* and *Chthonius* is associated with the maintenance of a liquid film between the false-scorpion and its prey, despite the fact that the chelicerae are moving.

Enemies

Owing to their secretive habits, false-scorpions have few enemies although Levi (1948) has recorded that they may be eaten
by ants. They do not often fall victim to spiders: their poison-
bearing pedipalps help them to hold their own against species
of their own size, whilst they are likely to remain unnoticed
by many spiders of a larger size. They do not appear to be
distasteful, however, and Bristowe (1941)* has fed *Chthonius
ischnocheles* and *Lamprochernes nodosus* to a number of spider
species. They may also be eaten by harvest-spiders (Cloudsley-
Thompson, 1955).

With the exception of six nematode worms of the genus
Hexameris found in a female *Roncus* sp. whose ovaries were
atrophied, no parasites of pseudoscorpions are known.

Mating habits

In male false-scorpions the galea or spinneret on the movable finger of the chelicerae is poorly developed compared
with that of the female; the abdominal tergites may be provided with strong lateral keels as in *Chelifer cancroides* and the
claws of the pedipalps are more robust and have a wider gape.
Lateral genital sacs are present under the genital operculum
close to the genital aperture. In some species these are capable
of being extruded. They reach their highest development in
the Cheliferidae where they can be completely evaginated and
constitute the 'ram's-horn organs' of many authors, a term
proposed by Menge.

The pairing of *Dendrochernes cyrneus* and *Dactylochelifer
latreillei* has been described by Kew (1914). The males are
differently equipped: *D. latreillei* has an elaborate genital area,
long ram's-horn organs and much-modified legs of the first

pair, while *D. cyrneus* has a less elaborate genital area, no ram's-horn organs and no modified legs. Both are destitute of intromittent organs of copulation and fertilisation is effected by means of a spermatophore. The male and female face one another in walking position, the male grasping one or both of the pedipalps of the female with one or both of his own. There is a forced courtship during which the male makes display of definite character. At length he extrudes a sperma-

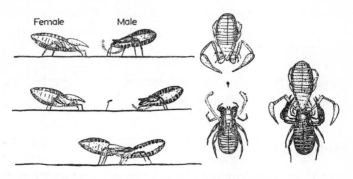

FIG. 26. Courtship dance of false-scorpions. (After Vachon, 1938.)

tophore which is attached to the substrate in front of the female where it stands erect or obliquely. The male then retires and the female moves forward until her genital opening comes into contact with the spermatophore, which is received without delay.

Courtship varies in the two species correlated with their morphological differences. *D. latreillei* holds the female with both palps and makes display with his ram's-horn organs, releasing her just before extruding a spermatophore. When she comes forward he seizes her by the genital opening with his first pair of legs and executes a series of pulling movements by which the reception of the male product is facilitated. The animals then separate and go their different ways. In *D. cyrneus* the male holds his mate with one pedipalp only, the other being shaken in her face, and his first legs are moved rapidly, being lifted and replaced in a peculiar fashion. The female, who is apparently 'much impressed' by these actions, is not released during extrusion of the spermatophore, which she takes quickly without the male seizing her genital opening. After a period of repose the whole process may be repeated a number of times and a large number of spermatophores are thus produced and received in quick succession.

In *Chelifer cancroides*, according to Vachon (1938), a nuptial dance takes place during which the male vigorously displays and retracts his ram's-horn organs and waves his pedipalps in the air like the arms of a swimmer. The dance consists of at least three set figures which are repeated rhythmically for some minutes or longer if the female is unresponsive. Still dancing, he approaches his mate, deposits a spermatophore and then retreats, slowly moving his palps. Obedient to this signal, the female advances until she stands above the spermatophore, which she introduces into her spermathecae. The male then lowers his head beneath that of his mate, grips the femurs of her palps with his own claws and taps her genital region with his anterior legs, thus ensuring that the spermatozoa from the spermatophore are properly secured.

Reproduction and life cycle

It has been known since the time of Fabricius in 1793 that the eggs of *Chelifer* were retained beneath the abdomen of the mother, but Lubbock in 1861 was the first to observe that they were enclosed in a transparent, structureless membrane attached to the abdomen and that large motionless young similarly retained were nourished by a milky fluid provided by the mother. Ten years later Metschnikoff discovered that development involved a metamorphosis including immobile larvae which were provided anteriorly with a strongly muscular sucking-apparatus and Barrois showed that the larvae underwent two distinct periods of embryogenesis.

The eggs and later the larvae may be arranged in a flat disc in those species where the female continues an active existence during gestation, for example in most of the Cheliferidae; but where the female constructs a nest in which she seals herself up and remains inactive until the development of the young is complete, they are usually in a mulberry-like mass. According to Kew (1929) in these false-scorpions the enormously distended females imprison themselves in brood nests where they remain hidden from view. A few hours before the eggs are laid an incubation chamber or brood-sac makes its appearance accompanied by peculiar muscular movements of the mother's body. It is a delicate, transparent membrane and looks like a minute mushroom, its stalk joined to the oviduct, and the eggs are laid into it. Their number may vary from five to forty or more. After a few days the young escape from the egg-membrane but stay inside the brood-sac.

These first larvae have a sucking beak and remain attached to the genital orifice of the female through which they are fed on a kind of uterine milk secreted by the transformed ovaries of the mother, whose abdomen gradually shrinks as the larvae grow. They swell so much that Vachon describes them as 'larvae gonflées' and the brood-mass becomes more bulky than the mother's body whence it projects broadly on each side and often also posteriorly. By degrees and without much further increase in size these deutembryos complete their development. Behind the old larval structures the chelicerae appear anteriorly and wide apart while dorsally the abdominal segments with their setae become distinct. Laterally and ventrally the palps

and legs become clearly differentiated. Four or five weeks after
the extrusion of the eggs some power of movement is attained
and the young emerge from the brood-mass, the débris of
which remains attached to their mother.

The young, or protonymphs, emerge within about a day. In
some species such as *Garypus minor* and the British *Chthonius
ischnocheles*, *Neobisium carpenteri*, *N. maritimum*, *N. muscorum*, *Toxochernes panzeri*, *Chernes cimicoides* and *Dendrochernes cyrneus*, 20 or more young are produced, in *Chelifer cancroides*, 7 to 39, but the families of the smaller *Cheiridium
museorum* number only 2 to 5 individuals.

In some species the protonymphs ride on their mothers'
backs like young scorpions and wolf spiders, but they are active, greedy little creatures and soon disperse.

When young pseudoscorpions emerge from the brood-mass
they resemble miniature copies of their parents. They moult
three times only, for which purpose they usually enclose themselves in moulting nests, before reaching the adult stage. During
this time they increase their length by about one and a half
times, the special structures of the chelicerae develop and the
number of hairs with which the body is covered increases considerably. A period of quiescence lasting some ten to fifteen
days precedes the actual moulting process and the animals do
not leave their nests until they are almost fully coloured; that
is to say, within ten or twelve days. Pairing may occur within
about a fortnight of the final moult.

According to Vachon (1947b) the different instars of false-
scorpions can be recognised as follows: the protonymph always
has four trichobothria (or long sensory hairs) on the chelae of
the pedipalps (one on the movable finger, three on the fixed
finger), the deutonymph has eight (two on the movable finger,
six on the fixed), the tritonymph has ten (three on the movable
finger, seven on the fixed) while the adult has twelve tricho-

bothria (four on the mobile finger and eight on the fixed finger). This rule holds good for all species in which the adult has twelve trichobothria on each of its claws.

In *Chernes cimicoides* females produce their eggs in the summer, but young may be found throughout the year. The larval stages are passed through in the autumn and the young usually hibernate before or after their second moult. They reappear the following spring and the final moult takes place in early summer, the entire life cycle lasting for a year. Levi (1948) found that in Wisconsin the life cycle of *Chelifer cancroides* also occupies a year, but Vachon (1938) found that in France the same species took two years to reach maturity. A pseudoscorpion has been known to live in captivity for approximately $3\frac{1}{2}$ years (Strebel, 1937).

BIBLIOGRAPHY

Identification

BEIER, M. (1932) Pseudoscorpionidae. *Das Tierreich*, **57**, 1–258; **58**, 1–294.

CHAMBERLIN, J. C. (1931) The Arachnid order Chelonethida. *Publ. Stanf. Univ. (Biol.)*, **7**, 1–284.

EVANS, G. O. and BROWNING, E. (1954) *Synopses of the British Fauna, No. 10—Pseudoscorpiones*. London: *Linn. Soc.*

KEW, H. W. (1911) A synopsis of the false-scorpions of Britain and Ireland. *Proc. R. Irish Acad.* (B), **29**, 38–64.

—— (1916) *Idem*. Supplement. *Ibid.* (B), **33**, 71–85.

ROEWER, C. F. (1937–40) Chelonethi oder Pseudoskorpione *in* H. G. BRONN's *Klass. Ordn. Tierreichs*, **5**, IV (6), 1–354.

Biology

BEIER, M. (1948) Phoresie und Phagophilie bei Pseudoscorpionen. *Öst. Zool. Z.*, **1**, 441–97.

CLOUDSLEY-THOMPSON, J. L. (1956) Notes on Arachnida, 25.—An unusual case of phoresy by false-scorpions. *Ent. Mon. Mag.*, **92**, 71.

GABUTT, P. and VACHON, M. (1963) The external morphology and life history of the pseudoscorpion *Chthonius ischnocheles* (Hermann). *Proc. Zool. Soc. Lond.*, **140**, 75–98.

—— (1965) The external morphology and life history of the pseudoscorpion *Neobisium muscorum*. *Ibid.*, **145**, 335–58.

GILBERT, O. (1951) Observations on the feeding of some British false-scorpions. *Proc. Zool. Soc. Lond.*, **121**, 547–55.

KEW, H. W. (1911) On the pairing of Pseudoscorpiones. *Proc. Zool. Soc. Lond.*, **1911**, 376–90.

—— (1914) On the nests of Pseudoscorpiones: with historical notes on the spinning organs and observations on the building and spinning of nests. *Ibid.*, **1914**, 93–111.

—— (1929) On the external features of the development of the Pseudoscorpiones: with observations on the ecdyses and notes on the immature forms. *Ibid.*, **1929**, 33–8.

LEVI, H. W. (1948) Notes on the life history of the Pseudoscorpion *Chelifer cancroides* (Linn.) (Chelonethida.) *Trans. Amer. Micr. Soc.*, **67**, 290–8.

STREBEL, O. (1937) Beobachtungen am einheimischen Bücherskorpion *Chelifer cancroides* L. (Pseudoscorpiones). *Beitr. naturh. Forsch. Südw. Dtsch.*, **2**, 143–55.

TURK, F. A. (1953) A new genus and species of pseudoscorpion with some notes on its biology. *Proc. Zool. Soc. Lond.*, **122**, 951–4.

VACHON, M. (1938) La reproduction et le développement des Pseudoscorpions. *Ann. Sci. nat. Zool.*, (11), **1**, 1–209.

—— (1947a) Nouvelles remarques à propos de la phorésie des Pseudoscorpions. *Bull. Mus. Hist. nat. Paris*, (2), **19**, 84–7.

—— (1947b) Comment reconnaitre l'age chez les Pseudoscorpions (Arachnides). *Ibid.*, (2), **19**, 271–4.

—— (1948) Quelques remarques sur la 'nettoyage des pattes machoires' et les glandes salivaires, chez les Pseudoscorpions (Arachnides). *Ibid.*, (2), **20**, 162–4.

—— (1954) Remarques sur un Pseudoscorpion vivant dans les ruches d'Abeilles au Congo Belge, *Ellingsenius hendrickxi* n. sp. *Ann. Mus. Congo. Tervuren*, **1**, 284–7.

WEYGOLDT, P. (1964) Vergleichend embryologische an Pseudoscorpionen (Chelonethi). *Z. Morph. Ökol. Tiere*, **54**, 1–106.

CHAPTER VIII

WHIP-SCORPIONS AND OTHERS

IN THE present chapter, five small orders of Arachnida are considered whose affinities have long been disputed, and whose natural history and way of life are still largely unknown. The

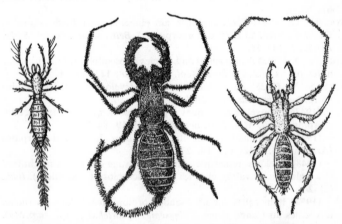

FIG. 27. Examples of Palpigradi, Thelyphonida and Schizomida.
(Drawings not to scale.) (After various authors.)

three orders Thelyphonida, Schizomida and Phrynichida were for many years recognised as sub-orders of the order Pedipalpi and were known as Uropygi Holopeltidia, Uropygi Schizopeltidia and Amblypygi or Tarantulidae respectively. However, in 1948, Petrunkevitch raised them to ordinal rank and thus they are here treated, although Millot (*in* Grassé, 1949)* still regards the Schizomida as a sub-order of the Uropygi.

Order PALPIGRADI

Classification and distribution

The Palpigradi or Microthelyphonida are tiny creatures resembling, as their alternative name suggests, miniature whip-scorpions. The prosoma appears to consist of only two segments when seen from above, the tergum of the segment bearing the fourth pair of appendages forming part of the carapace; but ventrally there are four sternites. The chelicerae are the only chelate appendages as the pedipalps are leg-like and terminate in a pair of claws. Eyes are absent and the mouth is a mere slit between the bases of the chelicerae. The abdomen is distinctly segmented and is terminated by a slender flagellum consisting of 15 segments. The external reproductive organs of the adults are quite complicated and are borne on the second and third abdominal segments.

The order comprises but a single family, the Koeneniidae, containing about twenty species in four genera. These minute Arachnida are widely distributed in southern Europe, Africa, America from California to Chile, Siam and Australia.

Biology

Palpigradi show a marked avoidance of light and are usually found under half-buried stones and in other damp and sheltered places in company with spring-tails, myriapods, woodlice and other retiring animals. A few species such as *Koenenia spelaea*, *K. draco* and *K. pyrenaica* are troglodytes and have particularly elongated limbs with abundant sensory hairs. Micro-whip-scorpions appear to be dependent upon moist conditions and are extremely susceptible to desiccation. During periods of drought they make their way deep into the soil.

Palpigradi can move with great agility, their pedipalps assisting the other limbs in locomotion while their flagellum is held horizontally behind the body. From the structure of their chelicerae it is evident that these animals are carnivorous, but in view of their minute size there can be few other animals small enough to be suitable as prey. Wheeler (1900) found that the alimentary canal of *Koenenia mirabilis*, a species occurring in Texas, contained only material resembling yolk particles and concluded that it was admirably constructed for sucking the eggs of other minute arthropods such as Symphyla and Pauropods, but this hypothesis has been contested. No predators have yet been recorded, although the same author found attached to the ventral surface of the prosoma of certain individuals, an ectoparasite of unknown nature, the young forms of which were uni-segmented and the adults three-segmented.

Of the mating habits and life cycle of the Palpigradi very little is known, though it is believed that individuals can recognise one another by scent. In certain species the males appear to outnumber the females, while in others, such as *K. mirabilis*, males are extremely rare. In the young stages of *Prokoenenia wheeleri* there are fewer hairs, fewer cheliceral teeth and fewer flagellar segments than in the adults. In certain species, a pair of eversible sacs have been described on each of the fourth to sixth abdominal sternites. These vary in number and position during growth and may represent a primitive and very simple type of breathing organ.

PLATE I*a*. A group of woodlice. Top row: *Ligia oceanica, Ligidium hypnorum, Hemilepistus reaumuri* and *Armadillidium vulgare*. Bottom row: *Oniscus asellus, Porcellio scaber, Androniscus dentiger* and *Philoscia muscorum*. The halfpenny gives the scale. (*Photo:* J. L. Cloudsley-Thompson.)

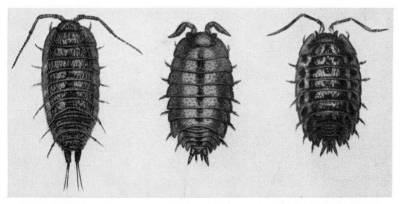

PLATE I*b*. *Ligia oceanica* (length 2–3 cm), *Platyarthrus hoffmannseggi* (length 3 mm) and *Oniscus asellus* (length 16 mm). (From Webb and Sillem, 1906.)

 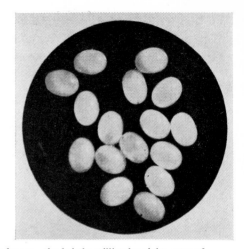

PLATE IIa. Left, *Polyxenus lagurus*, the bristly millipede; right, eggs of a woodlouse. (*Photos:* copyright, J. H. P. Sankey.)

PLATE IIb. Swarming millipedes (*Habrodesmus* sp.) in Nyasaland. (*Photo:* G. Fryer.)

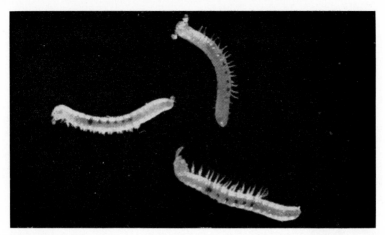

PLATE IIIa. Young spotted-snake millipedes (*Blaniulus guttulatus*).

PLATE IIIb. Black millipedes (*Tachypodoiulus niger*). (Shell photographs.)

PLATE IVa. Flat-backed millipede (*Polydesmus angustus*).

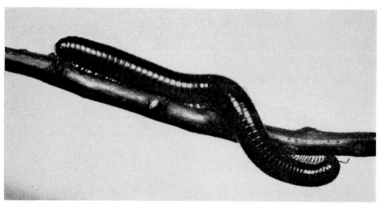

PLATE IVb. Giant tropical millipede (*Spirostreptus* sp.). (Shell photographs.)

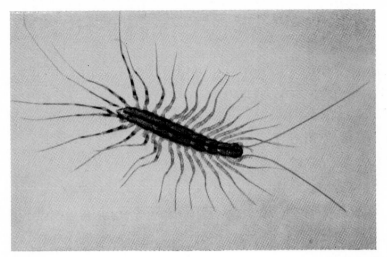

PLATE V*a*. American house centipede (*Scutigera forceps*). (*Photo:* Hugh Spencer.)

PLATE V*b*. The common centipede (*Lithobius forficatus*). The specimen
has lost some legs. (Shell photograph.)

PLATE VIa. *Scolopendra cingulata.*

PLATE VIb. Head of *S. cingulata.* (*Photos:* J. L. Cloudsley-Thompson.)

PLATE VIIa. Fat-tailed scorpion (*Androctonus australis*). The halfpenny gives the scale. (*Photo:* J. L. Cloudsley-Thompson.)

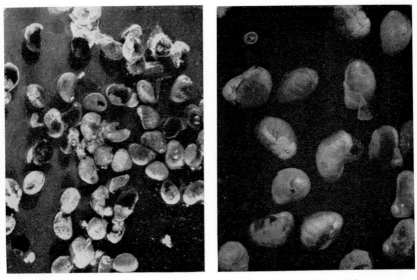

PLATE VIIb. Newly born scorpions escaping from their chorions. (*Photos:* E. A. Robins.)

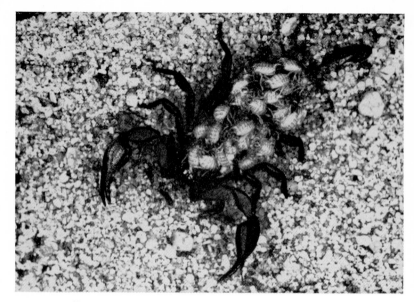

PLATE VIIIa. *Euscorpius italicus* with newly born young.

PLATE VIIIb. *E. italicus*, the same female protecting her young just after their first moult. The cast skins can be seen on the mother's back. (*Photos:* J. L. Cloudsley-Thompson.)

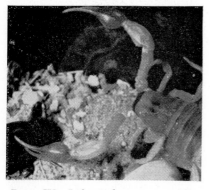 

PLATE IX*a*. Left, *Androctonus australis*, one of the most deadly species in the world. Right, ignoring a hard desert beetle (*Akis spinosa*). (*Photos:* J. L. Cloudsley-Thompson.)

 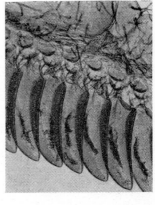

PLATE IX*b*. Left, black scorpion (*Androctonus æneas*). (*Photo:* J. L. Cloudsley-Thompson.) Right, pecten of scorpion much enlarged. (*Photo:* E. A. Robins.)

PLATE X*a*. Left, racquet organs of Solifugid; right, pecten of scorpion. (*Photos:* E. A. Robins.)

PLATE X*b*. *Solpuga caffra*, female depositing eggs. (*Photo:* R. A. Holliday.)

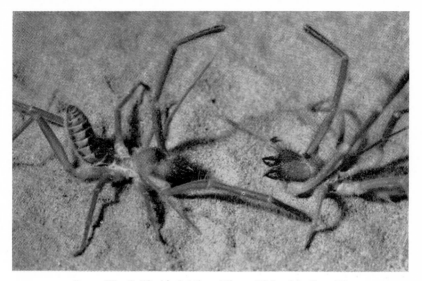

PLATE XI*a*. Solifugids fighting. (*Photo:* Richard L. Cassell.)

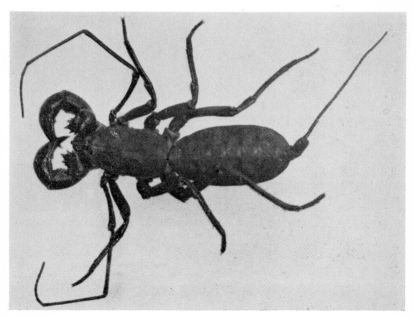

PLATE XI*b*. Whip-scorpion (*Thelyphonus caudatus*). (*Photo:* E. A. Robins.)

PLATE XIIa. Left, Mygalomorph spider; right, false-scorpion (*Toxochernes panzeri*).

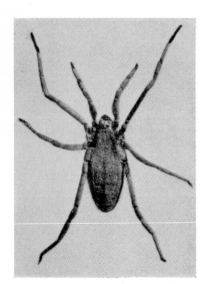
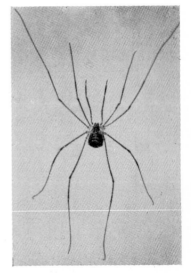

PLATE XIIb. Harvest spiders. Left, *Trogulus tricarinatus*; right, *Nemastoma chrysomelas*. (*Photos:* copyright, J. H. P. Sankey.)

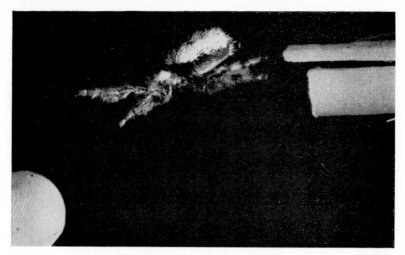

PLATE XIIIa. The jumping spider (*Phidippus audax*).

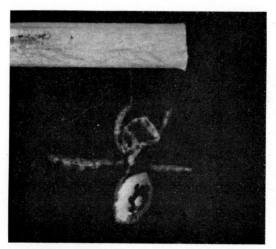

PLATE XIIIb. Jumping spider (*Phidippus audax*) climbing
up the safety-line. (*Photos:* Walker van Riper.)

PLATE XIV*a*. Wolf spider (*Lycosa* sp.) with egg sac.

PLATE XIV*b*. Left, *Amaurobius ferox* (male); right, *Scytodes thoracica* (female carrying egg sac). (*Photos:* J. L. Cloudsley-Thompson.)

PLATE XV*a*. *Argiope bruennichi* female on web. Left, ventral view; right, dorsal view. The narrow ribbons of silk or stabilimentum help to camouflage the spider. (*Photos:* J. L. Cloudsley-Thompson.)

PLATE XV*b*. Brown tick (*Rhipicephalus appendiculatus*). Male left; female right. (Shell photograph.)

PLATE XVI*a*. Bont tick (*Amblyomma hebraeum*). Close-up view of head and mouthparts of male.

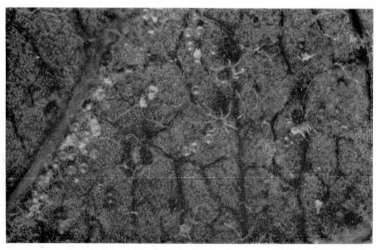

PLATE XVI*b*. Red spider mites (*Paratetranychus pilosus*). Adults, eggs and hatched egg cases on underside of apple leaf. (Shell photographs.)

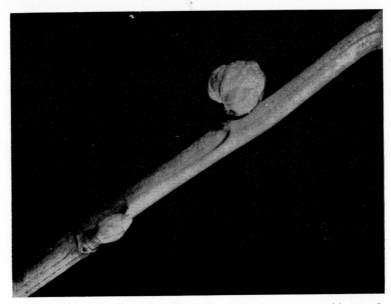

PLATE XVIIa. Big bud mite (*Eriophyes ribis*). Infected bud on top with normal bud underneath.

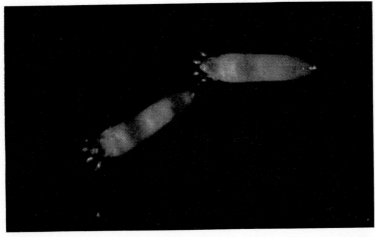

PLATE XVIIb. Big bud mite (*Eriophyes ribis*) removed from blackcurrant bud. (Shell photographs.)

Order THELYPHONIDA

Classification and distribution

In their general form, the Thelyphonida bear some slight resemblance to scorpions. They can easily be distinguished, however, by the form of the pedipalps, the first pair of legs and the abdomen, which bears a slender caudal appendage from which the name 'whip-scorpion' is derived. These strange Arachnids are generally of large size, varying from 25 to 70 mm in length. The elongated prosoma is covered by a dorsal carapace and has three thoracic sternites. The chelicerae are composed of two segments and are not chelate, while the pedipalpi are powerful limbs of six segments. Their coxae are fused below the mouth and have no masticating function, but each trochanter has a large semicircular process on its inner side armed with sharp teeth. The processes can be pressed against each other and are well adapted to crushing the prey, which is detected by the long anterior legs. These are not used for walking but are held stretched out in front as tactile organs. There is one pair of median and three pairs of lateral eyes but these are feeble and serve only to distinguish between light and darkness.

The abdomen is composed of 12 segments, of which the last three are small and annular, forming a pygidium which bears the long, whip-like telson.

Representatives of the order are dispersed somewhat unevenly throughout the tropics: the genus *Hypoctonus* is found in Malaya, *Typopeltis* in Cochinchina and Japan, while *Thelyphonus* has an Indo-oceanic distribution. The largest species belong to the genus *Mastigoproctus* which, appropriately enough, is exclusively American.

General behaviour

The Thelyphonida are nocturnal predators and usually spend the day-time hiding under logs and stones or sheltering in their burrows. According to Pergande (1886), *Mastigoproctus giganteus* appears to select a place for digging where there is already a small depression in the soil. With its front legs laid backwards, it then scrapes a quantity of sand into a heap with its powerful pedipalps, grasps this with both pedipalps and, moving backwards for some distance from its burrow, turns round and deposits its load. After patting and smoothing it somewhat with one or other of its palps, it rests for a moment with only the antennae-like first legs playing, 'as if in thought'. Then, turning round, it retraces its way to the opening, always using its long, slender legs cautiously to discover its path. On reaching the burrow it goes through the same performance as before. The channel when dug reaches a length of 7·5 to 10 cm and takes several days to complete, as the animal often rests motionless for hours, or goes out on a hunting expedition.

A small species, *Labochirus proboscideus*, is fairly abundant in the low-lying jungles of the Kandy district of Ceylon and is known to extend to a considerably higher altitude. It is found under stones and logs of decaying wood in the neighbourhood of watercourses and in other parts of the jungle where the soil is thoroughly moistened by the rains, but does not occur on marshy ground. This species digs a burrow for itself beneath the stones under which it lives (Graveley, 1911, 1915). *Thelyphonus sepiaris*, which also inhabits Ceylon is, however, much better able to withstand drought. It lives in drier situations and will survive in a dry cage without water for several weeks without apparent discomfort. It appears, too, to be of a somewhat less timid disposition.

Food and feeding habits

Whip-scorpions feed chiefly on insects such as cockroaches, grasshoppers, caterpillars and termites, as well as worms and slugs, which they seize quickly with their sharp pedipalps. According to Graveley (1915) it is almost impossible to observe the feeding of the nocturnal Ceylon species *Labochirus proboscideus* in its natural haunts. Even in captivity it is very shy of any light after emerging from its hiding place in search of food, but will eat as often as suitable prey is provided. It will accept winged termites, small locusts and roaches, especially when these are disabled, but is easily 'frightened' by larger insects and by very active ones. The prey is seized between the pedipalps and held between them and the prosoma: little use appears to be made of the chelae. The chelicerae are provided with brushes of hairs which may serve to filter the blood of the dismembered prey. They are also used in cleaning the terminal segments of the legs. The antenniform first legs are generally held directed forwards and usually somewhat outwards in an arched position. As the animal moves along they are lowered alternately from time to time until the tip comes in contact with the ground, and then raised again. It is not known for certain whether this species drinks water as so many others do, but it is highly probable.

When hunting, the large American *Mastigoproctus giganteus* moves slowly and cautiously with its formidable palps outstretched and open, feeling and touching all objects about it with its sensory first legs, until it discovers an insect which it grasps. The prey is then carried into the burrow as a cat carries a mouse. Alternate striking and grappling movements of the palps carry the attached prey firmly towards the chelicerae. This large species has been known to eat small frogs and toads, but on the whole Thelyphonida are very timid creatures.

Nevertheless, when introduced to one another in close quarters, they engage in fierce battles in which one or both of the contestants is frequently killed or mutilated.

In captivity, specimens of *Thelyphonus skimkewitchii* feed readily on dead insects, first carefully and slowly examining the object before taking it up in their chelae. Live insects are rarely caught and they do not attempt to interfere with beetles and grasshoppers larger than themselves. On the other hand a moth will be devoured almost completely and a dragonfly eaten all but the wings. Besides insects, they will eat small pieces of over-ripe banana (Flower, 1901). Marx (1892) found that very young *M. giganteus* would not eat flies but fed on small cockroaches.

The anterior legs of Thelyphonida serve as feelers: they are sensitive not only to touch, but also to chemicals and moisture. The delicacy of their response can be illustrated by breathing on them when they are at rest—even this slight stimulus in the case of *Mastigoproctus* is enough to send them into restless activity. If an animal which is aimlessly wandering about should happen to get the tip of one of these limbs into a dish of water, it will immediately swing about, thrust its other feeler into the water, clamber half into the dish and begin greedily to scoop water into its mouth with its chelicerae. If very dilute hydrochloric acid is substituted for water, a clear-cut avoidance reaction is obtained (Patten, 1917).

Although it is believed that none of the 'Pedipalps' is poisonous, and no poison glands have been found in any of these orders, *M. giganteus* is greatly feared in some of the southern United States on account of its supposedly venomous powers. It is given the local name of 'grampus' and can inflict wounds in the human skin with the sharp spines on its pedipalps. Thelyphonida protect themselves when disturbed by discharging from the anal region a dust-like cloud having a strong odour of acetic acid in species such as *Thelyphonus caudatus*, *T. sepiaris* and *Hypoctonus oatesi*, while the odour of the repugnatorial fluid from *T. linganus* is said to resemble that of chlorine gas. If a whip-scorpion be molested with a finger bearing a cut or raw scratch, this cut or scratch will probably begin to smart violently from acid ejected from near the base of the tail, but this is the worst they can do.

The name 'vinegarone' by which Thelyphonida are known in parts of the southern United States was originally bestowed on them by settlers from the French West Indies, and arose from the vinegar-like, acid secretion they exude when approached. A blacksmith in 1877 is reported to have crushed one to his upper left breast. Blisters resulted from the acid secretion which extended over the whole of his chest. Flower (1901) also had a curious experience with a specimen off *Thelyphonus skimkewitchii* in Bangkok. This species is known in Siamese as 'Mengpon-menn' (i.e. stinking scorpion): it is chiefly to be seen during the rainy season and gives off a faint and characteristic smell. He wrote: 'Seeing a *Thelyphonus* of this species running on the ground, I picked it up by the cephalothorax between the first finger and thumb off my left hand; it at once bent its thread-shaped tail over its back (as a scorpion does) and also scratched about my fingers with its legs, but the pincers did not touch me; I thought nothing of its tail, etc. until I felt a sharp pain and found the animal *had* somehow stung me. I went straight into my house, and already the first joint of my finger was very swollen and inflamed, there being a rapidly growing white lump, and the rest was red; at one spot was a fresh puncture as if a needle had been driven in, in a horizontal direction, and gone some little way under the skin. After cutting and squeezing the wound, I put my finger into a strong solution of permanganate of potash, which at once relieved the pain and stopped the swelling, but the little wound continued to smart for some hours. Since then I have been careful never to let a *Thelyphonus* touch me.'

Graveley (1915) however could hardly believe that this sting was really due to the *T. skimkewitchii* as he had frequently handled other species without receiving any harm and it is probable that the animal was blamed unfairly.

Mating habits and life cycle

The external appearance of the sexes is almost identical and they can often be distinguished only by means of small differences in the structure of the genital sternites. The courtship of *Thelyphonus sepiaris* has been described by Gravely (1915). It consists of a curious sexual parade reminiscent of that of the scorpions. The male grips the antenniform first legs of the female in his pedipalps and holds their extremities in his chelicerae. He then walks backwards, the female following. Before long she raises her abdomen in the air and the male commences to stroke her genital segment with his elongated front legs. These are usually passed between the third and fourth legs of the female, but sometimes pass behind her back legs. Their tips are generally crossed. At the same time the chelae of the male are held open and are moved slightly over the dorsal surface of the abdomen of the female. Klingel (1963) has described mating in *T. caudatus*. Courtship is essentially similar to that of *T. sepiaris*: the male produces a spermatophore of complicated structure which is held against the females' genital opening for some hours. Broods of 12 and 17 young have been observed. The behavioural components of the indirect transfer of spermatozoa by means of a spermatophore in *T. caudatus* are roughly comparable to what is found in Scizomida but have little resemblance to those of the Phrynichida which establish no close contact during mating.

When the female is pregnant, she seeks shelter. *Thelyphonus caudatus* digs a burrow some 40 cm in depth and slightly enlarged at its extremity. The entrance is concealed with leaves and other débris. The female installs herself at the bottom of the burrow where she lays some 20 to 35 yellowish eggs. These are retained in a transparent membrane fixed beneath her genital sternite. They are comparatively large, measuring about 3 mm in diameter, and are protected from desiccation by a quantity of liquid produced at the time of their emission.

The female remains motionless in her retreat for several weeks. The exact incubation period is not known however, as captive females usually devour their eggs. The young free themselves by cutting the egg-sac with special spines on their legs. They are yellowish-white in colour and very different in appearance from the adults. After a while they climb slowly on to their mother's back and cling to her opisthosoma and the base of her back legs by means of the adhesive discs with which their tarsi are furnished. Here they remain until after the first moult, when they acquire the typical form and resemble miniature adults. Now they leave their mother, who has become so thin and weak as a result of her prolonged vigil that she falls into a state of lethargy from which she does not recover. The development of the young is extremely slow. They undergo three more moults at yearly intervals before becoming adult (Strubell, 1926).

Order SCHIZOMIDA

Classification and distribution

Schizomida, sometimes known as Schizonotidae or Tartaridae, differ from the Thelyphonida, with which they are often grouped, in their small size—they measure from 5 to 7 mm in

length—and in having the carapace subdivided into three un-
equal divisions, the propeltidium, mesopeltidium and metapeltidium. The last two are present as free tergites, a primitive
condition, and belong to the segments bearing the third and
fourth pairs of legs respectively. Median eyes are lacking but a
pair of lateral eyes may be present which are reduced to small
pale areas of cuticle in some forms. The pedipalps are clawless,
raptatory, rather robust and often armed with characteristic
spines and setae, while the legs of the first pair are long and
slender and used like antennae as tactile sense organs. The
abdomen is again composed of twelve segments, the last three
being small, annular and forming a pygidium which bears a
short caudal appendage made up of one to three, or occasionally four, segments. In the males it is often fused into a single
rounded or elongate knob.

Three genera only are found in the order: *Schizomus* and
Trithyreus have a wide tropical and equatorial distribution,
while *Stenochrus* contains a single species from Porto Rico.
One or two species have been described from specimens introduced into hot-houses in temperate countries (Cloudsley-
Thompson, 1949). The genera *Schizomus* and *Trithyreus* can be
distinguished by the fact that the posterior free segment of the
prosoma is divided by a longitudinal suture in the latter.

Biology

Schizomida are absolutely nocturnal in their habits and
spend the day in damp, dark retreats under leaves, stones and
logs, or deep in the soil where the ground is moist. In Ceylon,
Schizomus crassicaudatus is found only under bricks, etc., on
or close to open ground more or less shaded by trees, while *S.
vittatus* and *Trithyreus paradenigensis* occur among dead leaves
especially where these form a layer of considerable depth and

are matted together by fungal hyphae. Although they make no attempt to drink, they are very susceptible to desiccation. In addition, they are strongly photo-negative and are very sensitive to tactile and vibratory stimuli. They can run surprisingly fast and, when touched in front, escape by a sudden jump backwards. Approaching objects appear often to be perceived —probably by means of vibrations—before they are actually touched. The elongated front pair of legs, highly sensitive tactile sense organs, are carried aloft and not used in walking. Little is known of the biology of Schizomida. They probably feed on small arthropods such as Collembola, Thysanura,

Fig. 28. *Schizomus crassicaudatus*, female guarding her eggs.
(After Gravely, 1915.)

Symphyla and possibly small ants such as *Monomorium pharaonis* with which they are frequently associated (Cloudsley-Thompson, 1949). In captivity they show cannibalistic proclivities. Anal stink glands produce acetic acid, or similar compounds, which are used in defence. The animals have no fixed abode, but live in natural holes and crevices in the soil.

Males of *Schizomus latipes* have not yet been found, although the writer has examined over forty specimens of this species. Possibly they have a short life and die soon after mating.

The breeding habits of Schizomida are little known and appear to have been observed only in the case of *S. crassicaudatus*. According to Graveley (1915) a captive specimen constructed a little cavity about 15 mm below the surface of the soil. The nest had no opening and the *Schizomus* never left it until the eggs disappeared three weeks later. It was lined with soil cemented together. The eggs were seven in number, flattened at their poles, glistening white and not enclosed in a brood pouch. They were arranged in a spherical mass attached to the abdomen of the female in the region of her genital aperture. As a rule she rested on the side of the nest, her body bent at right angles, with thorax vertical and abdomen horizontal. In *Trithyreus sturmi* the pair promenade one behind the other, the female linked by her chelicerae to the last segment of the male's abdomen. The male then deposits a spermatophore and cements it onto the substratum: from the top of this the female gathers sperm into her genital ducts (Sturm, 1958).

Order PHRYNICHIDA (= AMBLYPYGI)

Classification and distribution

The Phrynichida differ from other 'Pedipalps' in lacking any caudal appendage and in having the opisthosoma joined to the cephalothorax by a slender pedicel. The carapace is entire with a pair of median, and three pairs of lateral eyes, and there are three thoracic sternites. The pedipalps are stout raptatory organs armed with strong spines and terminating in a movable hook. The flexible tip of the legs of the first pair is very long and composed of many segments: it is used as a tactile sense organ.

With their flattened bodies and sombre colours, these animals bear a superficial resemblance to crab spiders. The abdomen is composed of twelve segments, the last one forming a pygidium. The size varies from 8 to 45 mm in length.

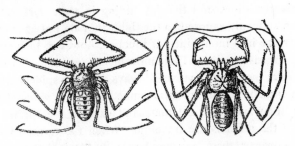

FIG. 29. Phrynichida (= Amblypygi), *Charon grayi* (after Kano, 1937) and *Charinus milloti* (after Millot, 1949). (Body lengths, 2 cm.)

The distribution of the tailless whip-scorpions is largely conditioned by their water requirements and they are found only in the more humid regions of the tropics and sub-tropics. There are two families, the Charontidae and the Tarantulidae. The former is composed mostly of smaller, cavernicolous forms having a distribution in southern and eastern Asia and the Pacific islands, while the latter contains three sub-families: the Phrynicinae which are found in Africa, India and Ceylon, the Damoninae which occur in Africa and South America, and the Tarantulinae which are entirely American.

Biology

As already mentioned, most of the Phrynichida live in humid regions under logs and stones, or in crevices among rocks, where they can move freely. Unlike the Thelyphonida which rest on the ground if the object under which they are sheltering is lifted up, they are usually to be found clinging to its under surface. They will dart round the stone beneath which they were hiding in order to evade capture, but seldom try to escape to other stones. The tailless whip-scorpions are again nocturnal carnivores and spend the day hiding in their dark retreats. When suddenly exposed to the light, they do not at once flee, but freeze into immobility. If touched, however, they can run with surprising speed. Their movements are somewhat unpredictable; they usually move sideways like crab spiders, walking with the six posterior legs extended sideways while the first pair are waved like antennae and explore the surface over which the animals are travelling. When the creatures are at rest, however, these legs may be slowly rotated, one forwards and the other backwards, so as to sweep a large area round the body. They resemble the writhing of tentacles rather than the more typical movements of arthropod antennae. The extreme tip is used to touch the surface which is being investigated and this is done with tapping movements of extreme delicacy.

Thanks to their tarsal pulvilli, the Charontidae can climb vertical surfaces and run about underneath the ceilings of caves. *Charinides bengalensis*, for example, can climb a vertical sheet of polished glass and even walk across the lower surface of a horizontal sheet while the Tarantulidae, lacking pulvilli, cannot do this.

A number of species have become domesticated and live in dark corners of houses in tropical regions. Examples are afforded by *Phrynichus ceylonicus* in India, *Paracharon caecus* in Portuguese Guinea, *Masicodamon allanteus* in Morocco and *Damon medius* and *D. variegatus* in French West Africa and South Africa respectively. According to Lawrence (1949) the last species probably occurs in all buildings in Pietermaritzburg in the ventilation areas below floor-level. Specimens are also very common in outhouses, beneath stored furniture, packing cases and other large wooden structures which have been left undisturbed. In parks and gardens they often live under old tree stumps or fallen trunks of trees, while in more open country they are common under stones and in crevices of rocks. It is probable that the more domesticated species are better able to withstand dry conditions, and *Phrynichus ceylonicus*, a species that does not burrow, can live for two or three weeks in a bare cage, while the variety *pusillus* appears to be confined to moist jungles of the lower hills of Ceylon and dies in a few days if not supplied with moist soil (Graveley, 1915).

All Phrynichida are predatory, feeding on a varied selection of insects such as cockroaches, crickets, grasshoppers, termites, woodlice and the like. They are very 'nervous' animals, approach their prey cautiously and then seize it suddenly, gripping it with their pedipalps. In *Phrynichus ceylonicus* both palps are shot forward in any attempt to catch the prey, but capture is usually effected between the terminal claw and the spine near the end of the tibia of the pedipalp on one side only. Spines are arranged to form a very effective 'hand', the terminal claw being apposable to the proximal of two long dorsal spines at the distal end of the tibia and the spine on the penultimate joint to the distal of these. As the claw and all three spines are rigid and sharply pointed it might be supposed that once the prey is grasped, escape would be quite impossible. The strength necessary to retain the prey appears to be lacking, however, and even a soft-bodied cricket may be attacked unsuccessfully, time after time. But once within reach of the chelicerae, all chance of escape vanishes.

The prey, which frequently remains alive for a time, is held between the pedipalps, often with the terminal finger embedded in its tissues, whilst parts of it are scooped into the mouth by the terminal segments of the chelicerae whose saw-like armature may be of use in severing pieces of suitable size from the main mass. Such pieces are masticated by combined vertical and longitudinal movements of these appendages which rub it against the gnathobases of the pedipalps.

Unlike *Phrynichus ceylonicus*, *Charinides bengalensis* captures its prey between the two second appendages as the terminal claw of the palp cannot be closed against the spines at the end of the tibia. The capture is extremely sudden and can only be observed with difficulty. When drinking, drops of water are conveyed by the palps to the chelicerae, or these organs may be inserted directly into the water which is taken up with movements like those employed in mastication.

The appendages are often cleaned by the chelicerae as in false-scorpions and great care is taken to keep their tips free from dirt. In the case of the pedipalps this may be correlated with the presence on the terminal segments of an elaborate system of spines, clubbed hairs and pits which may perhaps constitute an organ of taste. It is not unlikely too that the pulvillus on the tarsi of *C. bengalensis* and the pad in *P. ceylonicus* must be kept perfectly clean if they are to be used effectively and tactile organs may be concentrated in this region. That the antenniform first legs should be kept clean is clearly necessary on account of their function as feelers. The extent to which vision is used in seeking prey is uncertain (Graveley, 1915). Phrynichida usually fast for several days after each meal.

The secondary sex differences of the Phrynichida are extremely small, and in most species there is little to distinguish the males from the females. In *Charon grayi*, however, which has a wide distribution in eastern Asia, the femur of the pedipalp in the male is longer than those of the second, third and fourth walking legs, while in the female it is shorter. Mating habits have not yet been observed in any of the Phrynichida. During the breeding season, the females of the species carry an egg sac on their abdomens. The number of eggs may vary from 7 to 80 or more, depending on the size of the mother (Takashima, 1950). The eggs are quite large, measuring 2 to 3 mm in diameter and probably in all species are carried by the mother in a capsule attached to the ventral surface of her abdomen. Both eggs and embryos are closely packed in this egg sac, the pressure in the confined area giving a sub-angular outline to some of the contiguous eggs. The contents of the sac are not arranged in regular rows, either longitudinally or transversely, but in the South African *Damon variegatus* are two layers deep (Lawrence, 1949). In this species and in *Admetus barbadensis* of the West Indies, courtship involves tapping with the antenniform first legs and threatening with the pedipalps, but no mating grasp. Insemination consists of the male depositing a sper-

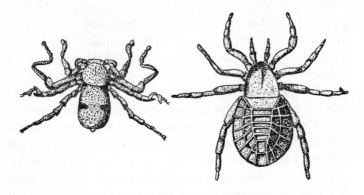

Fig. 30. Ricinulei. (After Berland, 1955, and Millot, 1949.)

matophore on the ground and loading its proximal end with the sperm which is afterwards collected by the female (Alexander, 1962).

According to Graveley (1915) all the Indian and Ceylonese species appear to breed at about the same time of year. The embryos are carried under the abdomen where they are supported by a membrane secreted for the purpose. The number of eggs varies from 15 to 60 or more. *Charinides bengalensis* breeds in July and August and sometimes earlier. The newly hatched young are entirely white: like young scorpions they cling to the dorsal surface and the sides of the abdomen of their mother until after their first moult. Immediately after the first moult the carapace is a little over 1 mm in width, but during the first year its width is doubled. During the second year it increases to about 2·5 mm and during the third to 3 mm or more. The adult size is approximately 3·5 mm.

Order RICINULEI

The Ricinulei or Podogonata are small Arachnids, 4 to 10 mm in length with a short massive body and a remarkably hard, thick and deeply granulated integument. The prosoma is covered by a non-segmented carapace at the front edge of which is a mobile hood or cucullus which fits down tightly over the chelicerae. No true eyes are present, but vague pale spots on each side of the carapace may well represent vestigial eyes. The pedipalps are of six segments and are remarkable in that their coxal segments are fused in the mid-line: they are chelate as are the two-segmented chelicerae. The prosoma is joined to the opisthosoma by a narrow pedicel, but this is hidden from view by expansions of the base of the abdomen which fits very closely against the prosoma, the juncture forming a coupling device. The living animal is able to disengage the carapace from the abdomen so that the genital orifice is exposed during mating and oviposition. The opisthosoma is composed of nine segments of which only the first four are well defined, while the last three form a small pygidium. The legs are short and stout, the third pair being modified as copulatory organs in mature males, a character otherwise found only in certain mites.

The order is limited to a single family, the Ricinoididae (or Cryptostemmidae) and contains only two genera, *Ricinoides* and *Cryptocellus*. Of these the first is represented by six West African species, the second by seven species having a distribution from Texas to the Amazon basin. After the discovery in 1838, of the first specimens of these very rare animals, only 32 were found until, nearly a century later in the British Cameroons no less than 317 specimens of *Ricinoides sjostedti* were obtained. It is not entirely surprising, therefore, that the biology of these peculiar creatures is practically unknown, although specimens have been kept alive at the British Museum (Natural History) for over a year (Finnegan, 1935).

Ricinulei appear generally to live under damp, fallen leaves in equatorial forests. Certain Mexican species are cavernicolous and specimens of *Cryptocellus dorotheae* have been found shortly after rains in the sandy soil of the Rio Grande River Valley. They were taken from under slabs of concrete, heavy sheet iron and roofing material which had not been disturbed for several years. The creatures are very sluggish and have a slow and curious gait. They move with considerable deliberation and seem to feel their way along with their front pair of legs, their movements resembling those of a tick crawling over the ground, Sudden illumination or slight vibrations of the soil send them into a cataleptic state. They are extremely sensitive to desiccation.

Ricinulei have never been observed to feed on non-living material and, in nature, their diet probably consists of termites, insect larvae and small spiders. Males court females by stroking and tapping them with their long second pair of legs. In the male the tarsal and metatarsal segments of the third pair of legs are modified: the second tarsal segment is large and drawn out dorsally into a spoon-like structure known as the lamina cyathiformis whose function is apparently to protect the delicate tarsal process which bears a short basal and longer distal portion. During mating, the male exposes his genital aperture by rotating the fourth coxae and tilting the abdomen upwards. In this position he sways one of the legs of the third pair forward, twisting it to bring the lamina cyathiformis into a horizontal plane, and inserts it beneath his body where it collects a spermaphore which is then applied to the genital opening of the female (Cooke, 1967).

This type of sperm transfer is also found in Solifugae and some Acari, whilst in Scorpions, Psuedoscorpions, Schizomida, Phrynichida, Thelyphonida and other Acari the spermaphore is a complex rod-like structure deposited on the ground. In these orders, mating involves the female walking over the spermaphore and gathering the spermatozoa into her genital orifice from the top of it. In spiders, sperms are transferred to the female by the palpal organs of the male (p. 215). The ancestral type probably used the claw at the tip of the pedipalp for this purpose, but later this evolved into the complex palpal organ that we find today. If, as seems probable, the third pair of legs in the Ricinulei has undergone analagous development, it means that, although the spermaphore is simple in structure, it is associated with an elaborate transfer organ. This indicates that the Ricinulei are not primitive, but a highly specialised group of animals.

Nothing is known of the life history and development of these rare Arachnids beyond the fact that they are oviparous. The eggs are laid singly and carried about by the female with her chelicerae. They hatch into a six-legged larvae known as Acari.

BIBLIOGRAPHY

Identification

EWING, H. E. (1929) A synopsis of the American Arachnids of the primitive order Ricinulei. *Ann. Ent. Soc. Amer.*, **22**, 583–600.

GRAVELEY, F. H. (1916) The evolution and distribution of the Indo-Australian Thelyphonidae, with notes on the distinctive characters of various species. *Rec. Ind. Mus.*, **12**, 59–89.

KÄSTNER, A. (1932) Pedipalpi Latreille *in* KÜKENTHAL, W. and KRUMBACH, T. *Handbuch der Zoologie*, Berlin, **3**, (2), 1–76.

—— (1932) Palpigradi Thorell. *Ibid.*, 77–98.

—— (1932) Ricinulei Thorell. *Ibid.*, 99–116.

KRAEPELIN, K. (1899) Scorpiones und Pedipalpi. *Das Tierreich*, **8**, 1–265.

—— (1901) Palpigradi. *Ibid.*, **12**, 1–3.

POCOCK, R. I. (1900) *The Fauna of British India, including Ceylon and Burma. Arachnida.* London.

ROEWER, C. F. (1934) Palpigradi *in* H. G. BRONN'S *Klass. Ordn. Tierreichs*, **5**, IV (8), 640–723.

WERNER, F. (1935) Pedipalpi. *Ibid.*, 317–490.

Biology

ALEXANDER, A. J. (1962) Courtship and mating in Ambylpygids (Pedipalpi, Arachinida). *Proc. Zool. Soc. Lond.*, **138**, 379–83.

CLOUDSLEY-THOMPSON, J. L. (1949) Notes on Arachnida, 11.—Schizomida in England. *Ent. Mon. Mag.*, **85**, 261.

COOKE, J. A. L. (1967) Observations on the biology of Ricinulei (Arachnida) with descriptions of two new species of *Cryptocellus*. *J. Zool., Lond.*, **151**, 31–42.

FINNEGAN, S. (1935) Rarity of the archaic Arachnids Podogona (Ricinulei). *Nature, Lond.*, **136**, 186.

FLOWER, S. S. (1901) Notes on the millipedes, centipedes, scorpions etc. of the Malay Peninsula and Siam. *J. Straits Brit. Asiat. Soc.*, **36**, 1–48.

GRAVELEY, F. H. (1911) Pedipalpi of Ceylon. *Spolia Zeylandica*, **7**, 43–7.

—— (1915) Notes on the habits of Indian insects, myriapods and arachnids. *Rec. Ind. Mus.*, **11**, 483–539.

KLINGEL, H. (1963) Mating and maternal behaviour in *Thelyphonus caudatus* L. (Pedipalpi, Holopeltidia Uropygi). *Treubia*, **26**, 65–70.

LAWRENCE, R. F. (1949) Notes on the whip-scorpions (Pedipalpi) of South Africa. *Trans. Roy. Soc. S. Africa*, **32**, 275–85.

MARX, G. (1892) Contributions to the life-history of Arachnida. *Proc. Ent. Soc. Wash.*, **2**, 252–4.

PATTEN, B. M. (1917) Reactions of the whip-tail scorpion to light. *J. Exp. Zool.*, **23**, 251–75.

PERGANDE, T. (1886) [Habits of a specimen of *Thelyphonus*.] *Proc. Ent. Soc. Wash.*, **1**, 42–4.

STRUBELL, A. (1926) *Thelyphonus caudatus L.*—Eine biologische Skizze. *Verh. Nat. Ver. Bonn.*, **82**, 301–14.

STURM, H. (1958) Indirekte Spermatophorenübertragung bei dem Gersselskorpion *Trithyreus sturmi* (Schizomidae, Pedipalpi). *Naturwiss.*, **45**, 142–3.

TAKASHIMA, H. (1950) Notes on Amblypygi found in territories adjacent to Japan. *Pacific Sci.*, **4**, 336–8.

WHEELER, W. M. (1900) A singular Arachnid (*Koenenia mirabilis* Grassi) occurring in Texas. *Amer. Nat.*, **34**, 837–50.

CHAPTER IX

HARVEST-SPIDERS

Classification and distribution

The order Opiliones or Phalangidea includes the harvest-men, the majority of which can be recognised by their long, slender legs and segmented abdomen which is joined to the cephalothorax across the whole breadth and not by a narrow pedicel as in spiders. The cephalothorax is composed of six segments and is often separated from the abdomen by a fairly deep groove. The carapace is usually smooth and, in most species, bears two eyes, although these may occasionally be absent. The eyes are nearly always situated on a prominent ocular tubercle near the middle of the cephalothorax, one looking out at each side. Near the anterior margin of the prosoma opposite the attachment of the first pair of legs there are two small openings leading to a pair of odoriferous glands: the glands themselves can, in some species, be seen through the carapace, when they look like an extra pair of eyes. The cheli-cerae are three-segmented, the last two segments forming pincers, while the pedipalps are of six segments. Their coxae bear gnathobases which form part of a complex mouth. The pedi-palps are short and leg-like; they are chiefly sensory organs for use in contact with objects close to the body, and they also help in grasping the food and bringing it to the jaws. In some genera they end in a claw which may be smooth or toothed, but in others no claw is found.

The bodies of harvest-spiders are usually covered with spines, pointed tubercles and bristles. There is often a double row along the centre of the ocular tubercle and in some genera of Palpatores (see below) a group forms a trident in the middle of the fore-edge of the cephalothorax and is an important diagnostic character. On the underside of the body the coxae of the legs almost meet in the middle so that there is no sternum as in spiders.

The abdomen is composed of ten segments, but these can be distinguished only in the most primitive sub-order, the Cyphophthalmi: in other Opiliones not more than nine tergites are apparent. A unique peculiarity of harvest-spiders lies in the fact

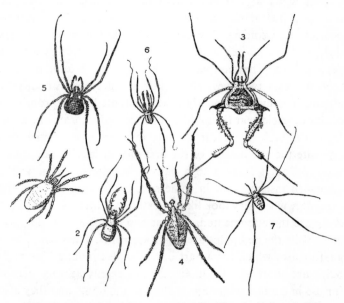

FIG. 31. Examples of harvest-spider families: 1. (Sub-order) Cyphophthalmi, 2. Phalangodidae, 3. Gonyleptidae, 4. Trogulidae, 5. Nemastomidae, 6. Ischyropsalidae, 7. Phalangiidae. (Drawings not to scale.) (After various authors.)

that the tergite and sternite of the same segment are not always placed vertically opposite one another. The anus has been brought forward ventrally so that the tergite primitively above it now lies behind, and the sternite primitively below is now placed immediately in front. Consequently most Opiliones have short and rounded bodies. The majority of species have cryptic, or concealing coloration, being usually brown or grey, often with a central dark band which serves to break up the outline of the animal's shape and renders it inconspicuous against its natural background. The size of the body varies from about 1 to 20 mm in length, but the majority are between 5 and 10 mm long.

The Opiliones are divided into three sub-orders, of which the Cyphophthalmi is the most primitive. It comprises some forty mite-like species varying in length between 1 and 3 mm, with short legs and repugnatorial glands opening at the ends of lateral prosomatic tubercles. The genitalia are not covered by an operculum but the body is protected by a shield resulting from the fusion of the cephalothorax and the abdominal tergites, excepting the last. The abdominal sternites are also fused in a similar manner and eyes are often absent.

The Cyphophthalmi have a very discontinuous distribution, species occurring in Corsica, Dalmatia, central France, parts of tropical Africa, Ceylon, Japan, the East Indies and the United States of Florida and Oregon. They are generally to be found in humid situations under more or less deeply buried stones. The genus *Siro* is represented in France by *S. rubens*, a species first discovered by Latreille at Brive and long mistaken for a mite until E. Simon established its true nature. *Siro duricorius* is known from the caves of Carniola in Yugoslavia and the related *Parasiro corsicus* from the neighbourhood of Porto Vecchio in Corsica. The genus *Stylocellus* occurs in the East Indies, *Ogivea* and *Paragovia* in Equatorial Africa and *Purcellia* on the

Cape of Good Hope, where the genus *Speleosiro* is represented by a single troglodytic species.

The second sub-order, the Laniatores, is more important than the preceding one and some 1500 species have so far been described, principally from southern latitudes. They are characterised by great development of the pedipalps which are armed with stout spines and strong claws and are used as raptatory organs for the capture of prey. The Laniatores have an almost exclusively tropical distribution, one family, the Phalangodidae, having a few representatives in Europe (*Scotolemon* spp.) and in North America (*Phalangodes* spp.). These are troglodytes inhabiting, amongst others, the Mammoth Cave in Kentucky. In addition, several genera occur in the tropics of the Old World, Australia, the Pacific islands and most of South America. The remaining families of Laniatores are entirely tropical: the Oncopodidae are found in India, the Assamiidae in India, and other parts of Asia and Africa excluding Madagascar, the Cosmetidae in the southern United States and the Triaeonychidae in Madagascar, Australia and America. The largest family is the Gonyleptidae which is almost entirely confined to South America where species live in damp forests under stones and fallen trees. They have particularly large, defensive spines on the last pair of legs.

The most important sub-order of the Opiliones is the Palpatores, to which all the British species belong. Four families are known, of which the Trogulidae are considered to be the most primitive. These are sluggish, short-legged, ground-living species to be found among grass roots, moss and even mud in chalky districts of Europe, Asia Minor, North Africa and North America. The fore-edge of the prosoma forms a bifurcated hood covering the mouth parts, there is no ocular tubercle and the body is dark coloured and habitually covered with particles of dirt and earth which render the animals extremely difficult to see. The Nemastomidae are also small, short-legged, dark, ground-living forms usually found among moss and dead leaves while the Ischyropsalidae are a small family limited to central Europe, where they live in damp moss in woods, mountain torrents and the caves of the Pyrenees. The largest family is the Phalangiidae which includes all the well-known long-legged harvestmen of Europe, North Africa and North America. These animals have typically rounded bodies, the palpal tarsus is longer than the tibia and its claw is well developed. They are to be found among litter and fallen leaves on the ground, on the trunks of trees and in vegetation (Todd, 1949).

The distribution of harvest-spiders in the British Isles has been described by Bristowe (1949) and Sankey (1949b), while the European forms have been studied by Stipperberger (1928).

General behaviour

The name Opilio means, in Latin, a 'shepherd' and may refer to the fact that in some countries shepherds walk about on stilts, the better to count their flocks. In our own land harvestmen were known as 'shepherd spiders' four centuries ago, but T. Muffett (1634) in his *Theatre of Insects*[†] explained this by saying 'the English call it Shepherd either because it is pleased with the Company of Sheep or because Shepherds think those fields that are full of them to be good wholesome Sheep-pasture ...'. Hooke (1658) in his *Micrographia* gave the alternative names 'shepherd or carter spider' and Bristowe (1949) quotes an old Essex superstition that it was unlucky purposely to kill a harvestman because of the belief that these creatures helped farmers with the scythe, rake and sickle which they were alleged to possess. In France they are known as

[†]*Insectorum sive minimorum animalium theatrum.* London.

faucheurs (reapers) because they give the appearance of reaping as they walk, while the German *Weber-knechte* may refer to the jerky movements made by the legs of these animals after they have become detached from the bodies of their owners.

Only two species, *Phalangium opilio* and *Leiobunum rotundum*, are at all conspicuous in our fields and are most noticeable at the harvest season, when they reach maturity. Consequently these, particularly *P. opilio*, are probably responsible for the name 'harvestmen'. Bristowe (1949) believes that '*Phalangium*' which is of eighteenth century origin, is derived from the Greek 'phalanx' and that the harvest-spider was likened to a formidable soldier in a phalanx because it was confused with the very poisonous 'Malmignatte', *Latrodectus* 13-*guttatus*, a relative of the notorious 'black-widow' spider which occasionally bites reapers in the fields of southern Europe. On the other hand, Sankey (1949b) has suggested that the name may be derived from *phalange*, a head or toe segment, for long limbs are one of the most conspicuous features of most harvest-spiders.

The biology of the Laniatores, so common in tropical regions, is practically unknown beyond the fact that they lead retiring lives in damp forests beneath bark, fallen trees and moss, and occasionally in caves. In New Zealand the harvestmen of the sub-order Laniatores are always found in forested country or in areas which have in recent times been forested but where the bush has been felled and cleared, leaving decaying logs and small pockets of forest which provide a favourable habitat. The great majority of species require a high and even relative humidity. They are nocturnal and are to be found during the day sheltering beneath logs and stones, in the débris on the forest floor, in moss growing in similar situations or on the trunks and branches of trees in the wetter areas. The leaf-mould fauna consists mainly of the smaller species of

Nuncia and species of *Pristobunus*. The species of *Synthetony-chia* are found only in leaf-mould and moss, while *Muscicola picta* and *Algidia viridata* appear to be restricted to moss and are distinguished by their striking green coloration. No altitudinal speciation has been observed: only a few species have been found above bush-line and then only in small numbers in sub-alpine scrub. They are more numerous near sea level and progressively diminish in number at higher altitudes. Very few are encountered above 2500 ft. and only Palpatores are found under alpine conditions (Forster, 1954). The Cyphoph-thalmi are rare and equally obscure, living like mites under stones, etc. in damp places, and are usually to be found only after rain has fallen. The only sub-order whose biology is known at all adequately is the Palpatores, thanks largely to the work of British naturalists.

The Trogulidae and Nemastomidae are inhabitants of the surface layers of the soil and appear to require a balanced microclimate as they are particularly susceptible to desiccation. The first named family is confined to chalky districts where they find the snails on which they feed, but members of both families avoid the light and crawl slowly into cover if exposed. Vibrations of the soil usually induce a death-feigning reflex. The British species *Trogulus tricarinatus* and *Anelasmocephalus cambridgei* are rare forms found only by careful searching in southern counties, but *Nemastoma lugubre* and *N. chrysomelas* are quite common and widely distributed.

'The study of harvestmen is a study of legs', wrote Savory (1938) and legs are indeed a feature that is bound to impress anyone observing the Phalangiidae. Although autotomy is frequently practised as an escape reaction, no regeneration of the limbs occurs in harvestmen. A minimum of four legs, provided one of the second pair remains, enables most species to lead a more or less normal life, but if both of the second pair are lost death soon follows. These second legs seem to be used for tactile purposes and possibly for smell reception and the sensory hairs on the first legs may also serve the latter purpose. It is interesting to note that the long-legged Phalangiidae possess two small spiracles on the tibia of each leg in addition to the usual spiracles which open near the coxae of the fourth pair of legs (Sankey, 1949b).

Like other Arachnids, harvestmen carefully clean their limbs. A leg is held in the chelicerae which open and shut as the long segments are pulled through them. By the time the tarsus is reached, the leg is bent almost into a circle, and finally shoots out like an unbent spring. The pedipalps are cleaned in the same way and the chelicerae are washed while drinking. A few species are able to stridulate but the sound is probably too faint to be audible to the human ear.

To the lyriform organs—button-shaped slits found singly or together in a lyre-shaped group—have been attributed the function of smell. They occur especially on the first segments of the chelicerae and on the coxae of the legs. Each is supplied with a nerve and they may well be proprioceptors analagous to the chordotonal sensillae of insects which serve to detect strains and stresses in the integument. Harvestmen respond to touch and chemical stimuli, and bunch together in captivity. Their eyes are simple and probably serve mainly for distinguishing light from darkness. It is doubtful if there is much form-vision in any of the Opiliones but some perception of movement may occur. Although harvest-spiders are susceptible to changes of temperature and humidity, the organs which serve these functions are not yet known. Todd (1949) has worked out the temperature and humidity preferences for some British species and found a strong correlation between the humidity preference of the species tested in the laboratory and their stratification in oak woodland. At the same time it was noted that those species with the highest temperature preference appeared to have a southern distribution or to live in drier or warmer habitats than others.

British harvest-spiders can be divided into various groups according to their vertical distribution. Thus the species which usually live on the ground under stones, logs and in moss or plant débris include those with short legs and small eyes such as *Trogulus tricarinatus, Anelasmocephalus cambridgei, Nemastoma lugubre, N. chrysomelas, Homalenotus quadridentatus, Oligolophus meadii* and *Opilio saxatilis*. The second group includes species which live mainly amongst low vegetation (the field layer) of grass and other herbaceous plants, but whose young stages occur on the ground, such as *Nelima silvatica, Leiobunum blackwalli, L. rotundum, Mitopus morio, Oligolophus tridens, Lacinius ephippiatus, Platybunus triangularis, Megabunus diadema* and *Phalangium opilio*. Finally certain species tend to live as adults above the field layer on bushes, trees, walls and fences while their young stages are found nearer the ground. These include *Oligolophus agrestis O. hansenii, Odiellus spinosus* and *Opilio parietinus*, but there is some overlap between all three groups and most species migrate upwards as they mature. This appears to be associated with the need for bigger prey, more space to move in, mating and probably different temperature and moisture requirements (Sankey, 1949b). In addition, Todd (1949) has shown that many species of harvestmen are most active at night when they show a tendency to migrate upwards on to trees where the air is damper. This activity is correlated with the decrease in light intensity, increase in relative humidity and decrease in temperature that occurs after dark. Thus in Wytham Woods, some $4\frac{1}{2}$ miles north-west of Oxford, *Leiobunum rotundum* hunts on the underside of *Mercuralis perennis* leaves during the day but passes the night on the trunks of trees.

A similar vertical migration was found to occur in *Oligo-lophus tridens*, and many other species show a vertical migration during their life histories, as already mentioned. At the same time there is usually a microhabitat separation in space and time, or both, between allied species of the same genus. *L. rotundum* and *L. blackwalli* resemble each other very closely but during their life histories there is no habitat overlap in time until they both appear on tree trunks at the age of six months. *L. rotundum* hatches about a month in advance of *L. blackwalli* and retains this lead as it ascends from one plant layer to the next. *L. blackwalli* is never abundant and is found on the lower parts of the tree trunks while *L. rotundum* is much more plentiful and is usually to be seen up to seven feet above ground level. Similarly *Oligolophus tridens* is a dominant field-layer form while the less abundant *O. agrestis* and *O. hansenii* are found predominantly on tree trunks and amongst the branches.

The floor-dwelling harvestmen are associated primarily with woodland and the vertical migration described above is claimed by Williams (1962) to be not an exodus from the ground but an upward spread. Although harvestmen are active through the 24 hours, most of their movement is at night, except when they are hungry. Then they are also active during the day, especially if the humidity is high.

Food and feeding habits

Harvest-spiders are primarily carnivorous and usually feed on fresh or recently dead animal tissues, but they will also eat a varied assortment of matter such as bread, fat, the gills of *Chanterelle* and other fungi, seeds and even chew pellets of miscellaneous vegetable matter which they have carried to a suitable feeding ground such as the top of a leaf. They have been recorded scavenging on bird droppings and dead animal material such as worms, millipedes, centipedes, ants, spiders, flies, beetles and vertebrates: indeed it seems that little organic material comes amiss to these omnivorous creatures (Sankey, 1949a). More often, however, they are seen to prey on woodlice, millipedes, centipedes, false-scorpions, spiders, mites and a wide variety of insects. A number of species, such as *Mitopus morio*, are habitually cannibalistic while the Trogulidae feed on snails such as *Cepaea* and *Oxychilus* spp. and are mainly found in the chalky districts where these are most numerous. The Ischyropsalidae also feed on Gasteropod molluscs and have extra long chelicerae with which the prey is drawn from its shell. When the snail is completely retracted the harvest-spider sometimes breaks off pieces of the shell until it can reach the body of the animal. The cavernicolous *Scotolemon* spp. are particularly ferocious and hunt other arthropods, particularly beetles, which they devour in great numbers. The sensitive second legs are of prime importance in the recognition of prey.

When eating, the chelicerae, pedipalps and legs may all be brought into use. Legs and palps help in subduing living prey and the pincers of the chelicerae serve to tear it to bits. Sometimes two or more Phalangids may be seen pulling and tearing at the same morsel of food. Water is of special importance in the economy of harvest-spiders and most species do not survive for long without it. They may fast for a fortnight or more without apparent discomfort but many will die in a couple of days if unable to drink. After rain many species, both diurnal and nocturnal, may be found abroad, but during periods of drought almost all will avoid direct light and forage only at twilight or early in the morning (Bishop, 1949b). According to Savory (1938) a very thirsty harvestman is stiff and torpid, but if placed on the surface of the water remains there sucking up the liquid like blotting paper.

Enemies

Adult harvest-spiders seem to have few enemies and most of their difficulties in life are probably of a physical nature such as changes of temperature and humidity: but according to one school of thought there must be some biological density-dependent factor to keep their numbers in check. For if a particular component of the environment is to regulate the population density of a species, it must be able to destroy a greater fraction of the population of that species when the density is high than when it is low. If destruction were merely proportional to population density, the factor causing it would not be a regulatory one. Parasites and predators are examples of the first category (density-dependent factors), climatic conditions of the second. Other writers suggest that natural control is achieved chiefly by climatic and edaphic factors and that it is unnecessary to invoke density-dependent factors to explain either the maximum or the minimum number occurring in a natural population. Perhaps the truth may lie somewhere between these extremes.[†]

The following predators have been recorded: fish (when harvestmen have been caught by the sudden flooding of streams), frogs, toads, lizards, birds, shrews, badgers, foxes and other mammals, centipedes, spiders, predaceous flies, beetles, earwigs, dragonflies, bugs and other insects, as well as cannibalistic Opiliones (Sankey, 1949a). However, the ground-living forms are exceedingly inconspicuous and probably seldom found by their potential enemies, whilst the long-legged species generally have cryptic coloration and can often stride out of harm's way. If caught they may escape by autotomising a limb. The leg breaks at the articulation between the coxa and tro-

[†] I have recently discussed these points; 1957, *Entomologist*, **90**, 195–203. See also MILNE, A. (1957) *Canad. Ent.* **89**, 193–213.

chanter and there is no bleeding. The detached portion may make spontaneous rhythmical movements which persist for an hour or more and serve to distract the predator's attention from its prey. Lost appendages are not regenerated however, and harvest-spiders appear to lack the ability to rid themselves of damaged members but continue to drag a crippled leg until it severs itself. It is interesting to note here that autotomy does not appear to occur in the Trogulidae.

Should a harvestman come to grips with an aggressor a fluid is extruded from its repugnatorial glands that is distasteful to most invertebrate predators. Thus few spiders will sustain an attack on adult harvestmen: usually they retreat after one bite and wipe their mouths on a leaf. In no British species is the odour discernible to man: the fluid is colourless and does not appear to have any marked flavour, but various Gonyleptidae in Brazil produce a strong, nauseating odour if handled, and in addition can deliver a sharp pinch by firmly drawing their hind femora together behind them. Odoriferous glands are found in both sexes of all species of harvest-spider and in their nature are very similar to those of millipedes. As already mentioned, there is a single pair of glands which opens at the margin of the cephalothorax above the coxa of the second leg. In the larger South African Laniatores such as *Larifugella natalensis*, the opening is protected and partly covered by a large flattened tubercle or process of the coxa. In some species the glandular secretion can be discharged in the form of a fine jet to a distance of more than an inch from the animal (Lawrence, 1937), but in most it merely flows from the gland opening. The colour of the secretion in the Laniatores is bright yellow or reddish brown: it is highly volatile with an acrid smell and may cause a smarting sensation in the eyes if a drop is brought too close to them.

Their repugnatorial fluid may be responsible for the fact

that if a number of phalangids are confined in a limited space they seem to be anaesthetised or narcotised by each other and remain for a long period in a state of insensibility. When thrown out upon the floor of a cage they promptly recover and run about normally (Savory, 1938). The same phenomenon has been observed by Bishop (1949b): the specimens lie in a tangled mass of legs and bodies, apparently without life, but when disturbed by shaking they recover and assume their normal activities.

The parasites of Opiliones include nematode worms and gregarines, while several species have been found with larval mites such as *Erythraeus phalangioides*, *Belaustium nemorum*, *Leptus* spp. and other Thrombidiidae which are a conspicuous bright red colour, attached to them. Phoretic false-scorpions are occasionally to be seen clinging to their legs. According to Forster (1954) the New Zealand Laniatores are not attacked by spiders but infestation by nematodes and Chalcid wasps has been noted. Specimens are often heavily infested with mites which cling to intersegmental membranes of abdomen and appendages.

Mating habits

Mating in harvest-spiders is as casual as eating or drinking. Mature males and females that encounter one another in the field ordinarily mate briefly, separate and continue their wanderings. A short time later they may mate again with one another or with different individuals. The necessity for frequent matings may perhaps be correlated with the fact that the eggs mature a few at a time and are deposited at intervals throughout, and in most British species towards the end of, summer. Secondary sexual differences are very slight. No true courtship has been observed in Opiliones, but some curious behaviour sometimes occurs in *Mitopus morio*, one of the dominant Arachnids in Iceland (Cloudsley-Thompson, 1948a, b). This species is particularly evident on sunny days. The male, recognisable by his smaller body, longer legs and paler colour, runs towards a moving female and takes up a position with his body just above and legs straddling hers. The two run in this position for several inches before stopping. The male then moves forward slightly so that his body is now in front of that of the female and turns about to face her. His long external genitalia are now thrust forward and mating takes place. In the majority of species, however, it is probable that copulation takes place at night.

Forster (1954) has observed mating in the New Zealand Laniatores of both *Nuncia* and *Algidia* spp. Copulation is direct with little prenuptial behaviour. The male approaches the female rapidly, touching her with the tarsi of the second pair of legs. When face to face he clasps her pedipalps with his own. Both bodies are then raised, bringing the genital openings in line. The long penis of the male is then exserted and placed directly into the genital opening of the female: in no case observed has the female exserted her ovipositor to receive the penis.

In *Leiobunum calcar*, a common, widely distributed species of Palpatores in North America, the males are easily recognised by the presence on the femur of the pedipalp of a large, ventro-lateral spur. The patella is short, strongly arched above and curved ventrally and its swollen base is armed with short dark denticles. Because of the shortness of the patella the spur on the femur may be apposed to the swollen base of the tibia to form an efficient grasping organ. When a male encounters a female he rushes at her without preliminary courtship, and grasps her firmly, holding the trochanters of her first legs

with the spur on his femur while copulation takes place
(Bishop, 1949a).

In the short-legged Trogulidae the male hangs beneath the
female clasping her with his legs, whose claws grip the rough
surface on her back so that the ventral surfaces of the two
are opposed (Pabst, 1953).

It has often been reported that at the breeding season male
harvest-spiders fight 'bloodless battles' with one another, but
Bristowe (1941)* has suggested that the explanation of these
fights has as its basis sexual excitement and mistaken identity.
The male's chemo-tactic sense is stimulated not only by a
female but also by a male of its own kind, as is shown by the
extrusion of the penis.

Reproduction and life cycle

Female harvest-spiders have very long ovipositors and generally lay their eggs in crevices in the soil, under stones, wood
and in other moist places. Among the New Zealand Palpatores
mating usually takes place in October and November and eggs
are laid between late October and December. No eggs appear
to be laid in the autumn for over-wintering as is the case in
some British Palpatores. In *Hendea myersi* and other Triaeonychidae the eggs are deposited in small groups numbering from
one to five among leafmould or more commonly in rotting
wood, and these receive no further attention. From 20 to 60
eggs may be laid in this way during two weeks. The species of
Soerensella, by contrast, select the under surface of a log or
occasionally a space beneath a loose-fitting rock for oviposition. A small group of eggs, from 10 to 20, is laid and this
is then guarded by the female. At intervals of a few days or a
week further eggs are deposited so that in some cases egg
masses of some 60 to 100 eggs may be found, some of which

are hatching, while others are found in all stages of development, often including newly laid eggs. It is probable that hatching normally takes about 20 days (Forster, 1954).

In *Phalangium opilio* among the Palpatores the first oviposition usually takes place about 18 days after the final moult, the second 2 to 22 days later and a third in another week. Virgin females can lay eggs, but do not usually do so (Gueutal, 1944). The eggs are usually white, devoid of sculpturing and adhere loosely together. Their number varies from over 200 in *Odiellus spinosus* according to Sankey (1949b) and 275 in *Platybunus pinetorum* (Stipperberger, 1928) to 400 to 600 in *Phalangium opilio* according to Gueutal (1944). Holm (1947) found that *Opilio parietinus* laid from 20 to 60 eggs at 20° C, and that there was no further development after an early blastoderm stage unless the eggs were transferred to a refrigerator, where they were kept at 6° C for two weeks and then, for a further week, at −6° C. In *Leiobunum blackwalli*, however, the percentage of eggs hatching was not significantly higher after cold treatment according to Todd (1949).

A faint mottling indicates the onset of development; the eyes appear at one pole and just before hatching the body segments and limbs can be seen neatly tucked away inside the egg. Hatching is a quick process, the young breaking the egg membrane by means of a powerful egg-tooth in front of the ocular tubercle. European Palpatores are about 1 mm in length on emergence. The newly hatched young resemble the adults in general, but are distinguished by the absence of a number of detailed characters which are gradually assumed with each moult. The first of these occurs almost immediately after eclosion and is followed by six or seven others at intervals of about ten days extending over a period of six to nine months. The young are at first soft-bodied and sluggish in their movements but there is a progressive hardening of the integument with each ecdysis. In those Laniatores and Palpatores which have numerous tarsal segments in the mature forms, the number is far fewer in the young stages and increases as they grow older.

Where known, the soft-skinned, delicate eggs of the Trogulidae are laid in the shells of snails in which they are sealed by a protective membrane secreted by the ovipositor of the female. The number varies from one to eight in each batch, but as many as 25 eggs may be laid by a single female during the year. Maximum activity takes place in the spring and autumn but eggs are produced during every month except December and January. The duration of ontogeny depends upon the season at which the eggs are laid, and development is slow between October and March, coming almost to a standstill between November and February, but in the summer months it lasts five to eight weeks. Post-embryonic development is completed after a constant number of ecdyses of which the first again takes place immediately after hatching. In *Anelasmocephalus cambridgei* and the *Trogulus* spp. there are five and six moults respectively. The animals do not moult after reaching maturity which in *A. cambridgei* is reached in one to two months and takes four to five months in *Trogulus* spp., although the adults may continue to live for another two years or more (Pabst, 1953).

Three types of life cycle can be recognised in the British Opiliones. The Trogulidae and Nemastomidae, which live in sheltered habitats, can be found both as young and adults throughout the year. Then there are the species that pass the winter as eggs and mature at the end of the following summer, such as *Oligolophus* and *Odiellus* spp. Finally a few, such as *Platybunus triangularis* and *Megabunus diadema*, mature in early summer and lay eggs from which hatch young that spend the following winter in an immature stage (Sankey, 1949b; Todd, 1949).

BIBLIOGRAPHY

Identification

FORSTER, R. R. (1954) The New Zealand Harvestmen (sub-order Lania-tores). *Canterbury Mus. Bull.*, No. 2, 1–329.

KÄSTNER, A. (1928) Spinnentiere oder Arachnoidea III. Opiliones *in* DAHL, F. *Tierw. Deuts.*, **8**, 1–51.

PICKARD-CAMBRIDGE, O. (1890) Monograph of the British Phalangidea or harvestmen. *Proc. Dorset Field Club.*, **11**, 163–216.

ROEWER, C. F. (1923) *Die Weberknechte der Erde*, Jena (with several supplements).

SAVORY, T. H. (1948) *Synopses of the British Fauna. No. 1. Opiliones (Arachnida) or Harvestmen.* 2nd Ed. London: *Linn. Soc.*

SIMON, E. (1879) *Les Arachnides de France*, Paris, **7**, 116–332.

TODD, V. (1948) Key to the determination of the British harvestmen (Arachnida, Opiliones). *Ent. Mon. Mag.*, **84**, 109–13.

Biology

BISHOP, S. C. (1949a) The function of the spur on the femur of the palpus of the male *Leiobunum calcar* (Wood) (Arachnida: Phalangida). *Ent. News Philad.*, **60**, 10–11.

—— (1949b) The Phalangida (Opiliones) of New York. *Proc. Rochester Acad. Sci.*, **9**, 159–235.

BRISTOWE, W. S. (1949) The distribution of harvestmen (Phalangida) in Great Britain and Ireland, with notes on their names, enemies and food. *J. Anim. Ecol.*, **18**, 100–14.

CLOUDSLEY-THOMPSON, J. L. (1948a) Notes on Arachnida, 4. Courtship behaviour of the harvester *Mitopus morio*. *Ann. Mag. Nat. Hist.*, (11), **14**, 809–10.

—— (1948b) Observations on the ecology of Arachnids in North-west Iceland. *Ibid.*, (12), **1**, 437–47.

GUEUTAL, J. (1944) La ponte chez un Opilion: *Phalangium opilio* Linné. *Rev. fr. Ent. Paris*, **11**, 6–9.

KÄSTNER, A. (1931) Biologische Beobachtungen an Phalangiiden. *Zool. Anz.*, **95**, 293–302.

LAWRENCE, R. F. (1937) The odoriferous glands of some South African harvest-spiders. *Trans. R. Soc. S. Africa*, **25**, 333–42.

HOLM, Å. (1947) On the development of *Opilio parietinus* Deg. *Zool. Bidr. Uppsala*, **25**, 409–22.

PABST, W. (1953) Zur Biologie der mitteleuropäischen Troguliden. *Zool. J. (Syst.)*, **82**, 1–46.

PHILLIPSON, J. (1960) The food consumption of different instars of *Mitopus morio* (F.) (Phalangida) under natural conditions. *J. Anim. Ecol.*, **29**, 299–307.

ROTERS, M. (1944) Observations on British Harvestmen. *J. Quek. Micr. Club.*, (4), **2**, 23–5.

SANKEY, J. H. P. (1949a) Observations on food, enemies and parasites of British harvest-spiders (Arachnida, Opiliones). *Ent. Mon. Mag.*, **85**, 246–7.

—— (1949b) British harvest-spiders. *Essex Nat.*, **28**, 181–91.

SAVORY, T. H. (1938) Notes on the biology of harvestmen. *J. Quek. Micr. Club.*, (4), **1**, 89–94.

—— (1949) Notes on the biology of Arachnida. *Ibid.*, (4), **3**, 18–24.

STIPPERBERGER, H. (1928) Biologie und Verbreitung der Opilioniden Nord-Tirols. *Arb. Zool. Inst. Univ. Innsbruck*, **3**, 12–79.

TODD, V. (1949) The habits and ecology of the British harvestmen (Arachnida, Opiliones), with special reference to those of the Oxford district. *J. Anim. Ecol.*, **18**, 209–16.

CHAPTER X

SPIDERS

Classification and distribution

Without doubt spiders are the best known and in many ways the most interesting of all the Arachnida. The diversity of their webs and the various and intricate methods used in

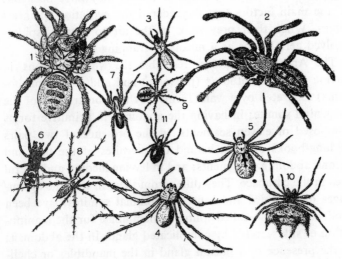

FIG. 32. Examples of spider families: 1. Liphistiidae, 2. Theraphosidae, 3. Gnaphosidae, 4. Sparassidae, 5. Thomisidae, 6. Salticidae, 7. Lycosidae, 8. Agelenidae, 9. Theridiidae, 10. Argiopidae, 11. Linyphiidae. (Drawings not to scale.) (After various authors and original.)

their construction have always attracted attention. Indeed, many people seem to notice only those species that capture their prey in webs such as the much maligned, long-legged house spiders (*Tegenaria* spp.) which spin cobwebs in the corners of rooms and outhouses; and the garden spiders (*Araneus* spp.) whose dew-spangled orb webs glistening in the sunlight lend their beauty to the autumn morning. All spiders spin silk, but by no means all of them live sedentary lives in webs: if they did, a large amount of potential food in the form of insects would not be exploited. In fact the more primitive species tend to use silk only for building their retreats and for weaving the cocoons in which they lay their eggs. Indeed, it has been suggested that predation by primitive hunting spiders upon early wingless insects may have been one of the main factors that engendered the evolution of insect wings. When their prey took to the air to escape, spiders evolved aerial webs as a means of trapping it in flight.

The Araneae or spiders resemble the whip-scorpions in having the cephalothorax (prosoma) and abdomen (opisthosoma) separated by a waist formed by the constriction of the pregenital somite; in having the abdomen in primitive forms composed of eleven segments, in the presence of two pairs of lung-books opening behind the sternites of the first and second abdominal segments; and in having median and lateral eyes in the carapace. They differ from them in that the appendages of the third and fourth abdominal somites have been retained as the so-called spinning mammillae for the manipulation of silk secreted by complicated glands in the abdomen; in the presence of a poison gland in the mandibles or chelicerae, the second segment of which forms a sharp, piercing fang with a single orifice at the tip for the exit of the poison; in the simple leg-like, non-prehensile palpi; and the conversion of the terminal segment of the palp of the male into a sperm-carrier.

Although the order is a homogeneous one, the phylogenetic and systematic problems involved in distinguishing the various families are often complex and several different classificatory schemes have been proposed (e.g. Bristowe, 1938; Petrunkevitch, 1933, 1939, etc.). Three sub-orders are now generally recognised. The first, Liphistiomorpha, is characterised by the fact that the abdomen has retained its primitive segmentation, being provided with eleven tergal plates and other atavistic qualities. The spiders of this sub-order belonging to the family Liphistiidae, of which the best known genus is *Liphistius*, are restricted to Burma, the Malay Peninsula and neighbouring countries. Several of the species such as *L. desultor* reach a fair size but very little is known of their habits. Some live exclusively in caves; all in burrows in the ground.

In the sub-order Mygalomorpha, which includes the so-called 'bird-eating' spiders of the tropics, the articulation of the mandibles with the prosoma is vertical so that they project forward, the fang or second segment closing straight backwards or nearly so. The spiders of this group are confined to temperate and tropical regions of the world where they are represented by large numbers of genera and species belonging to several families. The best known of these are the Theraphosidae, often erroneously spoken of as 'Tarantulas', which include the largest species known, the Ctenizidae or trap-door spiders which are famous for the perfection of their burrows, and the Atypidae which include the purseweb spider *Atypus affinis*, the sole British representative of the sub-order. This, one of our largest species, has a shining reddish black colour and is provided with enormous chelicerae. In the steaming jungles of South America live the largest spiders of all. A male *Theraphosa* sp. from French Guiana may measure three inches in length with a leg span exceeding ten inches, while an enormous female *Lasiodora* sp. from Brazil is recorded as having a body $3\frac{1}{2}$ inches long and a weight of almost 3 oz. (Gertsch, 1949).*

Bristowe (1947) relates that the hero of Milan is claimed to have slain a monstrous spider which had been lapping up the lamp oil of the Cathedral Church in 1751. 'After death, we are told, it weighed 4 lb. or somewhat more than a large Pekinese! Another, with similar oil-drinking habits, made its home in St. Eustace's Church in Paris, and I suspect the sexton was under grave suspicion of borrowing the oil himself until he reported seeing "a spider of enormous dimensions come down the chain by which the lamp was suspended, drink up the oil, and when gorged to satiety slowly retrace its steps".' The largest British house spider, *Tegenaria parietina*, has a body length of about $\frac{3}{4}$ inch and a leg span of about five inches. It has been recorded that, in 1936, a policeman on point duty at Lambeth Bridge held up the London traffic for some minutes to allow an outsize example to cross the road in safety—which it did, much to the delight of passers-by. There is an obscure legend that Cardinal Wolsey, who simply could not abide spiders, had a particular aversion to this species which was all too plentiful at Hampton Court and is still popularly known as the 'cardinal spider'.

The third sub-order, Araneomorpha, includes the most specialised spiders and comprises the majority of living species which exhibit a greater range in structural variation and in habits than any other order of Arachnida except, perhaps, the Acari. In the elaboration of complex instincts and habits they are unexcelled. The plane of articulation of the chelicerae to the cephalothorax is horizontal so that the mandibles point downward, the fangs closing obliquely inwards. These spiders are classified in families according to structural characters which are often correlated with the methods employed in the capture of prey. Thus the Dictynidae and Uloboridae coat their meshed webs with a bluish, sticky sheet of flocculent silk produced by a flat spinning organ or 'cribellum' lying close in front of the usual six spinnerets. The cribellum may be likened to the fused spinning fields of two spinnerets lying nearly flat against the ventral surface of the abdomen and is always accompanied by an accessory comb of hairs called the 'calamistrum' upon the metatarsi of the hind legs. The spider spins its composite hackled band by rubbing the calamistrum back and forth over the cribellum, drawing out two ribands that are attached to two lines of normal silk coming at the same time from the spinnerets. The Oonopidae, Dysderidae and Scytodidae are six-eyed nocturnal hunting spiders. Although the number of eyes is not such a fundamental character as was once thought, it is still a convenient diagnostic feature.

The members of the Gnaphosidae and Clubionidae are mostly nocturnal species that move stealthily as they feel for their prey with front legs outstretched. The Gnaphosidae are ground spiders of sombre coloration with few contrasting markings, the dull greys, browns and blacks deriving from a covering of short hairs that gives them a velvety appearance. More flattened than the Clubionidae, they differ from the latter in having the anterior lateral spinnerets widely separated. The Anyphaenidae and some Clubionidae live on plants, have well-developed claw tufts and are good climbers. Mostly whitish or brownish in colour, they dwell in flat tubular nests open at both ends, in rolled leaves or under bark. Some also live among vegetable débris and nest under stones. The Clubionidae that habitually live on the soil exhibit far more diversity in size, appearance and coloration than do the conservative plant-dwelling forms. Many smaller species such as the British *Phrurolithus festivus* are myrmecophilous and mimic ants.

Crab spiders or Thomisidae are sedentary animals that wait on the ground or in flowers and vegetation for passing insects which are seized by the powerful outstretched legs: they frequently possess markedly cryptic (concealing) coloration. The English name for this family derives from their habit of running sideways like crabs. The Salticidae or jumping spiders are small, rather squat animals with broad square heads, extremely large eyes and short, stout legs. They have very keen sight and stalk their prey from afar. This is one of the largest spider families and includes several thousand species which are found mainly in tropical countries where they almost rival the insects in the brilliance of their hues. Only thirty-two species are on the British list and most of these are rare and unlikely to be found, except by the most energetic collector. Our commonest species is the little 'zebra spider', *Salticus scenicus*, so named because it is conspicuously marked with black and white stripes. Though less brilliantly coloured than some of its exotic relatives, it is an attractive creature often to be seen walking on walls and fences in the sunshine.

Wolf spiders of the family Lycosidae have longer bodies and limbs and moderately large eyes and overcome their prey by sheer strength. Like the related Pisauridae, they are essentially ground-living forms and the majority of them hunt in the open by day. Two other families of hunting spiders, the Oxyopidae and the laterigrade Sparassidae, contain species which are usually found in low herbage whence they leap down on to their unsuspecting prey. They are represented in the British fauna by *Oxyopes heterophthalmus* and *Micrommata virescens*, respectively, and are more numerous in the warmer regions of the world where the giant crab spider, *Heteropoda venatoria*, is widely distributed.

The remaining families are all web-builders, the Agelenidae constructing funnel-shaped cobwebs consisting of a triangular sheet with its apex rolled into a tube in which the spider waits for its prey. The threads of which the web is constructed are not adhesive, but a tangled mass of scaffolding above trips passing insects which fall onto the sheet. Before they have time to recover, the owner of the web has darted from its tube and gathered them in.

The comb-footed spiders of the family Theridiidae are for the most part thickset, sedentary types that hang upside down from their irregular maze-like webs. Most are small spiders suspending their snares on plants with lines so fine that they are often unnoticed, or hiding them in burrows or fissures in the soil and under litter.

The two-dimensional orb web of the Argiopidae is the crowning achievement of the aerial spiders: it is the last stage in a series that has resulted in a circular design. Finally, the Linyphiidae build a horizontal platform upon which drop flying and jumping insects, usually after being halted in mid-air by a superstructure of criss-crossed lines guyed to adjacent vegetation. The spider clings upside down beneath it, runs over the surface with surprising rapidity and pulls its prey through the webbing. A second sheet is often present beneath the hanging spider and probably serves as a barrier to attack from below. In numbers of individuals, genera and species the Linyphiidae far exceed the total of any other family of spiders in the temperate zones where they are the dominant aerial types. The majority of these spiders are small, even minute, and they occur in vast, little noticed numbers under soil débris. Most of them are reddish or black creatures with somewhat elongated bodies and legs set with fine spines, but there are notable exceptions. The presence of a stridulating file on the side of the chelicerae and a scraping spine on the femur of the pedipalp serves to differentiate them from the orb weavers.

The spider fauna of the British Isles comprises some 24 families with over 570 species, nearly half of which are Linyphiidae. The population in late summer has been conservatively estimated by Bristowe (1939)* at some $2\frac{1}{4}$ millions per acre. He has calculated that if all the spiders from an acre of land were to combine to build one continuous thread, they would produce a strand in a single day's spinning that would just about circle the world at the equator: after ten days it would be long enough to reach the moon. The weight of insects destroyed each year by spiders in England and Wales must well exceed the total weight of the human population!

General behaviour

Spiders are seen in different lights by different people, but the superstitions regarding them, in both primitive and civilised countries, are extremely numerous. Bristowe (1945), who has written an interesting review of spider folklore, concludes that on the whole they are venerated and for a number of reasons. These include admiration for the spiders' skill as spinners of silk, admiration for their wisdom and cunning, fear of their venomous and sinister qualities, association of spiders with religious beliefs—in particular, that in spiders reside the spirits of the dead—belief in their ability to foretell and influence the weather, in their medicinal properties, and in the knowledge of the part they play in destroying insects.

Not all of these have given rise to superstitions, but the first four in particular provide the raw materials for folk tales as a result of which the spider's power for good and evil has become traditional throughout a large part of the world. In particular, there is a widespread legend of a fugitive who escaped his pursuers because a spider built a web across the mouth of his hiding place so that they thought he could not possibly be concealed therein. Among others this story has been told of the Infant Christ, who was thus saved from Herod, David, who escaped from the wrath of Saul, Mohammed from the

Coreishites, and Yoritomo, a twelfth-century Japanese hero, who hid in a hollow tree and was saved by a spider in similar fashion. Another and more famous myth is the ancient Greek story of Arachne, who, although deprived of her human form by Athene (Minerva) for daring to challenge the Goddess of Wisdom to a spinning contest, was nevertheless left with her skill as a spinner. This story is probably the origin of many superstitions which have survived in European countries although the myth itself has been forgotten. Thus there is a widespread belief that a spider found running over one's clothes has come to spin new ones: as a natural consequence of this it is unlucky to kill a spider. Whether the term 'money spider' should be applied to small scarlet mites or the small shiny-bodied black Linyphiid spiders, both of which are not infrequently found running over one's clothes on sunny days, is uncertain. As the mites do not spin silk, however, and the Linyphiids are responsible for the silver sheets of gossamer which cloak our fields in autumn it is appropriate that they and not the mites, should be awarded the title. (For a number of Red Indian superstitions and myths, see Gertsch, 1949*.)

Among the many remarkable traits of spiders, none has excited greater interest nor produced more fantastic speculation than that of 'ballooning'. The ancients were familiar with some of the phenomena attending the flight of spiders, for Aristotle believed that spiders could shoot out their threads, and Pliny wrote: 'In the year that L. Paulus and C. Marcellus were consuls, it rained wool.' Often during the late summer and autumn months on quiet, hazy days, the air is filled with shining strands and threads of gossamer, the silk produced by the spiders that have attempted to fly and failed. Sometimes one sees a field or meadow carpeted with silk and a host of little spiderlings spreading their lines in vain attempts to fly. On the other hand many are successful—Darwin, in 1839, recorded the arrival on H.M.S. *Beagle* of 'vast numbers of a small spider, about one-tenth of an inch in length, and of a dusky red colour' when the ship was sixty miles from the coast of South America—and ballooning is without doubt an important factor in the distribution of many species all over the world. Nor is it confined to any particular season. In Britain, aeronautic dispersal of immature spiders takes place mainly in summer, of adult Linyphiidae chiefly during the colder months when temperature is the most important micro-climatic factor, and ballooning is inhibited during unfavourable weather (Duffey, 1956).

The prosaic translate 'gossamer' as 'goose summer' in reference to the fanciful resemblance of the fragile skeins of silk to the down of geese which the thrifty housewife causes to fly when she renovates her feather beds and pillows; but gossamer translated as 'God's summer' refers to the legend that this gossamer 'is the remnant of Our Lady's winding sheet which fell away in these lightest fragments as she was assumed into heaven' (Bishop, 1945).

Much of the adventure and risk in the life of the spider is crowded into the first few days of freedom when the young spiderlings, having first left their egg sac, climb over the stems of plants and up the leaves of grasses, stringing their threads as they go. Soon a tangle of webs springs up, crossing in all directions and covering the vegetation. When the young spider has reached the summit of the nearest promontory—a weed, a bush or a fence—it turns to face the wind, extends its legs so that it appears to be standing on tiptoe and lets air currents carry the silk from its spinnerets. When the friction of the currents against the threads exerts sufficient pull, the spider loosens its hold and usually sails away: at the take off, at least, it is dragged backwards. Sometimes, after take-off, the spider climbs rapidly to the middle of its thread, which then sweeps forward and becomes doubled. Less frequently the spider makes a forward start. This method is employed by small spiders which make a weak attachment to a support and allow themselves to be blown outward and upward until the thread snaps near its hold (Braendegaard, 1938).

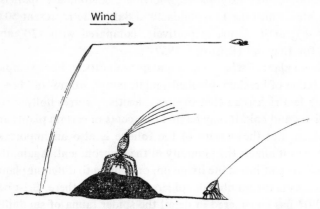

Wind

FIG. 33. Ballooning by young spiders.

The modes of life and the habitats of spiders are most varied: some are wanderers throughout their lives, others are almost entirely sedentary; some live in sunny, airy places, others are found in obscure caverns where the light never penetrates. A number of species inhabit desert regions, others are aquatic or semi-marine. Indeed, there are few parts of the world where spiders do not thrive. A number of generalisations can, however, be made. Some spiders such as the Mygalomorpha, Salticidae and Sparassidae flourish in the tropics and diminish progressively towards the cooler regions; the Gnaphosidae, Dysderidae, Agelenidae and various cribellate families thrive most successfully in the warmer temperate or sub-tropical areas, while others, including the Lycosidae and particularly the Linyphiidae, reach their greatest dominance in the arctic or sub-arctic regions. Even in such a small area as that covered by the British Isles there are marked differences between the spiders found in the north and south, differences which demonstrate the same trend as that outlined above: Scotland lacks Mygalomorpha, Oxyopidae, Pholcidae, Scytodidae, Sparassidae, etc., whilst the Linyphiidae and Salticidae represent 50% and 4% of its fauna respectively, compared with 42% and 6% for England (Bristowe, 1939)*.

Some plants harbour more spiders than others. For example, the fauna of bracken, bluebells, mint, laurel, willow and beech is far less rich than that of grass, heather, gorse, holly, yew, conifers and oak. It may be that the scents of certain plants are avoided, but the density of the foliage is also an important factor as it affects the humidity of the environment. Again, the abundance of insect life living on, or coming to different plants also affects the number of spiders that can live there. Bristowe (1939)* has considered in detail the spider fauna of sandhills, marshes, mountains, caves, mines and cellars, houses, towns, sewage works, ants' and termites' nests, beehives, birds' and mammals' nests, and other spiders' webs.

In recent years considerable attention has been devoted to solar orientation in various species of Lycosidae (for refs. see Cloudsley-Thompson, 1961*; Papi and Syrjamaki, 1963) from which it is known that, like many other animals, wolf spiders are able to maintain a steady direction at an angle to the sun and must therefore have a time sense to make the necessary corrections for solar movement.

A number of authors have stressed the importance of moisture on the distribution of spiders, and Nemenz (1954) has discussed its physiological significance. The conflict between the incompatible requirements of respiratory exchange and the prevention of water-loss has recently been demonstrated by the writer by a comparison of two common British species, *Amaurobius ferox* and *A. similis*, both of which have a cuticular wax-layer with a critical temperature at about 30° C, above which they quickly lose water by evaporation in dry air. At lower temperatures, however, the rate of water-loss in *A. ferox* is almost double that of *A. similis*. *A. similis* 'tires' very rapidly when forced to run at full speed without stopping and is almost always overcome in fights between evenly matched individuals of the two species. Both species can run for long periods when supplied with oxygen and it is suggested that the greater stamina of *A. ferox* depends upon a proportionately larger respiratory surface acquired at the expense of greater dependence upon environmental humidity (Cloudsley-Thompson, 1957).

In Britain, and in fact in the whole of the northern hemisphere, there is only one spider that is truly aquatic. This is the well-known *Argyroneta aquatica*, one of our largest species and somewhat exceptional in that the male is bigger than its mate. It swims under water clothed in a bubble of air that shines like quicksilver, and constructs a retreat in the form of a diving bell of silk filled with air which is carried down in bubbles from the surface. There are, however, several other species which live, like fishermen, by and on the water. Although most wolf spiders frequent dry and stony places and are particularly numerous in spring and early summer, the members of the genus *Pirata* are semi-aquatic, living at the margins of rivers and ponds, and are able to run on the surface of the water. *P. piscatorius* spins a silken tube in moss at the water's edge and will run beneath the water if it is alarmed. As the incoming tide creeps over the mud flats, *Lycosa purbeckensis*, an inhabitant of salt marshes, touches the water 'like a bather feeling the temperature with his toe before taking the plunge', and then deliberately walks down the stem of a sedge or other halophytic plant, taking with it a bubble of air caught by means of the hairs on its body (Bristowe, 1923). Various Theridiidae, such as *Oedothorax fuscus* and species of *Desis* (Agelenidae) from the shores of the Indian ocean, also live under semi-marine conditions.

To escape capture, the large *Dolomedes fimbriatus* (Pisauridae) will run down a plant stem beneath the surface of the water. This species, which lives in swamps and ditches, is sometimes called the 'raft-spider' on account of a popular fallacy that it makes a raft of fallen leaves on which to float downstream. Some of its foreign relations catch tadpoles and even small fishes to eat. No obvious features indicate that the Pisauridae are spiders of the water, but they can run on the surface with a grace almost equalling that of a water-skater and can remain submerged for long periods if necessary.

To summarise, aquatic spiders are known from several families including the Agelenidae, Lycosidae, Pisauridae, Argiopidae, Clubionidae, Linyphiidae, Salticidae and Thomisidae. The extent to which they live beneath the surface varies and some can walk about comfortably with a bubble of air surrounding their bodies whilst others rely on finding some cranny containing air or enclose themselves and a supply of air in a silken cell. The subject has been reviewed by Bristowe (1930b).

The majority of spiders live on the surface of the soil, some in burrows, others sheltering under stones, logs or beneath the débris of fallen leaves in forests. Most of the Theraphosidae choose any kind of retreat, living under stones or rubbish on the ground and in cracks in trees. Some dig a simple cell which they line with a slight web of silk. For the most part they are active forms and wander about at night in search of prey. The most perfectly constructed burrows are those of the Ctenizidae, which dig with the aid of a comb-like rake of large spines on the margins of their chelicerae. The walls of the tube in which the spider lives are lined with a waterproof coating of earth and saliva to which a layer of silk is applied: as the spider grows, it enlarges its burrow, the entrance to which is closed with a trap-door. The first description of this interesting device was given by Patrick Brown in his *Civil and Natural History of Jamaica*, London (1756). Seven years later the careful observations of the Abbé Sauvages on the nests of *Nemesia caementaria*, which he discovered near Montpellier, were published. Although trap-door spider nests attracted popular attention thereafter, it was not until Moggridge (1873) published his studies on the habits of these animals that any comprehensive treatment was accorded them.

Moggridge was able to distinguish four types of nest among the species he studied. The first was a simple cylindrical tube with a thick 'cork door', the second had a thin 'wafer door', the third a thin outer door with a second door part of the way down, while the fourth was the most complicated: a tube capped on the outside by a thin door and having an oblique side tunnel at the entrance to which was another trap-door. Since then several other types of nest have been discovered in different parts of the world; some of them of even more complicated design.

The majority of hunting spiders live in silken cells under stones, bark or fallen logs. Some of the smaller species seem to be absolute wanderers and have no home at all, spending the night under any suitable rock or stone that they come across, whilst the larger kinds live permanently in burrows from which they never go far. Habits vary considerably. One handsomely marked wolf spider, *Arctosa perita*, makes its silk lined burrows in dunes of firm sand and on heathland where the vegetation has been burned away. When alarmed it will seize with its chelicerae the rim of the silk that lines its burrow, and pull it across the entrance like a curtain. Then rapidly turning round it closes the last chink with a few sweeping strokes of its spinnerets (Bristowe, 1954). Sometimes several of these spiders live quite close together in a colony.

Web-building spiders usually construct a retreat amongst the vegetation from which their snare is suspended. Vibrations of a signal-thread connecting their shelter with the web enable

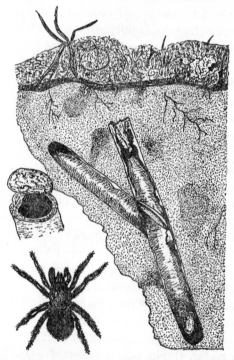

FIG. 34. Trapdoor spider and burrow. (After Moggridge, 1873.)

them instantly to detect the struggles of any insect that has been caught. Some species are peculiar in that they show a tendency towards social habits. This is apparent among a number of cribellate families and an Australian species *Amaurobius*

socialis from the Jenolan Caves constructs enormous communal and densely fabricated webs measuring as much as 12 feet
in length and 4 feet in width, which are inhabited by a large
number of individuals. In a similar way communal webs constructed by *Theridion socialis* and *Uloborus republicanus* have
been described.

The spider's web is unique among animal productions in
that (save one constructed by a caddis larva) it is the only trap
built by an animal. The web is so efficient for obtaining food
that its owner seldom makes use of any sense save that which
the action of the web demands, and the lives of web-building
species are almost entirely governed by responses to tactile and
vibratory stimuli supplemented by the development of the muscular sense. The methods of construction of the various types
of web have attracted a great deal of attention, in particular
from MacCook (1889–94), Peters (1933, etc.), Tilquin (1942)
and Wiehle. To review all this work would be beyond the scope
of the present volume, but fortunately much of it has been
summarised recently by Savory (1952), from whose book
further details can be obtained. Bristowe (1930) has suggested
that the origin of webs lies in the use of silk as a covering for
spiders' eggs which were then guarded by the mother and from
which random threads radiated but Savory thinks that they
have resulted from an accumulation of drag lines, laid down
by ancestral hunting spiders when their prey was captured and
which later gave the spiders warning of other insects passing by.

The typical procedure in the construction of an orb web is
the construction of a frame followed by that of the radii. A few
spirals around the centre hold the radii in place while the
spider travels outwards spinning a widely spaced temporary
spiral. Finally the spinning of viscid spirals starts at the outside
and works inwards with the simultaneous destruction of the
temporary spiral as it is reached. Many orb weavers renew their

webs, other than the framework, daily, but renewal may be postponed if the spiders are well fed or the weather unsuitable.

The chief economic use of spiders' silk lies in the construction of fine graticules for optical instruments. Cobwebs were used years ago as dressings for wounds to staunch the flow of blood, for which they were extremely effective. Moulds such as *Penicillium* were sometimes added, perhaps foreshadowing the present-day use of penicillin and other antibiotics. When several sheet-webs are superimposed they form a fine transparent silk fabric on which delicate and beautiful pictures were painted early in the nineteenth century by an Innsbruck family named Burgman. They are 'exquisite examples of an art that now ranks as scarcely more than a curiosity'.

Food and feeding habits

The food of spiders includes a variety of insects, woodlice, myriapods, false-scorpions, harvest-spiders and other Arachnida. Bristowe (1941)*, who has discussed the subject at some length, has shown that the potential food supply of different species varies within wide limits. A hungry spider is liable to accept an insect which it will reject when fully fed, thereby indicating that its distaste is relative and not absolute. By their mode of life, their hunting methods and the nature of their snares, different species of spiders become adapted within wide limits to the capture of particular insects and may refuse types to which they are unaccustomed. Thus, although *Amaurobius* spp. may investigate with their legs a woodlouse thrown into their webs, they nearly always retreat without harming it. Unlike *Segestria senoculata*, which will attack a blade of grass drawn across its web, and normally eats woodlice, *A. ferox* and *A. similis* will respond only to the vibrations of a tuning fork, and will attack a woodlouse if a vibrating tuning fork is placed on the web just beside it (Cloudsley-Thompson, 1956).

Atypus affinis, the sole British representative of the sub-order Mygalomorpha, burrows in the soil, but instead of making a trapdoor, it continues the silk lining of its burrow above the ground as a closed tube. When insects crawl on this, the spider seizes them from within and pulls them through the silk. The closed purseweb of this species clearly restricts its diet to crawling insects, worms and woodlice, whereas the orb webs of the Argiopidae are adapted to the capture of insects in flight. A parallel amongst hunting spiders is afforded by *Dysdera erythrina* or *Drassodes lapidosus*, which hunt mainly under stones or at the roots of herbage at night, whilst the flower-living habit of *Misumena vatia* and *Thomisius onustus* bring them into contact with winged insects.

Protective flavours have been evolved by many invertebrates which tend to render them distasteful to spiders. At least some species avoid earwigs, stoneflies, caddis flies, moths, beetles, bugs, ants and other Hymenoptera, harvest-spiders, mites, woodlice and millipedes, and many of these have developed warning movements since neither aposematic nor protective coloration is of any avail against spiders that respond to tactile rather than visual stimuli.

Although invertebrate animals, particularly Arthropoda, form the bulk of the diet of spiders, there are a number of records of vertebrates being eaten. As already mentioned some semi-aquatic Lycosidae and Pisauridae may catch fishes, while amphibia, lizards, young snakes, birds and small mammals not infrequently form the prey of larger spiders, especially the Theraphosidae. The subject has been reviewed by Millot (1943), to whom the reader is referred for further details.

Spiders are adapted to various habitats within which some attack large insects, others capture smaller kinds: some spiders attack diurnal insects, others hunt by night; some specialise in crawling insects, others in those that fly. Bristowe (1941)* discusses the means employed for the capture of prey and on this basis divides the various families into hunting spiders, tube builders, sheet-web builders, builders of scaffolding webs, meshed webs and orb webs.

Some hunting spiders seek their prey by day, trusting to their good sight, while others are active at night and depend mainly on the sense of touch. Jumping spiders (Salticidae) have the keenest sight of all and stalk their prey from afar. Our commonest species, *Salticus scenicus*, provides a convenient example of the group. Equally at home on a perpendicular surface or on the underside of a horizontal beam, it is able to maintain its position by means of an adhesive tuft of hairs, the 'scopula', on each of its feet. As it moves, the zebra spider trails behind it an exceedingly fine thread of silk which is attached at frequent intervals like a climbing rope, so that in the event of a slip the spider does not fall to the ground. The species has a curious way of exploring the surface over which it is working by successive short runs alternating with periods of absolute stillness. It will often patiently search a large area before it catches sight of an insect, when it can be seen to turn its head so as to bring its four large anterior eyes to bear upon the quarry. The four posterior eyes are smaller and less important. For a time it remains motionless, then begins to edge stealthily nearer until it is close enough for a sudden spring. The front pair of legs is used for seizing the prey and the remaining pairs for jumping. However, the jump is not always successful: often the insect sees its peril at the last moment and flies away, and the spider has to begin all over again. In contrast, the wolf spiders (Lycosidae) capture their prey by sheer strength and speed.

The typical crab spiders (Thomisidae) are seldom seen by

the ordinary observer, for their habits are retiring and many of them are rather small. They wait motionless for passing insects which are seized by the powerful outstretched legs, and having buried their jaws in the head or thorax of the prey, they draw their limbs backwards out of danger of the victim's bite or sting. Some species, however, are true rovers hunting by day and passing the night wherever they happen to find themselves. Those that lie in wait often show a remarkable degree of resemblance to the colour of their background. One East Indian species spins a white patch of silk on the upper surface of a leaf. Lying on this, it looks exactly like the dropping of some bird, and such droppings seem to be particularly attractive to butterflies! No doubt, however, predation by birds has been an even more important factor in natural selection. The Oxyopidae, sometimes called lynx spiders, are handsome hunting spiders that have become specialised for life on plants. They can run over vegetation with great agility and leap from stem to stem with a precision surpassed only by that of true jumping spiders. The only British example of this family is the rare *Oxyopes heterophthalmus*.

The remaining families such as the Theraphosidae, Dysderidae, Oonopidae, Gnaphosidae and Clubionidae contain mostly shortsighted nocturnal hunters that depend upon the sense of touch and grapple with any suitable insect they come across in their wanderings. *Harpactea hombergi*, a small grey species common under bark, holds its victims with its tarsal claws, while the large and formidable *Dysdera crocota* and *D. erythrina*, easily recognised by their red cephalothorax and yellow abdomen, feed mostly upon woodlice and lunge forward so quickly that few escape. Their chelicerae are especially adapted for dealing with this prey; they are exceptionally large and powerful, and by tilting the prosoma sideways one fang is intruded beneath the woodlouse and the other above it.

Herpyllus blackwalli is a mouse-coloured house spider that often falls into baths and sinks and then cannot climb out. Like many other Gnaphosidae and Clubionidae, it relies upon its speed for the capture of its prey, while the ferocious *Drassodes lapidosus*, frequently found under bark and stones, immobilises its prey by swathing it in bands of silk.

FIG. 35. *Dysdera* sp. eating a woodlouse. (After Bristowe, 1954.)

Perhaps the most interesting method employed in the capture of insects is that of the rare *Scytodes thoracica*. This slow-moving yellow-coloured species squirts poisonous gum from its jaws whilst on the move after the manner of a cruiser tank spraying infantry with machine-gun fire. The prey is stuck firmly to the ground while the spider advances and eats it at leisure.

The various uses of silk employed by spiders in the capture of prey have already been mentioned. The Ctenizidae dart from their tubes and capture insects passing near the trap-door while the Atypidae strike through their purse-webs at any small animal crawling over the exposed part. *Segestria senoculata* and other members of the genus make their tubes in crevices of walls and rock faces. The rim of the open entrance is stretched outwards by half a dozen or more long stout straight threads. When an insect or woodlouse touches one of these the spider darts forth to seize and retire with it. A similar method is employed by the Filistatidae, such as the well-known Mediterranean species *Filistata insidiatrix*.

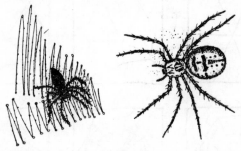

FIG. 36. *Scytodes thoracica* binding its prey with gum which it squirts from the fangs. (From Cloudsley-Thompson, 1953.)

Sheet-webs are built by several families, and in Britain by some of the Agelenidae, Linyphiidae and *Pholcus phalangioides* (Pholcidae). In the first family the spiders run in an erect position on the upper surface of the sheet, but in the other two they are suspended in an inverted position from the lower surface. Scaffolding webs are characteristic of the Theridiidae. In *Steatoda bipunctata*, for example, a sheet of wide meshes is kept taut from above and below by a number of threads extending vertically to the ground. These have viscid droplets for part of their length and break off easily at their point of attachment. As they are drawn very taut, an insect which blunders into one not only breaks the attachment but may be lifted into the air where its struggles bring it into contact with other viscid threads. The meshed webs of the Dictynidae and some Uloboridae with their typical calamistrated threads have already been mentioned. These threads entangle the legs of insects very securely and enable the spiders to capture prey often much larger than themselves.

Finally, typical orb webs are made by the Tetragnathidae and Argiopidae. During the daytime the garden spider *Araneus*

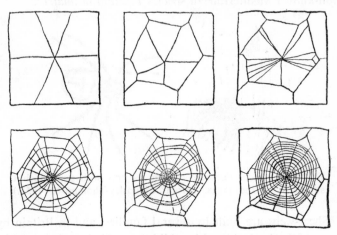

FIG. 37. Diagrammatic stages in the spinning of an orb-web.
(After Savory, 1952.)

diadematus generally abandons the hub of its web and rests in its retreat nearby, but towards evening it usually comes to the centre and remains there until early morning when it constructs a new web. Peters (1933) has shown that the prey is dealt with by means of a series of chain reflexes. The struggles of a victim in the web are the stimulus for a long bite and the taste experienced stimulates the enshrouding of the prey. The silk bands provide a tactile stimulus for the reflex of the short bite, which in turn produces a stimulus for the carrying reflex: small insects are carried to the hub of the web in the chelicerae, while heavier prey are carried on a thread from the spinnerets and supported by a hind leg. When a lifeless inedible object touches the web it is usually cut out and allowed to fall to the ground, as are formidable and dangerous insects such as wasps and bees, whereas suitable prey is bitten and then wrapped up. The behaviour which follows the biting of a distasteful insect is surprising: the spider makes its way, sometimes clumsily as if in distress, to the edge of its web where it gets rid of the distasteful liquid by pressing its mouth to the ground or wiping it on a leaf.

These brief descriptions of the methods employed by spiders for the capture of prey by no means exhaust the list of ingenious methods that have arisen in the course of evolution. The water spider *Argyroneta aquatica* no longer uses its web to entrap its prey, but hunts for small aquatic creatures which are eaten on dry land or in its bell, while a South African spider builds a small snare resembling a postage stamp in size and shape. The corners are held by the spider's long legs. When an insect approaches, the web is stretched to nearly five times its normal size and hurled over the prey. There can be few developments more remarkable however than that of certain Argiopidae in Australia and South Africa *(Dicrostichus magnificus* and *Cladomelea akermani)* which emerge at nightfall and whirl a thread weighted with a gummy globule until this strikes some passing insect which is then hauled in.

Enemies

So far only one side of the picture has been considered. In addition to the vast numbers killed as a result of unfavourable climatic conditions, spiders are beset with enemies throughout their lives. The infant mortality rate in particular is immense. Baby spiders do not feed until they have digested all the yolk with which the eggs from which they hatched were supplied, but after their first moult the little spiderlings develop their typical cannibalistic tendencies and many are eaten by their own kin. As Warburton (1912) wrote: 'The case of the survivor of the *Nancy Bell* in the Bab Ballads would be exceedingly commonplace in the araneid world.' In addition to the numbers devoured by other spiders, both of their own as well as of other species, spiders and their eggs are eaten by hosts of different kinds of animals. In this country the most important of these are probably toads and frogs, starlings and other insectivorous birds, shrews, wasps and centipedes. Invertebrate enemies are very much more numerous and probably destroy larger numbers of spiders than do vertebrates, but spiders enter largely into the diet of smaller birds, being fed especially to the nestlings. Moreover, many species of birds use spiders' egg cocoons to line their nests.

Social wasps often kill spiders to feed their larvae, and there are two British families of solitary digger wasps, the Pompilidae and Trypoxylinidae, which hunt spiders. The spiders are paralysed by stings, often in the principal nerve ganglia and are then dragged to previously prepared cells or burrows. After this the wasp lays an egg on each carcass and other paralysed spiders are added before the burrow is sealed up. These must provide enough food for the wasp grub, when it hatches, to last throughout the whole of its larval development, for the mother wasp never sees her offspring. Fabre, Hingston and other naturalists have written graphic accounts of the habits of spider-hunting wasps. All kinds of spiders are attacked, although wolf spiders are perhaps the most frequent victims of the Pompilidae, and in the tropics even large Theraphosidae fall prey to these terrible foes. The first action of one of these wasps when it attacks a spider is to remove the latter from its environment, for a garden spider is much more vulnerable when torn away from its web and a burrowing spider dragged into the open is nearly defenceless. It has been observed, however, that spiders appear completely 'panic-stricken' when confronted by a fossorial wasp. Their immediate reaction seems to be to flee, and they do not try to defend themselves even when cornered.

The parasites of spiders include Protozoa and Nematoda, but there are few records in the literature. Infinitely more important, especially in tropical climates, are 'parasitoids' or lethal parasites, particularly of the family Ichneumonidae. These insects probably paralyse a spider by means of their sting before laying an egg on its back. Although the most frequent victims of spider parasites are web-spinners, several different kinds of hunting spider have also been found with eggs or larvae on their backs. These larvae eventually cause the death of their victim by feeding on the contents of the abdomen. By some extraordinary instinct the vital organs are not eaten until last so that the spider does not die until the insect is ready to emerge from the now empty skin of its host. The Acroceridae (Diptera) are a family of flies which have evolved similar parasitic habits and members of several other fly families as well as the Pimplinae and Cryptinae (Hymenoptera) are parasitic on the eggs of spiders. Apparently cryptic coloration and other protective devices are of little avail against these creatures, but even so, Ichneumons and other parasitoids are probably a far less important factor in controlling the numbers of spiders than they are in controlling insect population.

With so many terrible foes it is not surprising to find that spiders have evolved all kinds of protective devices, including prickly spines, unpleasant flavour and scent: some even eject unpleasant fluids that deter predators. *Scytodes thoracica* squirts gum from its fangs for defensive purposes as well as when it is hunting. Many hunting spiders build silken protective cells in which they rest when not in search of prey. *Herpyllus blackwalli* has evolved the habit of retreating with abdomen raised, trailing behind it a ribbon of silk that serves as a protection against attack from the rear. Many spiders achieve concealment by means of cryptic coloration, closely resembling their natural background, whether this is a coloured flower, a leaf, lichen, sand or bark. The crab spiders provide numerous fine examples of such camouflage. Sometimes the outline of the spider is camouflaged by means of a 'dazzle-pattern', as in the case of *Salticus scenicus* whose irregular patches of contrasted colours tend to draw the attention of the observer from the shape that bears them. Egg cases too are frequently concealed with twigs and pieces of leaf. Poisonous and powerful species may show conspicuous colorations, while all kinds of poisonous and distasteful insects such as ants, wasps, bugs, beetles and even scorpions are effectively mimicked by various spiders (Bristowe, 1941)*.

For example, amongst the Argiopidae some species of the genus *Cyclosa* resemble small snails which, on account of the hardness of their shells, would be eaten by few birds and would certainly be neglected both by Pompilidae and Ichneumonidae, the principal enemies of spiders. One such species has been recorded from Ceylon, another from North America. The latter, when clinging to the underside of a leaf with its legs drawn up, is almost an exact copy in colour and shape of a small snail which is abundant in similar situations in the same locality during the warm months of the year. The resemblance is enhanced by the complete immobility the spider maintains when torn from its hold or when the plant is rudely shaken.

Apart from beetles, the insects most frequently mimicked by spiders are ants, and so numerous and perfect are the instances that all other examples of mimicry amongst spiders fall into insignificance beside them. A constriction on each side of the spider's carapace divides it into an anterior part resembling the head, a narrow intermediate part representing the neck and a posterior part representing the thorax of the insect. In many cases the appearance of slenderness about the neck is augmented by a strip of white hairs on each side of the constriction, which has the optical effect of cutting out an extra piece of the integument. The waist of the ant is reproduced by the conversion of the end of the carapace and often of the anterior end of the abdomen into a narrow stalk. In some cases the abdomen is itself shallowly constricted and even the abdominal segments of the insect may be represented by transverse bands of hairs. The legs are always slender, like those of an ant, and one of the anterior pairs is held up in front of the head as a substitute for antennae. Finally, it has been found that the spiders carry deception to the extent of copying the manners and gait of the insects (Pocock, 1909). As might be expected, ant-mimicry is of much commoner occurrence amongst ground-living species of spiders than it is amongst the sedentary web spinners, but instances are not unknown amongst the latter. Such mimicry represents a wonderful example of convergent evolution amongst spiders belonging to the families Salticidae, Gnaphosidae, Clubionidae, Thomisidae, Theridiidae, Argiopidae, etc. As in all cases of Batesian mimicry, the mimics exist in small numbers compared with their models.

Like scorpions and Solifugae, many of the larger spiders can stridulate, probably as a warning to enemies. In the case of smaller species in which sound-producing organs are confined to the males, their function is probably that of courtship. Chrysanthus (1953) has reviewed the subject of hearing and stridulation in spiders. He concludes that vibrations of the air are perceived, so spiders must possess a real faculty of hearing.

In conclusion, it should be remembered that of the enemies of spiders, man is in the first rank not only on account of the numbers destroyed by insecticides and in agriculture, but also for the numbers eaten by primitive peoples in all parts of the world. In Siam for example the Laos eat two different types, the giant orb webbed *Nephila* spp. and the large hairy Myga-lomorpha. The former are known by a Siamese name that means 'the golden one'. When roasted and dipped in salt the abdomen, which is the only part eaten, has a flavour of raw potato and lettuce mixed. Mygalomorpha are even more highly prized: their chelicerae are pulled out and the spiders are roast-ed on sticks which removes the hair, and then eaten with salt. Incidentally the hairs of these Mygalomorph spiders can cause very great discomfort, and if the face is touched after stroking one of these creatures, sight may even be endangered. On the other hand the bites of giant bird-eating Mygalomorpha are usually not serious. Far more dangerous are some of the Cte-nizidae, and the spiders of the genus *Latrodectus* such as *L. mactans*, the notorious 'black widow' of North America, whose bite causes agonising pain that develops and spreads within a quarter of an hour. This is often accompanied by profuse sweating, difficulty in breathing, vomiting, prostra-tion, convulsions and numerous other effects. Drop for drop the poison is said to be more virulent than that of the rattle-snake, but the amount injected by the spider is small and vari-able: death has occurred in about 5% of known cases of bites, but this figure is probably misleading as many cases are never recorded or diagnosed (Thorp and Woodson, 1945). The food of the 'black widow' includes very tough and resistant beetles and it has been suggested that the virulent toxicity of its venom may be correlated with the tough nature of its prey.

Mating habits

Spiders are nearly always on the offensive and are ready to kill and eat most animals of suitable size that come within range. They are inveterate cannibals, so it is obvious that mating must be a hazardous undertaking fraught with real danger, particularly to the male who is usually smaller and weaker than his intended mate. Indeed, he will almost certainly be devoured unless he succeeds in allaying temporarily the carnivorous instincts of the female, and this he must do before he ventures within reach of her rapacious jaws. Bristowe (1941,* etc.) has emphasised that it is of the utmost importance to the male to establish his identity so that he is not treated like an insect victim, and thereafter courtship must proceed until the female has been stimulated to a state in which her sexual instincts have been aroused so that she will permit mating to take place. Consequently, whichever of the senses is the one on which the species chiefly relies for the capture of its prey, is the sense most employed in courtship. Male jumping spiders and wolf spiders make use of visual signs, short-sighted and nocturnal species of contact stimuli, web spinners use distinctive tweaks and vibrations of the threads of the snare, and so on.

The mating procedure of spiders is quite unique, for when the male reaches maturity he weaves a small pad of silk on which a drop of sperm is deposited and this is sucked up by the specially modified 'pedipalps' or hands which in due course are inserted into the vagina of the female. Each species has a palp with its own distinctive shape, a diagnostic character essential for accurate identification.

Courtship is a subject of great interest and importance and the literature on the subject is immense.

In Theraphosid spiders such as *Dugesiella hentzi*, when a

restlessly wandering male happens to touch with his legs some part of the body or leg of a female, he at once stops short and begins to strike it simultaneously and violently with his anterior and sometimes with all four front feet. This continuous beating with the front legs upon the body or legs of the female constitutes the first step in courtship. At first the female assumes an attitude of defence, but after a while she rises high on her hind legs while still holding up her front legs. Finally she opens her fangs and the male catches them with the hooks on his front legs. He now forcibly pushes back the cephalothorax of the female, at the same time drumming on her sternum with the patellas of his pedipalps. Mating lasts only a minute or two, after which the two sexes part, the female making no attempt to attack (Petrunkevitch, 1911).

When the male *Atypus affinis* finds the tube of a female, he drums upon it with his palps and presumably is able to ascertain by the reactions of the inmate whether he is welcome. After a while he cuts open the tube and enters; the rent is afterwards repaired by the female. Mating occurs deep in the tube and the male is believed to live in the burrow for many months before his mate eventually eats him.

Amongst short-sighted hunting spiders the male's chemotactic sense often warns him of the presence of a female in the vicinity. He moves with caution and in some species vibrates his legs. *Drassodes* spp. take possession of their females before these have attained maturity or full strength. Some, such as *Pachygnatha* spp., avoid injury by seizing the chelicerae of the females and holding these with the aid of special adaptations, while others spar with their mates and rely on their outstretched legs and their agility to avoid injury from any initial attack resulting from the first contact. The nocturnal *Dysdera crocota* has a placid tactile courtship which apparently can be initiated by either sex. One spider approaches the other, quivering and gesticulating with front legs held aloft. During copulation the palps are inserted simultaneously and the two spiders stroke and caress each other with their forelegs.

Some of the sedentary spiders with inferior eyesight show few of the preliminary activities identifiable as true courtship. Even though the eyes of some of the Thomisidae are fairly large, the spiders make little use of sight in courting. When a male discovers a female of his species he immediately climbs upon her back or seizes an appendage with his chelicerae. He is more agile and can tickle and caress her body until he is able to accomplish his purpose. The male *Xysticus* sp. protects himself in mating by fastening his mate to the ground with a few silken threads (Bristowe, 1922, etc.), while in *Pisaura mirabilis* (Pisauridae) he catches and wraps an insect in silk before approaching the female and hands it to her as a preliminary to mating. This behaviour is unique in spiders but has a parallel amongst Empid flies.

The visual displays of the Lycosidae and Salticidae have been studied especially by Bristowe and Locket (Bristowe, 1929, 1941,* etc.), and more recently Crane (1948, 1949, etc.) has made detailed analyses of the behaviour of various tropical Salticidae such as *Corythalia* spp. In most wolf spiders the pedipalps and front legs are provided with an ornamentation of hair that contrasts sharply with the rest of the body. The male stands before the female waving these simultaneously or alternately in a kind of semaphore courtship. One species found on Staten Island, Argentina, makes a curious purring noise at mating time by drumming on dead leaves with its palps. It is probable that in this case the female appreciates the vibrations at some distance. Even more dramatic are the courting dances of male jumping spiders. In the tropical species *Hasarius adansoni* found in many hothouses in Britain, the male is a handsome, squat, glossy black and brown spider with conspicuous white markings on the pedipalps, abdomen and distal limb segments. During courtship he advances slowly in zig-zag fashion, waving his palps up and down. When the female, who is a sombre brown colour, turns towards him he stops and remains motionless with his large forelegs held horizontally above the ground. Then he moves forward again.

FIG. 38. *Hasarius adansoni*; the male in courting attitude. (From Cloudsley-Thompson, 1953.)

As he nears the female he may jump rapidly sideways or backwards. Again and again this display continues until at last he is permitted to insert first one and then the other of his pedipalps, and copulation takes place, the palps being inserted alternately (Cloudsley-Thompson, 1949).

Mock, bloodless battles not infrequently occur between rival male jumping spiders. Bristowe (1929) believes these to result from mistaken identity, one male being stimulated sexually by another of the same species, but Crane (1948) regards them as threat displays and she has shown that in *Corythalia* spp. such behaviour is distinct from courtship. The fringed, iridescent legs are always used in threat displays, but are never employed in courtship.

Among web-builders courtship usually consists of the male telegraphing to the female occupant of a web by tweaking the threads as he approaches, but in later stages a tactile stroking of the body precedes coition. This routine may constitute a tactile display almost equal in interest to the visual displays of the long-sighted hunting spiders.

In ethological terminology, the function of courtship is to provide releaser stimuli for the mating instinct which at the same time block hunger drives. The concept of recognition may not in fact be necessary.

Polygamy is the custom among spiders and it is indeed wise for the male to retreat hastily immediately copulation is finished. It is probable that the male *Atypus affinis* is not given any opportunity to escape from the female's lair, but there is no evidence that the widow will refuse admittance to a succession of husbands. In contrast, it seems probable that *Amaurobius ferox* females mate only once. Occasionally the sexes appear to live together peacefully, but experiment has shown that in the case of *Meta segmentata* this apparent faithfulness is fictional and males may visit the web of more than one female. In this species the males often kill one another. Since courtship is deferred until the female is engaged in trussing a victim or eating a meal, it is not uncommon to see it taking place over the dead body of a vanquished rival (Bristowe, 1941)*.

Life history

Spiders lay their eggs in retreats and cocoons which they construct of silk and often mount guard over them until the young have hatched. Theraphosidae prepare great flabby egg purses in their burrows and guard them assiduously, while the delicate silken sacs of the trap-door spiders often hang from the side of the tube. Wolf spiders (Lycosidae) carry their globular cocoons attached to their spinnerets wherever they go, and after hatching the young climb on their mother's back where they remain for several days. In the Pisauridae the mother spider carries her cocoon under her sternum: when the young are ready to emerge she fixes it to the end of a branch and mounts guard over it, while the female *Pholcus phalangioides* glues her few eggs together lightly and carries the mass in her chelicerae. Some of the most elaborate cocoons are spun by web-building spiders: the sac may hang from the web or may be fixed to the vegetation nearby.

The use of silk to protect the eggs was probably evolved early in the history of spiders and many refinements have since been added. The covering is often toughened and thickened with several layers of silk and may be plastered with layers of mud or embellished with bits of wood, leaves and other débris which render it inconspicuous. Some spiders spin a series of egg-sacs which are left singly here and there, thus minimising the risk of the whole brood being parasitised.

The number of eggs laid by different species varies enormously. *Theraphosa blondi*, the largest of all spiders, is said to lay as many as 3000 and the larger orb-weavers and Pisauridae may produce more than 2000. While the tiny *Oonops pulcher* lays only two, the majority of spiders probably lay about 100 eggs, and those producing more than one cocoon usually lay fewer eggs in each. The larger species tend to lay more eggs than the smaller species. Not only is there an obvious physical relationship, but there may be an ecological connection between size and egg number, for big spiders usually take longer to reach maturity than the smaller kinds.

The number of eggs laid is clearly related to the size of the mother spider where different species of the same family are concerned. Petersen (1950), in a discussion of the significance of this relationship in the evolution of size in various species of *Lycosa*, concludes that since larger spiders lay more eggs and the size of the mother is to a certain extent inherited, there must be a selection towards larger size which in nature is probably balanced by efficient counter selection. A similar relationship has also been shown to exist in *Amaurobius ferox* and *A. similis* by Cloudsley-Thompson (1956). In *A. ferox*, about three weeks elapse in the summer after egg laying before the young begin to leave their cocoon and the mother remains in the breeding nest until they have dispersed. Sometimes she dies and then the spiderlings appear to feed on her body before they leave the nest. In this species the life cycle occupies two or more years. Spiderlings hatching in the summer reach maturity in the autumn of the following year and lay their eggs when they are two years old. They may live for another season or even longer. After hatching, a period of some days may elapse before the spiderlings scatter, during which, as we have seen, they eat little or nothing. Bristowe (1947) states that the mother *Theridion sisyphium* feeds her young from her mouth. Whilst she hangs downwards, the babies jostle one another to reach the drops of fluid she regurgitates for their benefit, but this must be after the first ecdysis. For several days the procedure continues and then for some weeks afterwards mother and young feed simultaneously on the insects she catches.

The number of moults necessary to attain maturity varies widely in spiders. It has been shown that in most species, size is the determining factor: small spiders moult four or five times, those of medium size seven or eight times while some of the Theraphisodae may moult more than twenty times. Even within the same species there is variation in the number of ecdyses. For example, in *Dolomedes plantarius* the female may moult as few as nine or as many as thirteen times, the number being correlated with size and nourishment.

Most spiders that inhabit the temperate zones live only one

year, but the more primitive species tend to live longer. In the majority of species the life cycle varies from eight months to four years, and the record for longevity is held by a Theraphosid, *Eurypelma* sp., which lived for twenty years. The males mature in eight or nine years, and usually die a few months later.

The dispersal of young spiders of many species is achieved by 'ballooning', already mentioned. Those that survive the rigours of these perilous journeys and land in a suitable environment begin a life of toil and slaughter, of sacrifice and parental care which, for a small proportion of fortunate individuals, may culminate in the production of yet another batch of baby spiderlings.

BIBLIOGRAPHY

Identification

BLACKWALL, J. (1861) *A History of the Spiders of Great Britain and Ireland* **1.** London.
—— (1864) *Ibid.*, **2.**
BOSENBERG, W. (1901–3) Die Spinnen Deutschlands. *Zoologica Stuttgart*, **14,** 1–465.
BRISTOWE, W. S. (1938) The classification of spiders. *Proc. Zool. Soc. Lond.*, B **108,** 285–322.
BRYANT, E. B. (1940) Cuban spiders in the Museum of Comparative Zoology. *Bull. Mus. Comp. Zool.*, **86,** 249–532.
CHICKERING, A. M. (1946) The Salticidae (spiders) of Panama. *Ibid.*, **97,** 1–248.
DAHL, M. (1926) Spinnentiere oder Arachnoidea, 1: Springspinnen (Salticidae). *Tierws. Deuts.*, **3,** 1–55.
(Various other families have been treated subsequently by different authors under the general editorship of F. DAHL).
HOLM, Á. (1947) *Svensk Spendelfauna Araneae*, Fam. 8–10. Stockholm.
KASTON, B. J. (1948) Spiders of Connecticut. *State Geol. Nat. Hist. Surv. Hartford*, 70, 1–874.
LOCKET, G. H. and MILLIDGE, A. F. (1951) *British Spiders*, **1.** London.
—— (1953) *Idem.*, **2.**

LOHMANDER, H. (1942) Südschwedische Spinnen, 1. Gnaphosidae. *Medd. Göteborgs Mus. Zool.*, **98**, 1–163.

PETRUNKEVITCH, A. (1933) An inquiry into the natural classification of spiders, based on a study of their internal anatomy. *Trans. Conn. Acad. Arts Sci.*, **31**, 299–389.

—— et al. (1939) Catalogue of American spiders, Part 1. *Ibid.*, **33**, 133–338.

PICKARD-CAMBRIDGE, O. (1879) *The Spiders of Dorset*, Part 1. Sherborne.

—— (1881) *Ibid.*, Part 2.

SIMON, E. (1892–1903) *Histoire naturelle des Araignées*, 2me ed. Paris.

—— (1914–1937) *Arachnides de France*, **1–6**, 1–1298.

TULLGREN, A. (1944) *Svensk Spindelfauna Araneae*, Fam. 1–4. Stockholm.

—— (1946) *Ibid.*, Fam. 5–7.

WIEHLE, H. (1953) Spinnentiere oder Arachnoidea (Araneae) IX. *Tierw. Deuts.*, **42**, 1–150.

Biology

ANDERSON, J. F. (1966) The excreta of spiders. *Comp. Biochem. Physiol.*, **17**, 973–82.

BISHOP, S. C. (1945) Our Lady's threads. *Trans. Conn. Acad. Arts Sci.*, **36**, 91–7.

BRAENDEGAARD, J. (1938) Aeronautic spiders in the Arctic. *Medd. om Grønland*, **119**, (5), 1–9.

—— (1946) The spiders (Araneina) of East Greenland. *Ibid.*, **121**, (15), 1–128.

BRISTOWE, W. S. (1922) Spiders found in the neighbourhood of Oxshott. *Proc. S. Lond. Ent. Soc.*, **1922**, 1–11.

—— (1923) A British semi-marine spider. *Ann. Mag. Nat. Hist.*, (9), **12**, 154–6.

—— (1928) Facts and fallacies about spiders. *Proc. S. Lond. Ent. Nat. Hist. Soc.*, **1928–9**, 12–23.

—— (1929) The mating habits of spiders with special reference to the problems surrounding sex dimorphism. *Proc. Zool. Soc. Lond.*, **1929**, 309–58.

—— (1930a) Notes on the biology of spiders. I. The evolution of spiders' snares. *Ann. Mag. Nat. Hist.* (10), **6**, 334–42.

—— (1930b) Notes on the biology of spiders. II.—Aquatic spiders. *Ibid.*, (10), **6**, 343–7.

—— (1932) Insects and other invertebrates for human consumption in Siam. *Trans. Ent. Soc. Lond.*, **80**, 387–404.

—— (1945) Spider superstitions and folklore. *Trans. Conn. Acad. Arts Sci.*, **36**, 53–90.

—— (1947) *A Book of Spiders*. London.

—— (1954) The chelicerae of spiders. *Endeavour*, **13**, 42–9.

BRISTOWE, W. S. (1958) *The World of Spiders*. London.

CHRYSANTHUS, F. (1953) Hearing and stridulation in spiders. *Tijdscr. Ent.*, **96**, 57–83.

CLOUDSLEY-THOMPSON, J. L. (1949) Notes on Arachnida, 11. Mating habits of *Hasarius adansoni* Sav. *Ent. Mon. Mag.*, **85**, 261–2.

—— (1953) The biology of hunting spiders. *Discovery*, **14**, 286–9.

—— (1956) The life histories of the British cribellate spiders of the genus *Ciniflo* Bl. (Dictynidae). *Ann. Mag. Nat. Hist.*, (12), **8**, 787–94.

—— (1957) Studies in diurnal rhythms, V. Nocturnal ecology and water relations of the British cribellate spiders of the genus *Ciniflo* Bl. *J. Linn. Soc. (Zool.)*, **43**, 134–52.

—— (1968) The water-relations of scorpions and tarantulas from the Sonoran Desert. *Ent. Mon. Mog.*, **104**, 217–20.

CRANE, J. (1948) Comparative biology of Salticid spiders at Rancho Grande, Venezuela. Part 1. Systematics and life histories in *Corythalia*. *Zoologica*, **33**, 1–38.

—— (1949) *Idem*. Part IV. An analysis of display. *Ibid.*, **34**, 159–214.

DUFFEY, E. (1956) Aerial dispersal in a known spider population. *J. Anim. Ecol.*, **25**, 85–114.

ENGLEHARDT, W. (1964) Die mitteleuropäischen Arten der Gattung *Trochosa* C. L. Koch 1848 (Araneae, Lycosidae). Morphologie, Chemotaxonomie, Biologie, Autokologie. *Z. Morph. Ökol. Tiere*, **54**, 219–302.

MACCOOK, H. C. (1889–94) *American Spiders and their Spinningwork*, **1–3**, Philadelphia.

MERRETT, P. (1967) The phenology of spiders on heathland in Dorset. 1. Families Atypidae Dysderidae, Gnaphosidae, Clubionidae, Thomisidae and Salticidae. *J. Anim. Ecol.*, **36**, 363–74.

MILLOT, J. (1943) Les araignées mangeuses de vertébrés. *Bull. Soc. zool. Fr.*, **68**, 10–16.

MOGGRIDGE, J. T. (1873) *Harvesting Ants and Trap-door Spiders*. London.

—— (1874) *Ibid.* Supplement.

NEMENZ, H. (1954) Über den Wasseroushalt einiger Spinnen, mit besonderer Berücksichtigung der Transpiration. *Öst. Zool. Zeits.*, **5**, 123–58.

NIELSEN, E. (1932) *The Biology of Spiders*, **1, 2**. Copenhagen.

PAPI, F. and SYRJAMAKI (1963), The sun-orientation rhythm of wolf spiders at different latitudes. *Arch. ital. Biol.*, **101**, 59–77.

PECKHAM, G. W. and PECKHAM, E. G. (1889) Observations on sexual selection in spiders of the family Attidae. *Occ. Pap. Nat. Hist. Soc. Wisc.*, **1**, 1–60.

PETERS, H. (1933) Weitere Untersuchungen über die Fanghandlung der Kreuzspinne. *Z. vergl. Physiol.*, **19**, 47–67.

PETERSEN, N. (1950) The relation between size of mother and number of young in some spiders and its significance for the evolution of size. *Experientia*, **6**, 96–8.

PETRUNKEVITCH, A. (1911) Sense of sight, courtship and mating in *Dugesiella hentzi* (Gerard), a Theraphosid spider from Texas. *Zool. Jahrb. (Syst.)*, **31**, 355–76.

POCOCK, R. I. (1909) Mimicry in spiders. *J. Linn. Soc. (Zool.)*, **30**, 256–70.

SAVORY, T. H. (1952) *The Spider's Web*. London.

THOMAS, M. (1953) *Vie et Moeurs des Araignées*. Paris.

THORP, R. W. and WOODSON, W. D. (1945) *Black Widow: America's most Poisonous Spider*. Chapel Hill.

TILQUIN, A. (1942) *La Toile géométrique des Araignées*. Paris.

TRETZEL, E. (1961), Biologie, Ökologie und Brutpflege von *Coelotes terrestris* (Wider) (Araneae, Agelenadae). Teil 1. Biologie und Ökologie. *Z. Morph. Ökol. Tiere*, **49**, 658–745.

WARBURTON, C. (1912) *Spiders*. Cambridge.

[*Note:* A complete list of spider literature up to 1939, systematically classified by subject, will be found in the first volume of: P. BONNET (1945) *Bibliographia Araneorum*. Toulouse.]

CHAPTER XI

MITES AND TICKS

ON ACCOUNT of their economic and medical importance the order Acari which comprises the mites and ticks has attracted more attention than all the other Arachnida put together. Because of their vast numbers, small size and the enormous taxonomic difficulties involved, their study is very much a matter for the specialist, and in this chapter only the briefest outline of the biology of the group will be attempted.

Classification and distribution

The Acari do not represent a natural group, but comprise several heterogeneous and distinct phylogenetic lines. They are mostly of small size and possess four, six or eight legs: usually the larval stages have three pairs, the nymphal and adult four pairs of limbs. The shape of the body varies considerably and may be elongated and worm-like, short, rounded, elliptical or spherical. The more primitive forms show traces of segmentation which disappear completely in the more advanced groups. Six sub-orders are recognised by André (*in* Grassé, 1949)* and these are separated largely according to the position of the spiracles. The Notostigmata is a small group of primitive mites in which the segmentation of the body is manifest. The metapodosoma consists of two somites, the opisthosoma of nine. These animals resemble harvest-spiders

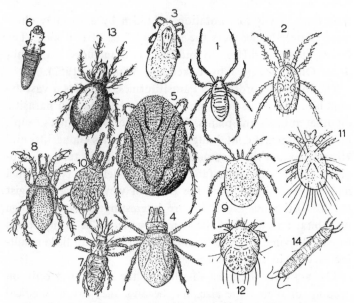

FIG. 39. Examples of various kinds of mites: 1. Notostigmata, 2. Dermanyssidae, 3. Halarachnidae, 4. Ixodid tick, 5. Argasid tick, 6. Demodicidae, 7. Bdellidae, 8. Halacaridae, 9. Hydrachnidae, 10. Thrombidiidae, 11. Tyroglyphidae, 12. Sarcoptidae, 13. Oribatei, 14. Eriophydiae. (From various sources.)

in general form but are brightly coloured and exhibit a combination of gold, blue and violet hues unknown elsewhere in the order. They are all referred to a single genus *Opilioacarus*, the species of which are found free-living under stones and are widely distributed in Europe, North Africa and South America.

The sub-order Holothyroidea again contains but a single genus of wide distribution found in the Seychelles, Mauritius, Australia, New Guinea and Ceylon. A few species of *Holothyrus* found in Papua are of interest because their size, which may reach 7 mm makes them the largest of all the mites, other than ticks. Their segmentation is hidden by a strongly chitinised plate which covers the upper surface of the body. The Notostigmata and Holothyroidea are both included in the sub-order Onychopalpida by Baker and Wharton (1952).

The third sub-order, the Parasitiformes, contains a vast assemblage of genera and species both free-living and parasitic on other animals and plants. They fall into two distinct groups, the Mesostigmata containing the super-families Gamasides and Uropodina and the Ixodoidea or ticks, which in turn are subdivided into three super-families, the Ixodei, the Nuttalliellei and the Argasides. From the point of view of the biologist the Mesostigmata are the more interesting, since the range of habitat and mode of life is more varied. The group seems to have become adapted to different habitats with little resulting change in fundamental structure.

The ticks are the most familiar of the mites, not only on account of their large size, but because they are of medical and veterinary importance. The majority of species are included in the family Ixodidae in which a scutum or shield is always present. The sexes are distinct: the males feed little or not at all, but the females and immature stages imbibe large quantities of blood so that the scutum becomes a mere patch on the anterior portion of their greatly distended bodies. They take several days to gorge themselves, and each stage feeds only once.

The Argasidae, on the other hand, are ticks with leathery integument, no portion being specially chitinised to form a scutum. When gorged there is no extravagant increase in size as in female Ixodidae.

The fourth sub-order is the Thrombidiformes or Trombidiformes which includes a very diverse group of mites probably derived from more than one ancestral type. A considerable degree of segmentation is retained in many species of the super-family Tarsonemini which contains a number of insect parasites. The super-family Prostigmata comprises a group known as the Eleutherengona in which are found a number of plant-feeding families, of which the most important economically are the 'red-spider' mites or Tetranychidae, the universal follicle-mites *Demodex* spp., the familiar Bdellidae or 'snout-mites' and the salt water Halacaridae.

The Parasitengona is the group of the Thrombidiformes which contains the fresh water mites, sometimes known as Hydracarina. These belong to a large number of families such as the Hydrachnidae, Limnocharidae, Eylaidae, Limnesiidae and Arrenuridae, etc. They are related to the irritating harvest-mites, chiggers or Thrombidiidae which are becoming increasingly important medically as they have been shown to transmit many forms of scrub-typhus (Audy and Harrison, 1951).

The fifth sub-order, the Sarcoptiformes, is probably the most specialised and external segmentation is reduced to a minimum. It contains two large and successful groups: the Acaridiae which includes the cheese-mites and other Tyroglyphidae which are often pests of stored products, as well as the itch-mite *Sarcoptes scabei*, and the Oribatei or beetle-mites. Generally speaking, the Acaridiae are soft and the Oribatei more or less armoured, but exceptions occur in both groups.

Finally, the Tetrapodili or Eriophyid mites are an aberrant sub-order of the Acari as they possess only the front two pairs of legs: the two posterior pairs are lacking or reduced to fine hairs. These include the gall-mites and other plant parasites, all of which have elongated, worm-like bodies in which the original segmentation is indistinguishable, for the ring-like appearance of the posterior part of the body is only an epidermal feature. A general characteristic is the possession of two long sinuous setae arising from the posterior part of the body.

The Acari are widely distributed all over the world from the north of Greenland to the antarctic. Terrestrial forms occur from sea level to the mountain tops, while marine and fresh water species are not uncommon. The distribution of parasites and commensals is intimately related with that of their hosts, but even free-living mites show marked degrees of adaptation to environments far removed from their original biotope.

General behaviour

Mites are found everywhere: many are present in damp soil and moss in shady places, where they live on small fungi, others live on plants, sucking the sap and sometimes causing gall-like tumours, while still more are the predators or parasites of insects, vertebrates and other animals. Whereas insects are numerically the leading group of animals inhabiting arable soils, in forests their place is taken by the Acari which, in humus are easily the most abundant invertebrates. It has been shown that they constitute 2–3% of the total weight of the invertebrate fauna in Danish beech woods and 5–7% in spruce woods. This difference, due to vast numbers of Oribatid mites which are practically limited to humus, appears to be a constant one.

Many mites are cavernicolous, others are myrmecophilous: of these some are scavengers, others eat the ants' food and still more feed on the ants themselves.

The Notostigmata are secretive and live under stones and other débris. Chitinous remains of arthropods have been found in their guts and it is probable that they are predatory, but so few specimens have been collected that little is yet known of their biology. The habits and life histories of the Holothyroidea too are virtually unknown. Many of the Mesostigmata live on plants and prey on small insects and other mites. A great many of the genera of Gamasides and Uropodina are found in damp places, in manure heaps and amongst moss and damp leaves, the Gamasides preying on smaller creatures. The Uropodina, which are slow-moving and sluggish, feed on fungi and vegetable matter. The members of the Parasitidae, for example, are found typically in accumulations of organic material such as rotting logs and litter. Other families, however, such as the Laelaptidae, are usually parasitic on vertebrates and to a lesser extent on invertebrates. Indeed, this family includes the most common ectoparasites of mammals, while the Halarachnidae live in the air passages of mammals, one genus occurring exclusively in the respiratory passages of seals of the family Phocidae, another parasitising the other Pinnipedia.

Ticks are comparatively large, leathery animals which are all parasitic on vertebrates. Even the larval forms or 'seed ticks' are visible to the naked eye and a fully gorged female may attain a length of half an inch. The Ixodidae are of great economic and medical importance. Heavy infestation by these creatures can cause anaemia in domestic animals, and they carry several noxious diseases to man and other vertebrates. Thus Rocky Mountain spotted fever and Texas fever of cattle in America are transmitted by *Dermacentor andersoni* and *Boophilus annulatus* respectively, while man is infected with Rocky Mountain fever, Kenya typhus, Q fever and Tularemia by the bites of various ticks. Tick paralysis of man and animals is believed to be due to toxins secreted in the saliva of the ticks. Though more frequently observed in tick-infested animals, a number of human cases have been reported in the United States, Canada and Australia. The ascending paralysis is caused by a rapidly engorging female tick attached to the base of the head where the hair may hide its presence for a long period. Complete recovery follows within a day or two of removal of the offending parasite, but death may occur if the paralysis has reached the respiratory centres of the human or animal victim before the tick has dropped off or been removed.

The ill effects of ticks on their hosts have been recognised since 200 B.C. when M. Porcius Cato referred to treatments whereby 'there will be no sores and the wool will be more plentiful and in better condition and the ticks (ricini) will not be troublesome'. Earlier, Aristotle in his famous *Historia Animalium* made some observations on the ecology of these ectoparasites and stated that the 'tick is generated from couch grass'. He was also aware of the harm that they caused. Despite the early realisation of the fact that ticks are ectoparasitic on mammals, it was not until the late nineteenth century that their role in the transmission of disease was first suspected.

The common sheep tick is *Ixodes reduvius*, found also on cattle and horses. Its distribution in Britain has been shown to be influenced by superficial soil deposits. Where good pasture occurs alongside 'islands' of damp ground, discrepancies in the distribution of the ticks are noted. Such 'islands' may harbour ticks while the rest of the pasture is free, and when cattle move into these 'islands' they are infested (Arthur, 1952). Milne (1945) has shown that the duration of the humidity level during daylight in conjunction with the temperature may decide the amount and extent of activity of these animals in summer.

During recent years considerable attention has been devoted to the physiology and behaviour of ticks. For example, Lees (1947) has shown that they owe their resistance to desiccation primarily to a superficial layer of wax in the integument: after exposure to increasing temperatures, water-loss increases abruptly at a certain 'critical temperature' as in insects. Species having higher critical temperatures are more resistant to desiccation at temperatures within the biological range. A broad correlation is possible between these powers of resistance and the natural choice of habitat: Argasidae infest dry, dusty situations, whereas Ixodidae occupy a wider variety of ecological niches. Unfed ticks are able to take up water rapidly through the wax-layer when exposed to high humidity. This water uptake is dependent on the secretory activities of the epidermal cells and is completely inhibited by abrasion of only a part of the total cuticle surface which suggests that the cells are functionally interconnected. Resistance to desiccation at low humidities is achieved by a dual mechanism: active secretion and the physical retention of water by the wax-layer.

The unfed sheep tick when at rest adopts either a questing attitude with the fore legs extended, or an attitude of repose with the legs folded. The ticks respond to gravity, humidity, temperature, smell, light and tactile stimuli. They climb upwards towards the tips of the leaves of the grass in which they live until they become desiccated when they become active and move downwards again to the moist air near the ground where they recover their water balance by active secretion through the cuticle: then they climb upwards again. If a suitable host happens to pass they are attracted by the moisture and scent of its body, and the vibrations caused by its movements, and respond by active questing. After feeding, the engorged ticks drop to the ground and are then strongly photonegative (Lees, 1948).

The main stimulus governing the ascent of grass blades by larvae of the Australian cattle tick, *Boophilus microplus*, is positive phototaxis to moderate light intensities: the ticks shelter from direct sunlight. In the field they are found to be more exposed in the early morning when they are often at the tops of grass stalks. The strongest questing behaviour occurs in response to odours, but vibration, air currents, interrupted

illumination, warmth and moisture all play a part in the reactions to the host (Wilkinson, 1953).

Argasid ticks are also of considerable economic and medical
importance. They occur on a wide variety of hosts including
reptiles, birds and mammals and in habits somewhat resemble
bed bugs. As a rule they are nocturnal, feeding moderately
and at frequent intervals. When fasting they are flat and readily
creep into narrow crevices. *Argas persicus* is not only a troublesome domestic pest in some places but it also infests poultry
all over the world, causing much damage by its bites and sometimes transmitting a spirochaete disease. Cattle are susceptible
to the spinose ear tick and relapsing fever is conveyed to
humans by the notorious *Ornithodorus moubata*.

The Thrombidiformes show a great diversity of form, life
history and behaviour and but a few selected examples can be
mentioned. Many of the Tarsonemini are parasitic on other
Arthropoda although the super-family also contains some
well-known plant pests. The family Scutacaridae are minute,
bizarre creatures found in moss and soil throughout the world,
as well as on ants and other insects. One species, *Acarapis
woodi*, infests the tracheal tubes of bees causing the fatal 'Isle
of Wight disease' found throughout Europe. The mites cause
injury by imbibing the hosts' body fluids, and by mechanically
blocking their tracheae.

The behaviour of the red-legged earth mite *Halotydeus destructor* (family Europidae) has been investigated experimentally by Solomon (1937) in Australia. The dry season is bridged
over by resting eggs produced in October. These eggs are laid
in great numbers on the surface soil, under clods of earth or
sticks and are highly resistant to heat, drought or desiccating
winds: moisture and sunshine are necessary for them to hatch.
The adult is a soft-bodied mite whose front legs act as sensory

organs. It lives from 25 to 50 days, prefers light, well-drained soils and is killed by heat and drought.

The Tetranychidae include the well-known red-spider mites, such as *Metatetranychus ulmi*, which are probably the most important economically of all the plant feeding mites. Populations may build up to such fantastic numbers if uncontrolled that trees may be completely defoliated and killed. These mites are often brightly coloured and do damage not only by sucking plant juices but also by spreading virus infections.

The follicle mites, *Demodex* spp., are responsible for various skin diseases in man and animals. Usually the general health of the host is not affected, but nodules or pustules are caused on the skin which, in the case of cattle parasites, may vary in size from the head of a pin to that of a hen's egg. One species causes red mange in dogs, which is accompanied by a foul and disgusting odour. The Cheyletidae, such as *Syringophilus* spp., are often found within the quills of birds and are correspondingly elongated, while others have stout claws with which they cling to the fur of mammals. It is probable that they feed on the detritus inside the quills and on the skin. The majority of the family however are free-living predators and have a world-wide distribution.

Bdellid mites are usually to be found in moss, lichen, leaf mould and débris, wherever there is an abundance of small insects and other mites. They are predaceous in habit and some species are said to capture their prey by squirting on to them a liquid silk which enmeshes their appendages while the mite sucks their body contents.

A few mites are littoral and run about the sand between tides, while others, the Halacaridae, are dredged from the sea. Newell (1947) records a total of 41 species, sub-species and varieties from North America and Greenland and has studied their ecology. He found that the fauna of the sub-tidal zone is more uniform than that of the inter-tidal zone, especially from a qualitative standpoint. There is a well-developed sand fauna, a fauna based upon molluscs and various algicolous faunas, while habitats characterised by low salinity have their own peculiar mite fauna containing but a small number of species.

Numerous species are found swimming in fresh water. These water mites constitute a far from negligible proportion of the fauna of all normal and permanent waters. Biologically and ecologically, two groups can be distinguished: the eurythermic forms which live mostly in standing waters naturally subject to wide variation of temperature, and the stenothermic forms which dwell in cold waters and are able to endure only slight variations of temperature. The latter are largely restricted to spring waters, streams and overflowings, but in addition to the temperature factor governing the choice of habitat, there is also a necessity for fast-flowing, richly oxygenated water. Viets (1940, etc.) has studied the distribution of some 219 species in Europe and has drawn some extremely interesting conclusions regarding the probable pre-glacial fauna and the possible routes and times of migration that took place after the ice age. About 220 species are represented in the British fauna, and their distribution is often peculiar. The dispersal of many of them depends upon the larvae attaching themselves to the bodies of various aquatic insects for transport.

The Thrombidiidae are extremely numerous in both numbers and kinds. They are of world-wide distribution and have been found on every land mass except those permanently covered by ice and snow. They are more abundant in the tropics than in temperate climates and constitute a conspicuous portion of the mite faunas of oceanic islands. On a dry, stony path on a sunny day in this country, one often find the adults of scarlet velvety mites *Thrombidium* sp. running about and feeding on small insects and their eggs, while others are common in leaf litter and under bark.

Adult giant velvet mites, *Dinothrombium tinctorium*, appear in the deserts of Africa after rain and probably feed on insects. The larvae are parasitic on grasshoppers. They are diurnal in habit, but become crepuscular in dry conditions. Their high rate of water-loss by transpiration suggests that they are not particularly well adapted to drought. They are positively photo-tactic and negatively geotactic in dry sand, but dig burrows where it is damp. Their scarlet coloration has an aposematic function and is associated with repugnatorial dermal glands (Cloudsley-Thompson,1962).

Much attention has recently been directed toward the biology of the minute hexapod mites which for ages have plagued man in various parts of the world, and which are known popularly as 'harvest bugs', 'harvest mites', 'bête rouge', 'rouget', 'chigger mites', etc. Great difficulty is usually experienced in obtaining the complete life history of these mites as the larvae alone are parasites. Jones (1950a) has investigated the sensory physiology of the harvest mite *Thrombicula autumnalis*. These animals are attracted to light and to moist air: they are very sensitive to touch but not to temperature although a range extending from 15° to 26° C appears to be preferred. The gregarious habit of the mites is primarily a response to the touch of each others bodies. The food of the harvest mite, *Thrombicula autumnalis*, consists of tissue, fluid and disintegrated cells of the malpighian layer partially liquefied by the action of injected saliva, a condition typical of extra-intestinal digestion. The physical factors of the skin have been shown to influence the choice of habitat upon the host. On birds the mites appear to favour the anal area and the lateral surface of the body between the wing and the thigh; but on man the factors which influence the choice are more varied, regions where the skin is thin and which provide the warmth and humidity favoured by the larvae being most likely to be attacked (Jones, 1950b).

Like the Thrombidiidae, the Acaridiae are notable for the extent of their distribution. They are found in all types of habitat from arctic tundra to tropical rain forest and wherever man in his wanderings has taken mites in his food and produce. Of the species attacking stored food, *Tyroglyphus farinae* is by far the most important. It infests all kinds of farinaceous material, not only eating the food but giving it a curious musty smell and taste so that it becomes unfit for human consumption. Not only is this species found in warehouses, but it also occurs in the nests and fur of small rodents which act as a natural reservoir of the mite. Grain which has become attacked by weevils or damaged mechanically is made more readily accessible to flour mites which are then able to penetrate the pericarp and consume the embryo. Grain that has become damaged by water seeping into the holds of ships is often attacked by another group of mites related to the forms that attack flower bulbs, particularly in badly-drained soil, while if the grain becomes completely saturated it may be infested with various other species which can live completely immersed in water.

Scabies of man is a condition produced by the itch-mite *Sarcoptes scabei* which burrows in the skin where it lays its eggs, the mite causing intense itching and irritation. In aggravated cases, an extensive crusting and scabbing results, particularly over the hands and arms.

Oribatid mites live in moss, in the humus of the forest floor, in lichens growing over tree stumps and trees, free on twigs and leaves, in decaying wood and in the sphagnum of marshes. A few are slightly aquatic and still fewer are known to inhabit the sea. They are found everywhere that plants decay with sufficient moisture and are penetrated by fungal mycelia (Willman, 1931). A number of species are important as vectors of tape-worms of sheep, etc. Apparently there is no taxonomic unit of mites that are vectors; the determining factor is which species is dominant on pasture and large enough to be able to swallow the eggs of the worms. On the whole very little is known of the habits of the Oribatei and there is much scope for further work.

The curious excrescences and abnormal growths which occur on the leaves and buds of plants are familiar to everyone. Various creatures are responsible for these deformities, many being the work of insects, but others are due to mites of the sub-order Tetrapodili. Though the galls caused by these mites are often outwardly similar to those of insect origin, they can at once be distinguished on close examination. Mite-galls contain a single chamber communicating with the exterior by a pore which is usually guarded by hairs. The mites live gregariously within, apparently feeding upon the hairs which grow abundantly on its inner surface, whereas in insect-galls each insect larva lives in a separate closed chamber.

Food and feeding habits

Mites live principally upon fluid nutriment, although this may be obtained from living animals and plants or from decaying organic matter. Some are entirely parasitic upon plants or other animals, others attach themselves to animals in their larval stage but are free when adult, while again others live an entirely independent and predaceous life. In the predatory forms the mandibles are chelate and masticatory, but in the parasitic forms the mouth parts are modified for sucking the blood or juices of the host. The largest and smallest examples of the order are found amongst the parasitic species.

The food and feeding habits of mites are closely related to their general behaviour and have already been discussed in some detail. Some species of mites rarely occur free-living but are found in association with mammals: here they feed, not on the host, but on other mites and insects living on it. It can readily be imagined that after a time, instead of living a blameless existence, some of these found an easy way to obtain food by sucking the blood of the animal on which they happened to find themselves, and thus developed the parasitic habit. In this way many families have become ectoparasitic on birds and mammals.

The majority of the mite-borne diseases of man were originally diseases of animals closely associated with humans, such as domestic rats and mice. At present some of these diseases, which include dermatitis, rickettsiosis, plague, various typhus and other fevers, phthiriasis, scabies and gastro-enteritis, tend to be encountered only in certain localities, but there is always a risk that they may be spread either by their original animal hosts, or by man, so that new foci of the disease are created. This important subject, somewhat beyond the scope of the present volume, has recently been reviewed by Zumpt and Graf (1950) to whose publication the reader is referred.

Halacaridae are either predaceous, lichen feeders or are parasitic (Newell, 1947). The basis of the behaviour of fresh water mites is a random locomotory activity in search of food such as Crustacea and aquatic insects which are detected by touch. A simple action system based on the principle of trial and error seems to be correlated with a simple mode of life. The predatory habit is often of economic importance and *Cheyletus eruditus* is the commonest predator of Tyroglyphid mites in stored products. Not infrequently mites are of ecological importance in controlling the numbers of insects, spiders and other mites by eating their eggs.

Enemies

The predators of mites include a large number of arthropods, including other mites, insects, spiders and so on, some of which appear to specialise in an acarine diet. Thus, species of Coniopterygidae (Neuroptera) appear to prey on the fruit-tree red-spider mite *Metatetranychus ulmi* both in the larval and adult stages. The larvae pierce the mites with their jaws and suck out the contents, leaving dry empty skins. The mite eggs are also sucked dry, their completely empty shells alone remaining. The adult insects pick up mites and devour them, bite off the top halves of the eggs and remove the contents. When hunting for food they move quickly and at random over a leaf, feeling the surface with their palps.

On the whole, despite this, mites tend to be avoided by many predators and their brilliant colours may well be a form of warning coloration. It is rare for spiders to kill or eat mites. According to Bristowe (1941)* this is in part due to their strong chitinous exoskeletons, but in the main to distastefulness. The Oribatei come into the former category. They move very slowly and draw in their legs at the first alarm. In this way they escape the attention of many spiders and most of those that do attack them find it impossible to pierce their strong armour. Of the remainder the majority are distasteful. Often they are rejected after one touch and a spider which bites a mite will not infrequently retire to wipe its mouth on the ground. Some species of *Holothyrus* produce a secretion which is poisonous to poultry.

The edibility of water mites has been investigated by Elton (1922) and Cloudsley-Thompson (1947) who have concluded that the bright colours of so many species may have a sematic function and be correlated with unpalatability if not distastefulness to predators. It is quite probable that the fact that so many species are bright red in colour and conspicuous against green vegetation, as the berries on holly, may be the result of Müllerian mimicry—the species tending to resemble one another so that numerical losses involved in teaching would-be predators to avoid them are reduced. The common colour facilitates the immediate recognition of undesirable prey. The predators investigated included various aquatic insects and fishes, most of which rejected the water mites, but sticklebacks and newts ate them with alacrity. A survey of the literature regarding the stomach contents of fishes and invertebrate predators has shown that water mites are seldom eaten in nature (Cloudsley-Thompson, 1947) and more recently it has been shown by experiment that nymphs of *Aeschna grandis* learn to avoid *Hydrachna* spp.

The integument of many Acari is provided with glands which may produce distasteful and poisonous secretions and these are particularly evident among the water mites. In addition, most mites are covered with hairs and setae. Many of these are no doubt sensory, but others serve to protect their owners from attack by predators in the same manner that the quills of a porcupine protect it. The shape and form of these setae are legion.

In contrast to many of the Acari, some of the ticks do not appear to be distasteful and may even be coloured so that they blend inconspicuously with the body of their host. In this way they may not only escape the attentions of the host itself, but also of tickbirds and other potential predators.

The eggs of the tick *Dermacentor andersoni* contain a toxic principle and, when inoculated in quantity into experimental animals, may cause death. It is not impossible that this may have been evolved as a deterrent to possible predators. No doubt further work would produce evidence to show that the bright colours of so many mite eggs are a form of warning advertisement, like the colours of the immature and adult stages.

Reproduction and life cycle

Nearly all mites lay eggs, although a few of the Oribatei are ovoviviparous. Occasionally the mother may die at a time when her abdomen contains a few ripe eggs, and these are able to complete their development internally so that fully-formed larvae emerge from the dead body of their parent. The young undergo metamorphosis varying in completeness in the different groups. Altogether five or six stages can be recognised, but they are seldom, if ever, all exhibited in the development of a single species. The life history normally consists of the egg which, is some cases is parthenogenetic, and hatches

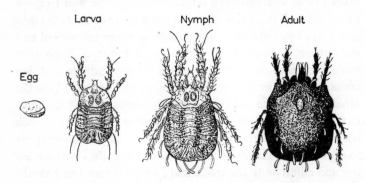

FIG. 40. Stages in the development of an Oribatid mite (*Pelops* sp.): 1. egg, 2. larva, 3. nymph, 4. adult. (After Michael, 1884.)

into a six-legged larva. This passes through from one to three nymphal forms before becoming adult, each stage in the life cycle being preceded by a resting period. In most mites the larvae, except for the absence of genital openings and the posterior pair of legs, somewhat resemble adults. In some Prostigmata, however, they are quite different and metamorphose into a nymph which is more like the adult in form. In the account given below a few typical examples of life histories will be given.

The life history and sensory behaviour of the Mesostigmatid snake mite *Ophionyssus natricis* has recently been investigated by Camin (1953) who found that development of the eggs takes from 28 to 98 hours; larvae 18 to 47 hours, protonymphs 3 to 14 days, deutonymphs 13 to 26 hours and adults 10 to 32 days within the range of temperatures 20° to 30° C, commonly occurring in snake cages in zoos. The adult female mite, after completing engorgement, crawls out from under the scale of the host, drops from the snake's body and wanders about until it finds some dark moist crevice where oviposition takes place. The emerging larvae remain in the moist region where there is little risk of desiccation and the protonymphs stay there too until their integument becomes sclerotised and the danger of death from water-loss is lessened. Then they wander at random until they come upon a suitable host, become concealed under a scale and commence feeding. If, on the other hand, a mite fails to meet with a suitable host it climbs to the top of some object such as a rock or the tip of a branch where it comes to rest with other nymphs. If a snake happens to crawl over a clump of these resting mites, they become active and climb on to the snake and conceal themselves beneath its scales. After feeding to engorgement, the protonymphs drop off and crawl about until they find a dark, moist crevice. Here males and females sometimes pair off and remain paired until they reach maturity. Ecdysis follows soon after repletion and the newly moulted deutonymphs, although active, usually remain in the humid area until the next ecdysis. The deutonymph males and females usually pair if this has not occurred in the previous stage. After moulting to the adult stage, the mites remain in the moist crevices until their integument has hardened and then begin to wander about until they come in contact with a suitable host, to which they respond by their reactions to gravity, temperature and odour. Male mites will copulate after feeding but are not attracted by replete females. These unfecunded females lay eggs which develop partheno-genetically into males. Females normally lay from 60 to 80 eggs, feeding two or three times at intervals of one or two weeks.

The blood-sucking mites of the genus *Haemolaelaps* are mammal and bird parasites and seem to show a preference for rodents. They are probably ovoviviparous and give birth to the first nymphal form. As in most parasitic mites the males probably do not feed on the blood of the host, but haemoglo-bin has been demonstrated in both proto- and deutonymphs which leave the host immediately after feeding and moult in the nest.

Ticks are parasitic during the greater part of their lives, but all leave the host in order to deposit their eggs. These are laid on the ground in enormous numbers and hatch into six-legged larvae. The young ticks remain clustered together for several days but then climb the nearest blade of grass and await the coming of their host. Many die in the attempt, but some suc-ceed in attaching themselves to a passing animal and proceed to gorge themselves with blood. After feeding for a few days the larvae drop off, seek a hiding place and moult into nymphs which behave in much the same way. The adult stage is reached after one more moult.

Lees and Beament (1948) have shown that the egg of the sheep tick *Ixodes reduvius* is water-proofed by an external covering of wax which is secreted by the female after the shell layers are complete. This waxy covering is first smeared over the egg as it passes down the vagina and a further layer of lipoid is applied when the egg touches Géné's organ, a glandular structure that is everted shortly before oviposition. In *Ornithodorus moubata* the wax is applied solely by Géné's organ: this difference may be related to the size of the egg which is relatively small in the Ixodoidea. The wax is probably secreted through pore canals distributed over a narrow zone of cuticle between the horns of the organ, and the cement covering layer of the epicuticle does not extend to this zone.

Sexual dimorphism is rare in Thrombidiform mites although it does occur in some genera of water mites, sometimes even affecting the nymphs. It is also to be found in the Tarsonemini and in the genus *Tenuipalpus* of the Tetranychidae and some few others. It is therefore of interest that Turk and Phillips (1946) found rudimentary sexual dimorphism in the slug mite *Riccardoella limacum* (family Ereynetidae), a species in which the adult stage is disappearing. The female deutonymph produces the eggs which are capable of fertilisation, but whether the larger adult female also lays eggs is undecided. The eggs mature in their own oocysts and some at least are fertilised in the ovary. Copulation takes place on the host and is probably confined to the early summer, the only time at which adult males are found. The eggs are commonly laid in the mantle cavity of the host, but may sometimes be found embedded in mucus on the skin. Viviparity and oviparity exist side by side and seemingly not all individuals retain an egg of retarded development over the winter, while some over-wintering larvae remain in the dry skin of the female.

In the Bdellidae the sexes are very similar. The eggs are slightly elliptical and are covered with clavate spines and projections. They are laid on the soil, in leaf mould or wherever the mite happens to be and hatch into a typical six-legged larva which develops through three nymphal stages to the adult.

The life cycles of the red-spider mites are comparatively well-known. The winter is passed as eggs which are deposited on branches and twigs and are bright red in colour. They hatch in spring to a larva which passes through various nymphal stages to the adult. During copulation the male crawls under the female from the rear and clasps his front legs about her abdomen and his second pair of legs about her hind legs. He then curves the end of his abdomen upward and forward until it meets the end of the female's abdomen. Copulation lasts from ten to fifteen minutes. Eggs are laid within a day or two days of emergence in hot weather: these summer eggs do not show diapause and hatch in about eight to ten days. The number of generations in a year depends on climate and latitude. Over-wintering, diapausing eggs are laid towards the autumn, their production being engendered by the decreasing length of daylight until cold weather kills the adult mites or causes the leaves on which they are feeding to fall (Lees, 1955).

The conditions of the micro-environment under which many parasitic mites can multiply are often limited. Thus 12° to 14° C represents the lowest temperature at which *Liponyssus bacoti* can reproduce and then only with a great lengthening of the cycle and an increase in mortality, and many other species that normally feed on the body of their host where they are protected from the cold are restricted in a similar way.

Most of the Cheyletidae and Demodicidae develop normally from egg, larval and nymphal stages to the adult, but in the water mites only three stages are noted subsequently to the egg, viz. the larva, nymph and adult or prosopon, between each of which metamorphosis takes place. The eggs are usually reddish in colour and laid on aquatic vegetation or stones to which they are fixed by a mucilaginous covering. In the genus

Hydrachna, the eggs are placed in cavities pierced in the stems of aquatic plants for their reception. The larval and nymphal stages are usually parasitic on aquatic insects and are separated by resting stages when the creatures are concealed in the axils of leaves or under stones. The adults are free living. For further details, see Soar and Williamson (1925, 1927, 1929).

The life cycle of the Acaridiae is similar to that of other mites, passing as it does through that of egg, hexapod larva and two nymphal stages before becoming adult. In some cases, however, an additional heteromorphic stage is introduced into the life history between the two nymphal stages. This is known as the *hypopus* and differs completely from all the others. Instead of having a flexible cuticle it is well chitinised and devoid of a mouth: it does not appear to be formed as the result of adverse conditions but acts as a means of dispersal. By means of a ventral sucker plate through which project a series of finger-like suckers, the hypopus attaches itself to a passing insect and is carried from one place to another. At the same time it is able to survive drier conditions than the adult.

It has been found that a temperature of 23° to 25° C is the optimum for rearing cultures of the furniture mite, *Glycyphagus domesticus* and temperature and humidity have a marked effect on the development of the egg and hypopus stages.

The life cycle of the feather mites, family Dermoglyphidae, is as follows: there are two types of egg, a hard shelled and a thin shelled one. The latter contain larvae while still within the mother who may be either viviparous or ovoviviparous. The six-legged larva hatches from the egg to moult to the eight-legged protonymph which in turn forms the deutonymph. When mating takes place the male always copulates with the female deutonymph which later moults to the adult stage.

Detailed knowledge of the development of the larvae and nymph of the Oribatid mites is virtually non-existent, but

Sengbusch (1954) has recently succeeded in timing the development of three American species of *Galumna* from egg to adult. Oviposition may occur in nature from spring to autumn and is probably correlated with temperature which also affects the time of development. This averages 63 days at 20° C in *G. nervosus*, but only 47 days at 25° C.

Finally, we come to the sub-order Tetrapodili. Not until Keifer's work (1946) on the alternation of generations of the buckeye rust mite *Oxypleurites aesculifoliae* was the life cycle of any of the Eriophyidae fully understood. The deutogynes become active in late winter and leave their hibernating quarters on twigs. When the buds swell in February they penetrate the outer scales and feed on the green inner tissue beneath. With the development of leaves, they lay eggs which hatch into nymphs producing primary mites on the leaves. These soon produce additional primary mites. In early May new deutogynes appear which when fully fed travel down the stem for six inches or more and then crawl into crevices of the previous season's wood. The primary mites are confined to the leaves and perish with them but the deutogynes, once they have attained a suitable crevice, become dormant during late summer. Winter rains and frost tend to break this diapause, however, and the deutogynes become active again the following spring. There is a high mortality amongst them, principally because of the limited number of suitable crevices.

BIBLIOGRAPHY

Identification

ANASTOS, G. (1950) The scutate ticks, or Ixodidae, of Indonesia. *Ent. Amer.* (N.S.), **30**, 1–144.
ARTHUR, D. R. (1965) *Ticks of the Genus Ixodes in Africa*. London.

Audy, J. R. (ed.) (1954) Malaysian Parasites, I–XV. *Stud. Inst. Med· Res. Malaya*, No. 26, 1–242.

Baker, E. W. and Wharton, G. W. (1952) *An Introduction to Acarology*. New York.

Beer, R. E. (1954) A revision of the Tarsonemidae of the Western Hemisphere (Order Acarina). *Univ. Kansas Sci. Bull.*, **36**, (2), 1091–1387.

Cooley, R. A. and Kohls, G. M. (1944) The Argasidae of North America, Central America and Cuba. *Amer. Midl. Nat. Monograph*, No. 1, 1–152.

—— (1945) The genus *Ixodes* in North America. *Bull. Nat. Inst. Health*, No. 184, 1–246.

Hammen, L. van der (1952) The Oribatei (Acari) of the Netherlands. *Zool. Verh. Leiden*, No. 17, 1–139.

Hoogstraal, H. (1956) *African Ixodoidea* **1**, *Ticks of the Sudan*. Cairo.

Hughes, A. M. (1948) *The Mites associated with stored Food Products*. London: *Min. Agric. Fish.*

—— (1961) *The Mites of Stored Products*. London.

Hughes, T. E. (1959) *Mites or the Acari*. London.

Keegan, H. L. (1951) The mites of the sub-family *Haemogamasinae* (Acari: Laelaptidae). *Proc. U.S. Nat. Mus. Wash.*, **101**, 203–68.

Michael, A. D. (1883) *British Oribatei*, **1**, London.

—— (1887) *Ibid.*, **2**.

—— (1901) *British Tyroglyphidae*, **1**. London.

—— (1903) *Ibid.*, **2**.

Nuttall, G., Warburton, C., Cooper, W. and Robinson, L. (1908) *Ticks. A Monograph of the Ixodoidea. Part* 1, *Argasidae*. Cambridge.

—— (1911) *Ibid.*, *Part* 2, *Ixodidae, the genus Ixodes*.

—— (1915) *Ibid.*, *Part* 3, *Ixodidae, the genus Haemaphysalis*.

Pritchard, A. E. and Baker, E. W. (1955) *A Revision of the Spider Mite Family Tetranychidae*. San Francisco.

Robinson, L. E. (1926) *Ibid.*, *Part* 4, *Ixodidae, the genus Amblyomma*.

Senevet, G. (1937) Ixodoidés. *Faune de France*, No. 32, 1–100. Paris.

Soar, C. D. and Williamson, W. (1925) *The British Hydracarina*. **1**. London.

—— (1927) *Ibid.*, **2**.

—— (1929) *Ibid.*, **3**.

Toumanoff, C. (1944) *Les Tiques* (*Ixodoidea*) *de l'Indochine*. Saigon.

Viets, K. (1955) *Die Milben des Sußwassers und des Meers*, **1**. Jena.

Vitzhtum, G. H. (1940–43) Acarina *in* H. G. Bronn's *Klass. Ordn. Tierreichs*, **5**, IV (5), 1–1011.

Willman, C. (1931) Moosmilben oder Oribatiden (Oribatei). *Tierw. Deutsch.*, **22**, 79–200.

Biology

ARTHUR, D. R. (1951) The bionomics of *Ixodes hexagonus* Leach in Britain. *Parasitology*, **41**, 82–90.

—— (1952) Economic importance of ticks. *Discovery*, **13**, 379–83.

—— (1962) *Ticks and Disease*. Oxford.

ATALLA, E. A. R. and HOBART, J. (1964) The survival of some soil mites at different humidities and their reaction to humidity gradients. *Ent. Exp. & Appl.* **7**, 215–28.

AUDY, J. R. and HARRISON, J. L. (1951) A review of investigations on mite typhus in Burma and Malaya, 1945–1950. *Trans. R. Soc. Trop. Med. Hyg.*, **44**, 371–404.

BOTTGER, K. (1965) Zur Ökologie und Fortpflanzungsbiologie von *Arrenurus valdiviensis* K. O. Viets 1964 (Hydrachnellae, Acari). *Z. Morph. Ökol. Tiere*, **55**, 115–41.

CAMIN, J. H. (1953) Observations on the life history and sensory behaviour of the snake mite, *Ophionyssus natricis* (Gervais) (Acarina: Macronyssidae). *Spec. Publ. Chicago. Acad. Sci.*, No. 10, 1–75.

CLOUDSLEY-THOMPSON, J. L. (1947) The edibility of Hydracarina. *Naturalist*, **1947**, 116–18.

—— (1962) Some aspects of the physiology and behaviour of *Dinothrombium* (Acari). *Ent. Exp. & Appl.*, **5**, 69–73.

EFFORD, I. E. (1965) Ecology of the watermite *Feltria romijni* Besseling. *J. Anim. Ecol.*, **34**, 233–51.

ELTON, C. S. (1922) On the colours of water mites. *Proc. Zool. Soc. Lond.*, **1922**, 1231–40.

EVANS, G. O., SHEALS, J. G. and MACFARLANE, D. (1961) *The Terrestrial Acari of the British Isles*. **1**, *Introduction and Biology*. London.

HUGHES, A. M. (1951) A general survey of the Acari (Arachnida). *J. Quek. Micr. Club*, (4), **3**, 247–60.

JONES, B. M. (1950a) The sensory physiology of the harvest mite *Trombicula autumnalis* Shaw. *J. Exp. Biol.*, **27**, 461–94.

—— (1950b) The penetration of the host tissue by the harvest mite, *Trombicula autumnalis* Shaw. *Parasitology*, **40**, 247–60.

KEIFER, H. H. (1946) A review of North American economic Eriophyid mites. *J. Econ. Ent.*, **39**, 563–70.

LEES, A. D. (1947) Transpiration and the structure of the epicuticle in ticks. *J. Exp. Biol.*, **23**, 379–410.

—— (1948) The sensory physiology of the sheep tick, *Ixodes ricinus* L. *Ibid.*, **25**, 145–207.

—— (1955) *The Physiology of Diapause in Arthropods*. Cambridge.

LEES, A. D. and BEAMENT, J. W. L. (1948) An egg-waxing organ in ticks. *Quart. J. Micr. Sci.*, **89**, 291–332.

MILNE, A. (1945) The ecology of the sheep tick *Ixodes ricinus* L. The seasonal activity in Britain with particular reference to northern England. *J. Exp. Biol.*, **36**, 142–52.

NEWELL, I. M. (1947) A systematic and ecological study of the Halacaridae of eastern North America. *Bull. Bingham Oceanogr. Coll.*, **10**, (3), 1–232.

SENGBUSCH, H. G. (1954) Studies on the life history of three Oribatoid mites with observations on other species (Acarina, Oribatei). *Ann. Ent. Soc. Amer.*, **47**, 646–67.

SOLOMON, M. E. (1937) Behaviour of the red-legged earthmite, *Halotydeus destructor*, in relation to environmental conditions. *J. Anim. Ecol.*, **6**, 340–61.

—— (1962) Ecology of the flour mite, *Acarus Siro* L. (=*Tyroglyphus farinae* De G.). *Ann. Appl. Biol.*, **50**, 178–84.

TURK, F. A. and PHILLIPS, S-M. (1946) A monograph of the slug mite *Riccardoella limacum* (Schrank). *Proc. Zool. Soc. Lond.*, **115**, 448–72.

VIETS, K. (1940) Ausbreitungswege und nacheiszeitliche Verbreitung der Kaltwasser und Strömung liebenden Wassermilben in Europa. *Arch. Hydrobiol.*, **37**, 278–319.

WALLWORK, J. A. (1960) Observations on the behaviour of some Oribatid mites in experimentally-controlled temperature gradients. *Proc. Zool. Soc. Lond.*, **135**, 619–29.

WILKINSON, P. R. (1953) Observations on the sensory physiology and behaviour of larvae of the cattle tick, *Boophilus microplus* (Can.), (Ixodidae). *Austr. J. Zool.*, **1**, 345–56.

WOODROFFE, G. E. and SOUTHGATE, B. J. (1951) Birds' nests as a source of domestic pests. *Proc. Zool. Soc. Lond.*, **121**, 55–62.

ZUMPT, F. and GRAF, H. (1950) Medical importance of mites. *S. Afr. J. Clin. Sci.*, **1**, 196–212.

EPILOGUE

IN THE introduction to this volume the complexity of factors influencing the ecology and distribution of animals was indicated, and the interactions with their environments of the species mentioned have been stressed throughout. Ecology can be studied from the point of view of the species (autecology) or from that of the particular habitat in which numbers of species occur (synecology). The former is a simpler approach and more suited to the activities of the individual natural historian: the latter usually involves team work. Whichever is adopted, however, the other should constantly be borne in mind or else the picture will become unbalanced and distorted. (Cloudsley-Thompson, 1967*).

Considerable uniformity is apparent throughout the groups that have been considered here: this is not altogether surprising in members of the same phylum. Arthropods have an exoskeleton which, in all classes, seems to be basically similar although it may vary greatly in complexity. An exceedingly thin outer epicuticular layer of 'cuticulin', a condensed lipo-protein tanned with quinones, is always present but only in insects and Arachnids does this support the impervious layer of wax to which their success on land is largely due.

It would be a mistake, however, to regard the absence of a discrete cuticular wax layer as a primitive characteristic, although the forms that lack one are so restricted in their choice of environment that they cannot be regarded as entirely successful land animals. Rather, it seems that a particular method has been exploited for surviving the conditions of life on land. The primitive respiratory organ is the skin, but special respiratory structures have been evolved in all but the smallest and simplest of the Arthropoda. In insects a system of minute air tubes or 'tracheae' lead into even finer 'tracheoles' that carry oxygen directly to the tissues where metabolic processes take place, while the Arachnida possess both tubular tracheae and lung-books. Scorpions have lung-books, while spiders are passing through a primitive lung-book stage from which none have yet emerged. Two pairs of lung-books without tracheae occur in the more primitive families while most others have an anterior pair of lung-books and a posterior pair of tracheae. Lung-books provide a localised respiratory area from which oxygen is distributed by the respiratory pigment, haemocyanin, in the blood. Insects possess no respiratory pigments as all their tissues are supplied with oxygen directly by the tracheoles.

The entrance to both lung-books and tracheae is guarded by spiracles closed by means of special muscles. In this way the minimum quantity of air necessary for respiratory purposes is allowed to circulate and consequently water-loss is much reduced. When an insect or Arachnid is placed in an atmosphere containing an abnormally high proportion of carbon dioxide the spiracles are kept open to their fullest extent and the rate of water-loss in dry air is then considerably increased.

In all organisms growth tends to be a cyclical process, periods of rest alternating with activity. In no animals, however, is it more marked than in the Arthropoda whose development is punctuated by a series of moults or ecdyses, each of which is preceded by a period of active growth and followed by one of apparent inactivity. All parts of the integument are moulted together, independently of nerve supply: the stimulus for this is hormonic in nature, metamorphosis too being under hormone control.

During moulting the old endocuticle is digested by enzymes in the moulting fluid and withdrawn in solution through the 'pore canals'. These are numerous fine tubes, sometimes numbering over a million per sq. cm of surface, which penetrate the exo- and endocuticle. A new epicuticle is always laid down beneath the old one before moulting takes place, so that this process is accompanied by little loss of water and a high degree of economy is achieved.

Woodlice and millipedes are almost entirely vegetarian, while centipedes and Arachnids, with the exception of certain mites, are primarily carnivorous; but different species of insects seem to be able to thrive on almost any kind of organic matter capable of supporting metabolism. In most of these animals water conservation is of prime importance; insufficient water is obtained with the food to allow for much excess to be lost during excretion.

The function of excretion, like that of osmotic regulation, is the maintenance of a constant internal environment within the animal body. An aquatic animal surrounded by a large volume of water can excrete toxic nitrogenous compounds with impunity, but the necessity for water economy in terrestrial forms generally requires the excretion of some compound less poisonous than ammonia. Woodlice are essentially ammonotelic since over half of their soluble non-protein nitrogen is excreted in the form of ammonia, but the retention of this primitive character has been attended by a general suppression of nitrogenous metabolism. In higher insects, as in myriapods, birds and reptiles, uric acid is the chief excretory compound. This substance has in the first place been evolved in response to the conditions of embryonic life. Uricotelic metabolism is correlated with the possession of 'cleidoic' eggs provided with water and enclosed in a comparatively impermeable shell. Ammonia is toxic as we have seen and is only suitable as an excretory compound for eggs developing in water: it cannot be converted to urea as this would cause ureamia, and in excess upset the osmotic relationships of the egg. Hence uric acid, a non-toxic, highly insoluble substance, has been evolved which can accumulate within the egg without causing any ill effects.

The chief excretory compound of the Arachnida is guanine which, like uric acid, is very insoluble, but the physiology of its excretion has not been studied in the same detail.

Throughout the Arthropoda entirely mechanistic patterns of behaviour are found, involving rigid but comparatively simple responses to the stimuli of the environments in which they live. Indeed it would seem that the typical arthropodan nervous system is capable only of stereotyped reflex behaviour patterns and that this perhaps restricts them no less than their rigid integument!

Nevertheless, within the limits imposed by their basic morphology and physiology, every conceivable type of modification and specialisation occurs within the Arthropoda and herein lies the great interest of these animals to the serious student of natural history.

GENERAL BIBLIOGRAPHY

In addition to the special bibliographies that follow each chapter, the following more general works will be found to be useful. References to them in the text have been marked by an asterisk.

BERLAND, L. (1932) *Les Arachnides*. Paris.

BONNET, P. (1945) *Bibliographia Araneorum*, **1.** Toulouse.

BRISTOWE, W. S. (1939) *The Comity of Spiders*, **1.** London.

—— (1941) *Ibid.* **2.**

BRUES, C. T., MELANDER, A. L. and CARPENTER, F. M. (1954) Classification of Insects. Keys to the living and extinct families of insects, and to the living families of other terrestrial Arthropods. *Bull. Mus. Comp. Zool.*, **108,** 1–917.

CLOUDSLEY-THOMPSON, J. L. (1961) *Rhythmic Activity in Animal Physiology and Behaviour*. London and New York.

—— (1967) *Microecology*. London.

CLOUDSLEY-THOMPSON, J. L. and CHADWICK, M. J. (1964) *Life in Deserts*. London.

CLOUDSLEY-THOMPSON, J. L. and SANKEY, J. (1961) *Land Invertebrates*. London.

COMSTOCK, J. H. (1940) (edited by W. J. GERTSCH). *The Spider Book* (revised ed.). New York.

DONISTHORPE, H. ST. J. K. (1927) *The Guests of British Ants*. London.

EDNEY, E. B. (1957) *The Water Relations of Terrestrial Arthropods*. Cambridge.

GERTSCH, W. (1949) *American Spiders*. New York.

GRASSÉ, P–P. (ed.) (1949) *Traité de Zoologie Anatomie, Systématique, Biologie*, **6,** Paris.

HARMER, S. F. and SHIPLEY, A. E. (eds.) (1909) *The Cambridge Natural History*, **4,** London.

KAESTNER, A. (1956) *Lehrbuch der Speziellen Zoologie*, **1** (13), 485–658. Berlin.

KEVAN, D. K. MCE. (ed.) (1955) *Soil Zoology*. London.

KEVAN, D. K. McE. (ed.) (1962) *Soil Animals*. London.

KÜHNELT, W. (1950) *Bodenbiologie*. Wien

—— (1961) *Soil Biology*. London.

LAWRENCE, R. F. (1953) *The Biology of the Cryptic Fauna of Forests*. Cape Town.

PATTON, W. S. and EVANS, A. M. (1929) *Insects, Ticks, Mites and Venomous Animals of Medical and Veterinary Importance*, **1**. Liverpool.

PHISALIX, M. (1922) *Animaux venimeux et Venins*, **1**. Paris.

POCOCK, R. I. (1928) *Guide to the Arachnida, Millipedes and Centipedes exhibited in the Department of Zoology, British Museum (Natural History)*. London.

SAVORY, T. H. (1928) *The Biology of Spiders*. London.

—— (1935) *The Arachnida*. London.

—— (1964) *Arachnida*. London.

SMART, J. and TAYLOR, G. (1953) *Bibliography of Key Works for the Identification of the British Fauna and Flora*, 2nd ed., London.

Zoological Record, London. (Published annually since 1865.)

CLASSIFICATORY INDEX

IN THE following summary of classification are included all species, families, sub-orders, orders and classes mentioned in the text. Thus, although it is not absolutely comprehensive, reference has been made in it to most, if not all, of the more important groups known. Page references to text-figures are given in heavy type.

*British genera and species.

GLOSSARY AND INDEX OF
SCIENTIFIC TERMS

IN THE following glossary, references to pages on which scientific terms have been more fully described are indicated by heavy type. Page references are not given where words are in constant use. When a word is in general use in more senses than one, it is explained below in relation to the sense in which it is used in the text of the present volume, and with reference to the particular groups of animals considered.

Aktograph—apparatus for recording locomotory activity 31, **32**
Anamorphosis—development involving transformation, characteristic of millipedes, during which additional segments appear at each moult or ecdysis. Cf. Epimorphosis (*q.v.*) **45**, 70, 77
Apophysis—projecting outgrowth or process
Aposematic coloration or sound—conspicuous warning or advertising coloration or sound, found in or produced by distasteful, poisonous or otherwise formidable animals and their mimics. Cf. Cryptic (*q.v.*) **96**, 97, 203, 212, 235, 241–3
Arolium—median tarsal lobe forming a pad or sucker beneath the claws of the leg of false-scorpions, etc. 128
Asparagine—amino-acid found in plant tissues and known to be strongly attractive to wireworms and other insects 34
Autotomy—reflex separation of part of the body; self-amputation 61, 64, 171, 176

Basiconic sensillae—conical sense-organs found in Arthropoda **29,** 33, 81
Batesian mimicry—imitation of the conspicuous appearance of a distasteful, poisonous or otherwise formidable species by a harmless one 212–13
Berlese funnel—apparatus for extracting small animals from leaf litter and other débris which is placed in a horizontal sieve above a funnel.

Heat from an electric light or a water-jacket dries the débris so that the fauna is driven downwards and eventually falls through the sieve and funnel into a bottle of preservative   128

Calamistrum—comb of short spines on the metatarsi of the fourth legs of some spiders   **149,** 208

Carapace—covering of the anterior upper surface in arthropods   87

Carina—lateral keel-like projection from the body segments of some millipedes   24

Cavernicolous—cave-dwelling

Cephalothorax—fore-part of the body of an Arachnid, corresponding to the head and thorax of an insect; more properly called the prosoma (*q.v.*)

Chelate—pincer-like, as the claw of a lobster. The last segment of a limb apposed to that preceding it so that the appendage is adapted for grasping

Chelicerae—jaws of an Arachnid; carrying the poison fangs in spiders

Chiggers—parasitic larvae of Thrombiculid mites   229, **237**

Chitin—nitrogenous polysaccharide forming the basic material of the integument or cuticle in the Arthropoda. Usually hardened by impregnation with calcium or sclerotin (*q.v.*)

Chiton—a mollusc that clings to rocks on the sea-shore   27

Chordotonal organs—integumental sensillae with auditory or propreoceptive function   172

Chromatophore—colour pigment cell   8

Clavate—club-shaped

Cleidoic egg—one containing enough water for development and enclosed in a comparatively impermeable membrane or shell   **255**

Clypeus—narrow strip of prosoma between the eyes and bases of the chelicerae in spiders

Collum—first post-cephalic segment of myriapods   78

Commensal—an animal living in a loose association with another and from which only one partner derives benefit   30, 129, 230

Compound eye—eye composed of numerous visual elements, found in many of the arthropods   49

Coxa—first segment of the limb attaching it to the body

Cribellum—sieve-like plate in front of the spinnerets in some spiders **189,** 195, 200

Cryptic coloration—colour pattern making for inconspicuousness. Cf. Aposematic (*q.v.*)   **167,** 176, 190, 203, 211

Cucullus—mobile hood at front edge of carapace of Ricinulei   160

Cuticle—hardened integument of arthropods

Dermal light sense—appreciation of light stimuli through the integument 29

Deutogyne—secondary female Eriophyid mite differing from the primogyne or primary type and having no male counterpart   249

Deutonymph—second nymphal stage following the larval instar of a mite or false-scorpion   139, 248

Diapause—dormant state usually characterised by temporary failure of growth or reproduction, by reduced metabolism and often by enhanced resistance to climatic factors such as cold, heat or drought   247–9

Digitigrade—walking on the toes or claws. Cf. Plantigrade (*q.v.*)   56

Distal—part of limb or segment farthest from the centre of the body

Ecdysis—moulting, casting of the outer skin in growth

Endite—lateral lobes on inner side of crustacean limb

Endocuticle—inner layers of the integument   255

Endogenous rhythm—rhythm of activity that persists under constant conditions   31

Endopodite—inner ramus of a primitively forked arthropodan limb or mouth part

Epicuticle—thin outermost chitin-free layer of the integument or cuticle xii, 255

Epigyne—external genitalia of the female Arachnid

Epimorphosis—development characteristic of centipedes in which slow growth takes place but the number of segments does not increase   **70**

Eurythermic—able to tolerate considerable variations in temperature. Cf. Stenothermic (*q.v.*)   236

Exocuticle—outer layers of chitinous endocuticle beneath epicuticle (*q.v.*) 255

Femur—third segment of an Arachnid's leg or palp

Flagellum—a whip-like extension of the body, a limb or antenna. In false-scorpions, a structure composed of setae on the chelicerae

Galea—spinneret on movable finger in false-scorpions   130, 135

Genital operculum—chitinous plate covering reproductive opening

Geotaxis—directed movement in response to the stimulus of gravity

Gnathobase—projection from the coxa of a limb used to crush food

Gnathochilarium—mouth parts of millipedes composed of fused maxillae **22, 23, 29,** 33, 34, 81

Gonopod—limb modified for sexual reproduction   25, 39–40, 46

Guanine—insoluble nitrogenous excretory compound characteristic of Arachnids   **526**

Haemocyanin—respiratory pigment found in Crustacea and Arachnids in which the metallic element is copper and not iron as in haemoglobin 254

Hypopus—resistant, dispersal stage of some mites 248

Instar—larval, nymphal or other developmental stage of an arthropod. Instars change at moulting and metamorphosis (*q.v.*)

Ion—electrically charged atom or group of atoms 31

Kinesis—non-directed locomotory response to a stimulus. Cf. Taxis (*q.v.*)

Kinetic reaction—kinesis (*q.v.*)

Labium—lower 'lip' or lower surface of mouth between the maxillae of an arthropod

Labrum—upper 'lip' of an arthropod 91, 133

Lacuna—space among the tissues serving in place of vessels for the circulation of the blood 47

Lamella—one of an aggregate of thin plates which compose gills, lungbooks, etc.

Lamina—blade-like stucture. On fingers of false-scorpions 125

Laterigrade—able to run side ways

Luciferase—enzyme in the presence of which luciferin is oxidised and light produced 32

Luciferin—substance oxidised in the presence of luciferase to form oxyluciferin. The reaction is accompanied by the production of light 32

Lyriform organ—lyre-shaped sensillae of harvest-spiders **172**

Malleoli—organs of unknown function on the legs of the fourth pair in Solifugae, otherwise known as 'racquet organs' **107**

Mandibles—modified anterior limbs of arthropods forming jaws primitively adapted for chewing. The chelicerae of Arachnids

Marsupium—brood pouch of woodlice **1**, 15

Maxilla—one of the anterior appendages of insects and other arthropods modified so as to serve the purpose of mastication

Maxillipede—poison claw or toxocognath of centipedes, literally 'jawfoot' 49, 50–4

Mesopeltidium—central portion of carapace in Schizomida 152

Metachronal wave or rhythm—wave of rhythmic movement of similar objects, such as cilia or the legs of a millipede in which each is slightly and equally out of phase with the next 26

Metamorphosis—ecdysis accompanied by a change in form from larva to nymph, or nymph to adult instar (*q.v.*)

Metapeltidium—posterior portion of carapace in Schizomida 152

Metapodosoma—posterior part of prosoma of mites, bearing third and fourth pairs of legs   226

Metasoma—hind region of opisthosoma of scorpions, etc., forming a tail region   86, 124

Metatarsus—penultimate segment of an Arachnid's leg

Müllerian mimicry—imitation of the conspicuous or aposematic appearance of one distasteful animal by another, resulting in a reduction in the losses required to teach would-be predators to avoid this particular appearance or colour pattern and thus benefiting both species equally   242

Myrmecophilous—living in company with ants

Ocellus—simple type of eye, sometimes occurring in groups, but which, by itself, cannot provide form-vision   49, 54, 58, 172

Ocular tubercle—prominence bearing the eyes in harvestmen and some spiders, etc.   165–6, 168, 181

Odoriferous glands—repugnatorial glands (*q.v.*)

Ontogeny—origin and development of an individual living being as distinguished from phylogeny (*q.v.*)

Operculum—exoskeletal plate forming a lid or cover. See genital operculum

Opisthosoma—posterior region of the body of Arachnids, often known as the abdomen

Osmosis—flow of water from a weaker to a stronger solution through a semi-permeable membrane   256

Ovoviviparous—retaining the eggs inside the body of the mother, although within the egg-membrane, until the embryos are fully developed so that living young are produced

Palp—pedipalp (*q.v.*). Also tactile head appendage of insects, crustaceans, myriapods, etc.

Papilla—a projection

Parasitoids—parasitic insects which, like Ichneumon wasps, eventually kill their host   15, 211

Parthenogenesis—the development of unfertilised eggs

Patella—short leg segment between femur and tibia

Pecten—comb-like sense-organ on ventral surface of abdomen in scorpions   **86**, 93–6, Pl. IX*b*, X*a*

Pedicle—the narrow 'waist' of an Arachnid uniting the prosoma and opisthosoma

Pedipalp—leg-like tactile organ in front of the legs of an Arachnid forming claw of scorpions, reproductive organ of male spiders, etc.

Penolic tanning—sclerotisation (*q.v.*)

Phoresy—utilisation of another animal for transport   38, 127, **129,** 178

Phototaxis—directed response in relation to the stimulus of light

Phylogeny—evolutionary change in the ancestry of a living organism. Cf. Ontogeny (*q.v.*)

Planidium larva—active larva of parasitic Hymenoptera developing from an egg laid away from the host. It is a migratory form adapted to seek out the latter   38

Plantigrade—walking on the sole of the foot or on a flat termination of the limb and not on the toes or claws. Cf. Digitigrade (*q.v.*)   56

Pleopods—plate-like, respiratory endopodites of abdominal limbs of crustaceans   2, 7

Pleurite—chitinous plate forming the side of a body segment

Propeltidium—front portion of carapace in Schizomida   152

Proprioceptors—sense organs that detect the positions and movements of different parts of their possessor's body   172

Prosoma—anterior region of the body of an Arachnid, sometimes called the cephalothorax (*q.v.*)

Prosopon—adult or imago stage in Hydracarina   247

Protonymph—first nymphal stage following the larval instar of a mite or false-scorpion   139-40, 244, 248

Pseudo-tracheae—respiratory tubules in pleopods of woodlice   2, 7, 9

Pulvilli—lateral tarsal lobes forming suckers beneath the bases of the claws in Phrynichida, etc.   156, 158

Pygidium—posterior part of the body forming a distinct division   145, 152, 154, 160

Racquet organs—malleoli (*q.v.*)

Ram's-horn organ—extrusible reproductive organ of some male false-scorpions   135-7

Reflex—simple, automatic and involuntary response to a stimulus

Repugnatorial gland—gland secreting distasteful or unpleasant liquid whose function is to deter aggressors

Sclerite—sclerotised or chitinous plate on the body of an arthropod

Sclerotin—product of sclerotisation (*q.v.*)

Sclerotisation—chemical process analogous to the tanning of leather by which a protein combines with a phenol or quinone to form sclerotin, a tough, resistant and somewhat impervious component of the arthropodan integument   26

Scopula—brush of hairs or setae at the end of the tarsus   204

Scutum—dorsal plate in ticks and some mites formed by a fusion of tergites   228

Sensilla—arthropodan sense-organ

Serrula—row of chitinous teeth as on the maxillae or chelicerae   123, 130, 134

Seta—hair, bristle or spine, often sensory, on the body of an arthropod

Somite—segment of the body

Spermathecae—female organs in which are stored the spermatozoa received from the male 137

Spermatophore—envelope or bag containing spermatozoa and secreted
by some male arthropods 68, 101–2, 118–19, 136–7, 162

Spinneret—spinning organ at rear of body in spiders and on chelicerae of
false-scorpions 130–1, 186, 199–200, 220

Spiracle—respiratory aperture, the orifice of a tracheal tube 21, 51, 52,
54, 172, 254,

Stabilimentum—narrow ribbon of silk on a spider's web which helps to
camouflage the spider Pl. XV*a*

Stadium—developmental stage

Stenothermic—unable to tolerate wide variations in temperature. Cf.
Eurythermic (*q.v.*) 236

Sternite—chitinous plate on the ventral side of a body segment

Sternum—chitinous plate behind the labium, forming the underside of
the prosoma of an Arachnid

Stink gland—repugnatorial gland (*q.v.*)

Stridulation—sound production by the mechanical friction of one part
of the body agains another; usually by means of a number of file-like
ridges which rub against another set of ridges or a cluster of chitinous
granules or pegs

Systole—contraction of the heart or arteries forcing the blood through
the system 57

Tarsus—terminal segment of an arthropodan limb which bears the claws

Taxis—direct orientation in response to a stimulus. Cf. Kinesis (*q.v.*)

Tergite—chitinous plate on the dorsal side of a body segment

Thigmotaxis—directed response to the stimulus of contact 88

Tibia—segment of arthropodan limb between patella and metatarsus (*q.v.*)

Toxocognath—maxillipede (*q.v.*)

Tracheae—fine tubes carrying air from the spiracles and branching into
the tracheoles of most terrestrial arthropods 21, 51, 54, 75, 234, **254**

Tracheoles—fine tracheal capillaries which conduct air from the tracheae
to the tissues in most terrestrial arthropods **254**

Trichobothrium—very fine seta or hair usually believed to have an auditory as well as tactile function 92, 139

Tritonymph—third nymphal stage following deutonymph (*q.v.*) 139

Trochanter—the second, ring-like segment of an arthropodan limb

Uric acid—insoluble excretory compound characteristic of insects 255–6

Uropod—terminal abdominal appendage of Crustacea 10

Vulva—external reproductive organ, especially the orifice or opening of
that organ 39

INDEX OF GENERAL TOPICS